OXFORD WORLD'

KU-603-379

AUTHORS IN CONTEXT

General Editor: PATRICIA INGHAM, University of Oxford
Historical Adviser: BOYD HILTON, University of Cambridge

WILKIE COLLINS

AUTHORS IN CONTEXT examines the work of major writers in relation to their own time and to the present day. The series provides detailed coverage of the values and debates that colour the writing of particular authors and considers their novels, plays, and poetry against this background. Set in their social, cultural, and political contexts, classic books take on a new meaning for modern readers. And since readers, like writers, have their own contexts, the series considers how critical interpretations have altered over time, and how films, sequels, and other popular adaptations relate to the new age in which they are produced.

LYN PYKETT is a Professor of English and Pro Vice-Chancellor at the University of Wales, Aberystwyth. She is the author of numerous books and essays on nineteenth- and twentieth-century literature and culture, including: *Emily Brontë* (1989), *The Improper Feminine: The Women's Sensation Novel and the New Woman Writing* (1992), *Engendering Fictions: The English Novel in the Early Twentieth Century* (1995), and *Charles Dickens* (2002). She has also written on Collins in *The Sensation Novel from 'The Woman in White' to 'The Moonstone'* (1994) and *Wilkie Collins: Contemporary Critical Essays* (1998).

AUTHORS IN CONTEXT

OXFORD WORLD'S CLASSICS

══

LYN PYKETT

Wilkie Collins

══

OXFORD
UNIVERSITY PRESS

OXFORD
UNIVERSITY PRESS

Great Clarendon Street, Oxford OX2 6DP

Oxford University Press is a department of the University of Oxford.
It furthers the University's objective of excellence in research, scholarship,
and education by publishing worldwide in

Oxford New York

Auckland Cape Town Dar es Salaam Hong Kong Karachi
Kuala Lumpur Madrid Melbourne Mexico City Nairobi
New Delhi Shanghai Taipei Toronto

With offices in

Argentina Austria Brazil Chile Czech Republic France Greece
Guatemala Hungary Italy Japan Poland Portugal Singapore
South Korea Switzerland Thailand Turkey Ukraine Vietnam

Oxford is a registered trade mark of Oxford University Press
in the UK and in certain other countries

Published in the United States
by Oxford University Press Inc., New York

British Library Cataloguing in Publication Data

Data applied for

Library of Congress Cataloging in Publication Data

Pykett, Lyn.
    Wilkie Collins / Lyn Pykett.
        p. cm. – (Oxford world's classics)
    Includes bibliographical references (p.   ) and index.
    1. Collins, Wilkie, 1824–1889.   2. Novelists, English – 19th century – Bibliography. 3. Authors and
publishers – Great Britain – History – 19th century.   4. Literature
publishing – Great Britain – History – 19th century.   I. Title.   II. Oxford world's classics (Oxford
University Press)
    PR4496.P94 2005   823'.8–dc22   2005001541

        ISBN 0–19–284034–7   978–0–19–284034–9

                                1

Typeset in Ehrhardt by
RefineCatch Limited, Bungay, Suffolk
Printed in Great Britain by
Clays Ltd, St Ives plc

CONTENTS

LIST OF ILLUSTRATIONS

A CHRONOLOGY OF WILKIE COLLINS

	Life	*Historical and Cultural Background*
1824	(8 Jan.) Born at 11 New Cavendish Street, St Marylebone, London, elder son of William Collins, RA (1788–1847), artist, and Harriet Collins, née Geddes (1790–1868).	Death of Byron. Scott, *Redgauntlet*
1825		Stockton–Darlington railway opened.
1826	(Spring) Family move to Pond Street, Hampstead.	Hazlitt, *Spirit of the Age*
1827		Death of Blake; University College London founded.
1828	(25 Jan.) Brother, Charles Allston Collins, born.	Birth of Meredith, D. G. Rossetti; Catholic Emancipation Act.
1829	(Autumn) Family move to Hampstead Square.	Balzac's *La Comédie humaine* begins publication
1830	Family move to Porchester Terrace, Bayswater.	Death of George IV and accession of William IV; July Revolution in France. Hugo, *Hernani* Tennyson, *Poems Chiefly Lyrical*
1831		British Association for the Advancement of Science founded; Britain annexes Mysore.
1832		Deaths of Bentham, Crabbe, Goethe, Scott; First Reform Bill passed.
1833		Slavery abolished throughout British Empire. Carlyle, *Sartor Resartus*
1834		Deaths of Coleridge, Lamb; new Poor Law comes into effect; Tolpuddle Martyrs.
1835	(13 Jan.) Starts school, the Maida Hill Academy.	Dickens, *Sketches by Boz* (1st series)
1836	(19 Sept.–15 Aug. 1838) Family visits France and Italy.	

	Life	Historical and Cultural Background
1837		Death of William IV and accession of Victoria. Carlyle, *The French Revolution* Dickens, *Pickwick Papers*
1838	(Aug.) Family move to 20 Avenue Road, Regent's Park. Attends Mr Cole's boarding school, Highbury Place, until Dec. 1840.	Anti-Corn Law League founded; Chartist petitions published; London–Birmingham railway opened; Anglo–Afghan War. Dickens, *Oliver Twist*
1840	(Summer) Family move to 85 Oxford Terrace, Bayswater.	Birth of Hardy; marriage of Victoria and Albert; penny postage introduced. Browning, *Sordello* Darwin, *Voyage of H.M.S. Beagle* Dickens, *The Old Curiosity Shop*
1841	(Jan.) Apprenticed to Antrobus and Co., tea merchants, Strand.	Carlyle, *Heroes and Hero-Worship*
1842	(June–July) Trip to Highlands of Scotland, and Shetland, with William Collins.	Child and female underground labour becomes illegal; Chartist riots; Act for inspection of asylums. Browning, *Dramatic Lyrics* Comte, *Cours de philosophie positive* Macaulay, *Lays of Ancient Rome* Tennyson, *Poems*
1843	(Aug.) First signed publication 'The Last Stage Coachman' in the *Illuminated Magazine*.	Birth of Henry James; Thames Tunnel opened. Carlyle, *Past and Present* Dickens, *A Christmas Carol* Ruskin, *Modern Painters* begins publication
1844	Writes first (unpublished) novel, 'Iolani; or, Tahiti as it was; a Romance'.	Factory Act. Chambers, *Vestiges of the Natural History of Creation* Elizabeth Barrett, *Poems*
1845	(Jan.) 'Iolani' submitted to Longman and to Chapman and Hall, rejected.	Boom in railway speculation; Newman joins Church of Rome. Disraeli, *Sybil* Engels, *Condition of the Working Class in England in 1844* Poe, *Tales of Mystery and Imagination*
1846	(17 May) Admitted student of Lincoln's Inn.	Repeal of Corn Laws; Irish potato famine. Lear, *Book of Nonsense*

Life	Historical and Cultural Background
1847	(17 Feb.) Death of William Collins.	Ten-hour Factory Act; California gold rush. Emily Brontë, *Wuthering Heights* Charlotte Brontë, *Jane Eyre* Tennyson, *The Princess*
1848	(Summer) Family move to 38 Blandford Square. (Nov.) First book, *Memoirs of the Life of William Collins, Esq., RA* published.	Death of Emily Brontë; Pre-Raphaelite Brotherhood founded; Chartist Petition; cholera epidemic; Public Health Act; revolutions in Europe. Dickens, *Dombey and Son* Gaskell, *Mary Barton* Marx and Engels, *Communist Manifesto* Thackeray, *Vanity Fair*
1849	Exhibits a painting at the Royal Academy summer exhibition.	Ruskin, *Seven Lamps of Architecture*
1850	(27 Feb.) First published novel, *Antonina*. (Summer) Family move to 17 Hanover Terrace.	Deaths of Balzac, Wordsworth; Tennyson becomes Poet Laureate; Public Libraries Act. Dickens, *David Copperfield* Charles Kingsley, *Alton Locke* Tennyson, *In Memoriam* Thackeray, *Pendennis* Wordsworth, *The Prelude* Dickens starts *Household Words*
1851	(Jan.) Travel book on Cornwall, *Rambles Beyond Railways*, published. (Mar.) Meets Dickens for the first time. (May) Acts with Dickens in Bulwer Lytton's *Not So Bad As We Seem*.	Death of Turner; Great Exhibition in Hyde Park; Australian gold rush. Ruskin, *The Stones of Venice*
1852	(Jan.) *Mr Wray's Cash-Box* published, with frontispiece by Millais. (24 Apr.) 'A Terribly Strange Bed', first contribution to *Household Words*. (May) Goes on tour with Dickens's company of amateur actors. (16 Nov.) *Basil* published.	Death of Wellington; Louis Napoleon becomes Emperor of France. Stowe, *Uncle Tom's Cabin* Thackeray, *Henry Esmond*

Life	*Historical and Cultural Background*
1853 (Oct.–Dec.) Tours Switzerland and Italy with Dickens and Augustus Egg.	Arnold, *Poems* Charlotte Brontë, *Villette* Dickens, *Bleak House* Gaskell, *Cranford*
1854 (5 June) *Hide and Seek* published.	Birth of Wilde; outbreak of Crimean War; Working Men's College founded. Dickens, *Hard Times*
1855 (Feb.) Spends a holiday in Paris with Dickens. (16 June) First play, *The Lighthouse*, performed by Dickens's theatrical company at Tavistock House. (Nov.–Dec.) 'Mad Monkton' serialized.	Death of Charlotte Brontë. Browning, *Men and Women* Gaskell, *North and South* Trollope, *The Warden*
1856 (Feb.) *After Dark*, a collection of short stories, published. (Feb.–Apr.) Spends six weeks in Paris with Dickens. (Mar.) *A Rogue's Life* serialized in *Household Words*. (Oct.) Joins staff of *Household Words* and begins collaboration with Dickens in *The Wreck of the Golden Mary* (Dec.).	Birth of Freud, Shaw; Crimean War ends. E. B. Browning, *Aurora Leigh* Reade, *It Is Never Too Late to Mend*
1857 (Jan.–June) *The Dead Secret* serialized in *Household Words*, published in volume form (June). (6 Jan.) *The Frozen Deep* performed by Dickens's theatrical company at Tavistock House. (Aug.) *The Lighthouse* performed at the Olympic Theatre. (Sept.) Spends a working holiday in the Lake District with Dickens, their account appearing as 'The Lazy Tour of Two Idle Apprentices', serialized in *Household Words* (Oct.). Collaborates with Dickens on *The Perils of Certain English Prisoners*.	Birth of Conrad; Matrimonial Causes Act establishes divorce courts; Indian Mutiny. Dickens, *Little Dorrit* Flaubert, *Madame Bovary* Trollope, *Barchester Towers*

	Life	Historical and Cultural Background
1858	(May) Dickens separates from his wife. (Oct.) *The Red Vial* produced at the Olympic Theatre; a failure.	Victoria proclaimed Empress of India. Eliot, *Scenes of Clerical Life*
1859	From this year no longer living with his mother; lives for the rest of his life (with one interlude) with Mrs Caroline Graves. (Jan.–Feb.) Living at 124 Albany Street; (May–Dec.) Living at 2a New Cavendish Street. (Oct.) *The Queen of Hearts*, a collection of short stories, published. (26 Nov.–25 Aug. 1860) *The Woman in White* serialized in *All the Year Round*. (Dec.) Moves to 12 Harley Street.	War of Italian Liberation. Darwin, *Origin of Species* Eliot, *Adam Bede* Meredith, *The Ordeal of Richard Feverel* Mill, *On Liberty* Samuel Smiles, *Self-Help* Tennyson, *Idylls of the King* Dickens starts *All the Year Round*
1860	(Aug.) *The Woman in White* published in volume form: a best-seller in Britain and the United States, and rapidly translated into most European languages.	British Association meeting at Oxford (Huxley–Wilberforce debate). Eliot, *The Mill on the Floss*
1861	(Jan.) Resigns from *All the Year Round*.	Death of Albert, Prince Consort; Offences Against the Person Act (includes provisions on bigamy); outbreak of American Civil War. Dickens, *Great Expectations* Eliot, *Silas Marner* Palgrave, *Golden Treasury* Reade, *The Cloister and the Hearth* Ellen Wood, *East Lynne*
1862	(15 Mar.–17 Jan. 1863) *No Name* serialized in *All the Year Round*, published in volume form (31 Dec.).	Mary Elizabeth Braddon, *Lady Andley's Secret* Clough, *Poems*

	Life	Historical and Cultural Background
1863	*My Miscellanies*, a collection of journalism from *Household Words* and *All the Year Round*, published.	Death of Thackeray. Eliot, *Romola* Huxley, *Man's Place in Nature* Lyell, *Antiquity of Man* Mill, *Utilitarianism* Reade, *Hard Cash*
1864	(Nov.–June 1866) *Armadale* serialized in *The Cornhill*. (Dec.) Moves to 9 Melcombe Place, Dorset Square.	Albert Memorial constructed. Braddon, *The Doctor's Wife* Newman, *Apologia pro Vita Sua*
1865		Birth of Kipling, Yeats; death of Gaskell. Arnold, *Essays in Criticism* (1st series) Carroll, *Alice's Adventures in Wonderland* Dickens, *Our Mutual Friend* Tolstoy, *War and Peace* Wagner, *Tristan und Isolde*
1866	(May) *Armadale* published in two volumes. (Oct.) *The Frozen Deep* produced at the Olympic Theatre.	Birth of Wells. Dostoyevsky, *Crime and Punishment* Reade, *Griffith Gaunt: or Jealousy* Swinburne, *Poems and Ballads* Wood, *St Martin's Eve*
1867	(Sept.) Moves to 90 Gloucester Place, Portman Square. Collaborates with Dickens on 'No Thoroughfare', published as Christmas number of *All the Year Round*; dramatic version performed at the Adelphi Theatre (Christmas Eve).	Second Reform Bill passed; Paris Exhibition. Bagehot, *English Constitution* Marx, *Das Kapital*
1868	(4 Jan.–8 Aug.) *The Moonstone* serialized in *All the Year Round*; published in three volumes (July). (19 Mar.) Mother, Harriet Collins, dies. Collins forms liaison with Martha Rudd ('Mrs Dawson'). (29 Oct.) Caroline Graves marries Joseph Charles Clow.	Report of Royal Commission on the Laws of Marriage. Browning, *The Ring and the Book*
1869	(Mar.) *Black and White*, written in collaboration with Charles Fechter, produced at the Adelphi Theatre.	Suez Canal opened. Arnold, *Culture and Anarchy* Mill, *On the Subjection of Women*

Life	*Historical and Cultural Background*
(4 July) Daughter, Marian Dawson, born to Collins and Martha Rudd, at 33 Bolsover Street, Portland Place.	

1870 (June) *Man and Wife* published in volume form.
(Aug.) Dramatic version of *The Woman in White* tried out in Leicester.

Education Act; Married Women's Property Act; Franco-Prussian War; fall of Napoleon III.
D. G. Rossetti, *Poems*
Spencer, *Principles of Psychology*

1871 (14 May) Second daughter, Harriet Constance Dawson, born at 33 Bolsover Street.
(May) Caroline Graves again living with Collins.
(Oct.) *The Woman in White* produced at the Olympic Theatre.
(Oct.–Mar. 1872) *Poor Miss Finch* serialized in *Cassell's Magazine*.
(25 Dec.) *Miss or Mrs?* published.

Trade unions become legal; first Impressionist Exhibition held in Paris; religious tests abolished at Oxford, Cambridge, Durham.
Darwin, *Descent of Man*
Eliot, *Middlemarch*

1872 (Feb.) *Poor Miss Finch* published in volume form.

Butler, *Erewhon*

1873 (Feb.) Dramatic version of *Man and Wife* performed at the Prince of Wales Theatre.
(9 Apr.) Brother, Charles Allston Collins, dies.
(May) *The New Magdalen* published in volume form; dramatic version performed at the Olympic Theatre.
Miss or Mrs? And Other Stories in Outline published.
(Sept.–Mar. 1874) Tours United States and Canada, giving readings from his work.

Mill, *Autobiography*
Pater, *Studies in the Renaissance*

1874 (Nov.) *The Frozen Deep and Other Stories*.
(25 Dec.) Son, William Charles Dawson, born, 10 Taunton Place, Regent's Park.

Factory Act; Public Worship Act.
Hardy, *Far from the Madding Crowd*

	Life	Historical and Cultural Background
1875	Copyrights in Collins's work transferred to Chatto & Windus, who become his main publisher. *The Law and the Lady* serialized in *The London Graphic*; published in volume form.	Artisans' Dwellings Act; Public Health Act.
1876	(Apr.) *Miss Gwilt* (dramatic version of *Armadale*) performed at the Globe Theatre. *The Two Destinies* published in volume form.	Invention of telephone and phonograph. Eliot, *Daniel Deronda* James, *Roderick Hudson* Lombroso, *The Criminal*
1877	(Sept.) Dramatic version of *The Moonstone* performed at the Royal Olympic Theatre. *My Lady's Money* and *Percy and the Prophet*, short stories, published.	Annexation of Transvaal. Ibsen, *The Pillars of Society* Tolstoy, *Anna Karenina*
1878	(June–Nov.) *The Haunted Hotel* serialized.	Whistler–Ruskin controversy; Congress of Berlin; Edison invents the incandescent electric lamp. Hardy, *The Return of the Native*
1879	*The Haunted Hotel* published in volume form. *The Fallen Leaves—First Series* published in volume form. *A Rogue's Life* published in volume form.	Birth of E. M. Forster. Ibsen, *A Doll's House*
1880	*Jezebel's Daughter* published in volume form.	Deaths of George Eliot, Flaubert; Bradlaugh, an atheist, becomes an MP. Gissing, *Workers in the Dawn* Zola, *Nana*
1881	*The Black Robe* published in volume form. A. P. Watt becomes Collins's literary agent.	Death of Carlyle; Democratic Federation founded. Ibsen, *Ghosts* James, *Portrait of a Lady*
1882		Birth of Joyce, Woolf: death of Darwin, D. G. Rossetti, Trollope; Married Women's Property Act; Daimler invents the petrol engine.
1883	*Heart and Science* published in volume form. *Rank and Riches* produced at the Adelphi Theatre: a theatrical disaster.	Deaths of Marx, Wagner. Trollope, *An Autobiography*

Life	*Historical and Cultural Background*
1884	*'I Say No'* published in volume form.	Fabian Society founded; Third Reform Bill.
1885		Birth of Lawrence; Criminal Law Amendment Act (raising age of consent to 16). Maupassant, *Bel-Ami* Pater, *Marius the Epicurean* Zola, *Germinal*
1886	*The Evil Genius* published in volume form. *The Guilty River* published in *Arrowsmith's Christmas Annual*.	Irish Home Rule Bill; Contagious Diseases Acts repealed. Hardy, *The Mayor of Casterbridge*
1887	*Little Novels*, a collection of short stories, published.	Victoria's Golden Jubilee; Independent Labour Party founded. Conan Doyle, *A Study in Scarlet* Hardy, *The Woodlanders* Strindberg, *The Father*
1888	(Feb.) Moves to 82 Wimpole Street.	Death of Arnold; birth of T. S. Eliot. Kipling, *Plain Tales from the Hills*
1889	*The Legacy of Cain* published in volume form. (23 Sept.) Dies at 82 Wimpole Street.	Deaths of Browning, Hopkins; dock strike in London. Booth, *Life and Labour of the People in London* Shaw, *Fabian Essays in Socialism* Ibsen's *A Doll's House* staged in London
1890	*Blind Love* (completed by Walter Besant) published in volume form.	Death of Newman; Parnell case; first underground railway in London. Booth, *In Darkest England* Frazer, *The Golden Bough* William James, *Principles of Psychology*
1895	(June) Caroline Graves dies and is buried in Wilkie Collins's grave.	Morris, *News from Nowhere*
1919	Martha Rudd (Dawson) dies.	

ABBREVIATIONS

Letters   *The Letters of Wilkie Collins*, ed. William Baker and William
                      M. Clarke (New York: St Martin's Press, 1999), 2 vols.

Memoirs   Wilkie Collins, *Memoirs of the Life of William Collins, Esq.,
                      RA* (2 vols. repr. in 1; Wakefield: E.P. Publishing, 1978)

My Miscellanies   Wilkie Collins, *My Miscellanies* (Farnborough: Gregg, 1971)

Pilgrim   *The Letters of Charles Dickens*, ed. Madeline House, Graham
                      Storey, and Kathleen Tillotson (Pilgrim Edition, Oxford:
                      Clarendon Press, 1965–2002), 12 vols.

CHAPTER I

THE LIFE OF WILKIE COLLINS

My life has been rather a strange one. It may not seem particularly . . . respectable . . . but it has been, in some respects adventurous.

A Rogue's Life, Chapter 1

FROM his second published novel (his first 'story of modern life'), *Basil* (1852), to his last, the posthumously published *Blind Love* (1890), Wilkie Collins's stories and novels were preoccupied with the interconnections of the world of respectable society, the *demi-monde*, and the criminal 'underworld'. They were concerned with the plight and progress of professional men, and also with the adventures of rogues, and outsiders; with respectable families and their often unrespectable secrets, with irregular liaisons, and the disreputably chaotic state of the marriage laws which were the cornerstone of respectable society; with doubles and with questions of social and psychological identity. These fictional concerns were by no means exclusive to Collins, indeed they were common preoccupations in the Victorian novel. However, they did have particularly close links with the circumstances of Collins's own life. The family into which he was born and the families which he created for himself in his adult life were marked by a curious combination of respectability and social fragility, of orthodoxy and unconventionality. Throughout his adult life—and especially as a young man—Collins paradoxically combined a taste for footloose bohemianism with the order and discipline associated with the professions, as he strove first to establish himself and then to maintain his position as a successful professional writer. His origins, his occupation, and his private life all made his own respectability and class position rather ambivalent. The son of educated parents who had descended in the social scale before they rose by their own efforts, Collins did not attend a public school or a university, and thus did not belong to the main Victorian homosocial

networks of middle- and upper-class power and influence. His own
social views and conduct excluded him from 'polite' society. Nevertheless, he mixed easily with bankers, lawyers, and doctors, as well as
with actors, painters, and writers. He also included a number of their
wives among his friends. Collins was thus both an insider and an
outsider, or, perhaps more accurately, he was neither an insider nor
an outsider, but occupied a position somewhere in between—a liminal position. It was a position which gave him a very interesting
perspective on Victorian society, and what he described in his Preface
to *Armadale* as its clap-trap morality.[1] From his liminal position
Collins did not so much hold up the glass of satire to his contemporaries, as refract or re-present contemporary society through his
peculiarly angled lens.

Childhood and the Education of a Storyteller

William Wilkie Collins was born in London on 8 January 1824 to
Harriet Collins (née Geddes) and William Collins, a successful
landscape painter who had been elected to membership of the Royal
Academy in 1822. Collins's second name, and the name by which he
chose to be known as a young man, was that of his godfather, his
father's friend and in some respects his mentor, the painter Sir
David Wilkie. Collins had one sibling, a brother, Charles Allston
Collins, who was born on 25 January 1828. The brothers enjoyed a
generally happy and secure childhood as the offspring of intelligent,
creative, and upwardly mobile parents. Both of Collins's parents
adopted an evangelical position on religion and his father was a Tory
in politics. William Collins—unlike his elder son—was also much
concerned with maintaining a respectable position in society. This
concern with respectability was, in part, religious and moral, but
William Collins also regarded respectability as the necessary condition for success in his chosen field. Lucrative commissions depended
on cultivating connections and making one's way in respectable and
wealthy society: as he noted in his journal in 1816, '[a]s it is impos-
sible to rise in the world without connection, connection I must
have' (*Memoirs*, i. 83).

Collins's parents' concern with financial success and social
acceptance was, no doubt, also linked to the downward mobility of
the families in which they had been brought up. Harriet Geddes, the

daughter of an army officer, had been brought up in conditions of genteel poverty, cushioned to some extent from the adverse effects of her father's financial position by joining in activities with her better-off cousins. However, her father's financial failure during her teenage years made it necessary for her to earn her own living. A talented actress, she was on the point of taking up a professional engagement at the Theatre Royal, Bath—a socially compromising move for a woman at this time—when she was 'saved' by an evangelical clergyman and his wife, who converted her to their religious views and educated her for a career as a governess. Harriet maintained herself by working as a teacher in a London school, and then as a governess in several private households, before marrying William Collins in September 1822, some eight years after their first meeting. The lengthy period between their first meeting and their marriage was the result of William's need to recover from near destitution and to make his way in the world before embarking on matrimony, his own father having died a bankrupt in 1812. The life of Wilkie Collins's grandfather reads rather like the life of a fictional character created by his grandson. As an impoverished youth William Collins the elder had moved to London from County Wicklow in Ireland, and had earned an uncertain living restoring and dealing in paintings. Like his grandson, he had literary aspirations, and he published, among other things, a poem against the slave trade and a novel, *Memoirs of a Picture* (1805). This book, which details counterfeiting and other shady practices in the world of art-dealing, and draws on the colourful and scandalous life of his friend, the painter George Morland, provided the inspiration for Wilkie Collins's novella *A Rogue's Life* (1856). Collins discusses his grandfather's narrative at some length in his *Memoirs of the Life of William Collins, Esq., RA* (1848).

Although Wilkie Collins grew increasingly impatient with his parents' (and particularly his father's) evangelicalism and social conformity, it is clear that he regarded them with affection and admiration. In later life he described his mother as a 'woman of remarkable mental culture', and named her as the source of 'whatever of poetry and imagination there may be in my composition'.[2] His regard for his father can be seen in the memoir that he wrote immediately after William Collins's death in 1847. This memoir also reveals something of Collins's attitudes to his father's snobbery and to his conservative political and social views, as when he quotes his father's view of 'the speculation of marriage' as 'the most momentous risk in which any man can engage' (*Memoirs*, i. 209). Elsewhere, Collins recounts the delight which he took as an 8-year-old in lighting up the front windows of the family house in support of the pro-Reform Bill demonstrators in 1832—to avoid having their windows broken—and his father's discomfiture as a ' "high Tory" and a sincerely religious man' who 'looked on the Reform Bill and the cholera (then prevalent) as similar judgements of an offended Deity punishing social and political "backsliding" ' (*Letters*, ii. 541). The 8-year-old radical, on the other hand, cheered with 'the sovereign people' when they cheered for the Reform Bill (*Letters*, ii. 541).

If his father's evangelical and Tory sympathies cast a shadow on Collins's childhood, and particularly on his Sundays, they do not appear to have prevented Willie (as he was known to his family in childhood) from reading widely and enthusiastically. The young Collins immersed himself in his mother's collection of Anne Radcliffe's Gothic romances and the poetry of Shakespeare, Pope, Scott, Shelley, and Byron, as well as the usual fictional fare of the middle-class boy of the nineteenth century: tales of Robin Hood, *Don Quixote*, *The Vicar of Wakefield*, *The Arabian Nights Entertainment*, and the novels of Frederick Marryat and Sir Walter Scott. Willie was not sent to school until January 1835, when he went to the Maida Hill Academy. His formal schooling was cut short in September 1836, when his father followed Sir David Wilkie's advice and realized a long-held ambition to travel to Italy to experience Italian landscape, art, and architecture at first hand and to paint Italian scenes. The Collins family set out for Paris on 19 September 1836, and from there travelled to Nice, Florence, Rome, Naples, and Venice. Collins later claimed that in the two years he spent in Italy between the ages of 12 and 14, he learnt more 'which has since been of use to me, among the pictures, the scenery and the people, than I ever learnt at school'.[3] He learnt to speak and write Italian, became familiar with the art galleries of France and Italy, and mixed with many of the leading artists of the day. This adolescent version of the Grand Tour customarily undertaken by upper-class young men in the eighteenth and nineteenth centuries apparently also served as a sexual initiation for Collins, as it did for those other Grand Tourists. According to the tales that he later told to his friends Augustus Egg and Charles

Dickens, it was during his stay in Rome that the 12- or 13-year-old Collins also fell in love for the first time—with a married woman. Indeed, in some versions of his exploits Collins claims to have seduced her.

When the family returned to England in August 1838, Collins was sent to a boarding school in Highbury, North London, which he attended for the next three years. With a total of no more than four years' formal schooling at two London schools, Wilkie Collins seems to have avoided the conventional education and socialization of the relatively well-to-do middle-class English male. In most respects, his period at Henry Cole's Highbury school was uneventful. Collins kept up his Italian by writing letters home in that language. The Reverend Cole regarded him as a lazy pupil who did not pay attention to his classes. Collins, in turn, felt rather out of place—perhaps because of his recent cosmopolitan experience, perhaps because he was self-conscious about his appearance: he was very short, with extremely small feet and hands, and a misshapen forehead (having been born with a bulge on its right side), and he was also very short-sighted. Perhaps the most notable aspect of Collins's stay at the Highbury school was his induction into the role of storyteller—if we are able to believe the account he gave in 'Reminiscences of a Story-Teller' (published, with some omissions, in the *Universal Review*, 1888). This account closely resembles Dickens's description of David Copperfield's formation as a storyteller by his school-fellow James Steerforth in Chapter 7 of *David Copperfield* (1849–50). Collins describes his initiation at the hands of a 'great fellow of seventeen' who was 'as fond of hearing stories in bed, as the oriental Despot to whose literary tastes we are indebted for the Arabian Nights': 'On the first night, my capacity for telling stories was tested at a preliminary examination—vanity urged me to do my best—and I paid the penalty . . . I was the unhappy boy appointed to amuse the captain from that time forth.'[4] It was as a result of this experience that Collins 'learnt to be amusing at short notice', a lesson from which he 'derived benefit . . . at a later period of my life'. Despite being thrashed on the older boy's instructions when he refused to tell a story, or when invention failed him, Collins claimed (on another occasion) that he owed a 'debt of gratitude' to the 'brute who first awakened in me, his poor little victim, a power of which but for him I might never have been aware. Certainly no-one in my own home credited me with it; and when I left school I still continued story-telling for my own pleasure.'[5]

Collins's Literary Apprenticeship

An author I was to be, and an author I became in the year 1848.

(*Letters*, i. 207)

The first location in which Collins continued his pleasurable story-telling was the Strand office of the tea merchant Edward Antrobus, 'Teaman to Her Majesty'. It was here that William Collins found a post for his son, when Wilkie declined to take up his father's suggestion that he should go to Oxford as a preparation for entering the Church. As he put it in a 'memorandum, relating to the life and writings of Wilkie Collins' which he sent to an unknown correspondent in 1862: 'I had no vocation for that way of life, and I preferred trying mercantile pursuits. I had already begun to write in secret, and mercantile pursuits lost all attraction for me' (*Letters*, i. 206). Wilkie's own career preference was for writing books. As he recalled in an interview in 1887:

I told my father that I thought I should like to write books, though how to write, or on what subjects, I don't believe at the time I had the smallest conception. However, I began to scribble in a desultory kind of way, and drifted, I hardly know how, into tale-writing. . . . This went on for some time, till an intimate friend of my father's remonstrated with him on the folly of allowing me to waste my time on a pursuit which could never lead to anything but the traditional poverty of the poor author and he mentioned an eligible opening in a tea-merchant's firm as a suitable position for me.[6]

Collins's position at Antrobus's seems to have been that of an unpaid apprentice, and something of his attitude to the office which he came to regard as his 'prison on the Strand', can be seen in his account of the experience of Zack Thorpe in *Hide and Seek* (1854). After three weeks at a tea broker's office, Zack declares: 'They all say it's a good opening for me, and talk about the respectability of commercial pursuits. I don't want to be respectable, and I hate commercial pursuits' (*Hide and Seek*, Book I, Chapter II). Despite his own dislike of respectability and commercial pursuits, Collins

worked at the tea merchant's for the next five years, punctuated
by extended breaks for a tour of Scotland with his father in the
summer of 1842 (vividly recalled in the *Memoirs*), and two visits to
France—a five-week visit with his friend Charles Ward in 1844, and
an unaccompanied trip to Paris in 1845. These French expeditions
were the first of many such trips that Collins was to make during his
lifelong love affair with France, and particularly with its capital city.
Collins's period of employment at the office on the Strand was prolonged by his father's inability to find him a better position in the
Civil Service (through appeals to his former patron Sir Robert Peel)
and the Royal Academy (through Landseer). And perhaps the office
on the Strand was not such a bad place to be for an aspiring writer. It
was convenient for theatres and booksellers, and more importantly, it
was close to the centre of the publishing world. The offices of the
Saturday Magazine were next door to Antrobus's, and nearby were
the offices of *Punch*, the *Illustrated London News*, Bell's *Life in London*,
the *Observer*, and Chapman and Hall, the publisher of several monthly
magazines.

In some ways, during this period of his life Collins bore some
resemblance to the hero of Mary Elizabeth Braddon's *Lady Audley's
Secret*, Robert Audley (during his French-novel-reading phase), or
to those young men of Dickens's novels—Richard Carstone and
Eugene Wrayburn, for example—who live on their expectations
while they wait for an opening. Collins, however, was doing more
than biding his time; he was actively preparing himself for a literary
career. According to his friend Edmund Yates, Collins quickly got
through his office duties in order to devote himself to 'tale-writing'
and experimenting with 'tragedies, comedies, epic poems and the
usual literary rubbish invariably accumulated about themselves by
"young beginners" '.[7] By 1843 'The Last Stage Coachman' (a fantasy
about the plight of the stagecoach in the railway age) appeared over
the signature of 'W. Wilkie Collins' in Douglas Jerrold's *Illuminated
Magazine*, and other articles and stories had begun to find their way
into the periodicals. Collins also used his office hours to write his
first novel 'Iolani; or, Tahiti as it was', a Gothic romance in which, as
Collins put it, 'my youthful imagination ran riot among the noble
savages'.[8] In the late summer of 1845 Collins's father offered the
novel to Longman's and to Chapman and Hall, but both publishers
turned it down. It remained unpublished in Collins's lifetime, and

was thought to have been lost altogether until 1991; it has since been published by Princeton University Press (1997).

Following this peremptory 'shut[ting] of the gates of the realms of fancy in my face',[9] Collins agreed to the suggestion of a friend of his father's that he should read for the Bar, and was duly admitted as a student of Lincoln's Inn on 17 May 1846. Embarking on a similar course, one of Collins's fictional creations confides: 'At that time . . . I had no serious intention of following any special vocation. I simply wanted an excuse for enjoying the pleasures of a London life' ('Miss Jeromette and the Clergyman', II).[10] However, according to Collins's own account of this period in his own life, he 'worked hard and conscientiously' at his legal studies in the beginning, but 'at the end of two months I had conceived such a complete disgust for the law that I was obliged to tell my father that I could endure the drudgery no longer'.[11] Certainly, there is little evidence that Collins did any more than keep the legal terms, eat the legal dinners,[12] and make some legal friends who would later be the source of comradeship, journalistic contacts, and useful information for his fiction. After the first flurry of activity to equip himself as a student of the Bar (including acquiring a ticket for the British Museum Reading Room), Collins returned to work on the novel that he had begun about a month before enrolling at Lincoln's Inn.

This work was *Antonina*, an often lurid and violent historical novel based on Gibbon's account of Alaric's conquest of Rome in AD 410 in the *Decline and Fall of the Roman Empire*, Collins's own visit to Rome in 1837, and his reading of the historical novels of Sir Walter Scott and Bulwer Lytton's *The Last Days of Pompeii* (1824). As Catherine Peters notes, Collins's manuscript indicates that from the outset he worked on this novel in a meticulous and professional way, carefully planning and pacing his plot.[13] The manuscript also clearly indicates the point (in the third chapter) at which the novel was temporarily abandoned following the death of his father in February 1847, after a few years of declining health. Collins did not return to work on his novel until 25 July 1848, when he had completed work on what was to be his first published book, a biography of his father entitled *Memoirs of the Life of William Collins, Esq., RA: With Selections from his Journals and Correspondence*.

In writing this commemorative work, Wilkie Collins was fulfilling a filial duty which his father had planned and prepared for him. As early as 1 January 1844 William Collins had noted in his journal that he thought it 'quite possible that my dear son, William Wilkie Collins, may be tempted . . . to furnish the world with a memoir of my life' and that he therefore had the intention of 'occasionally noting down some circumstances as leading points, which may be useful'. The writing of the memoir also served as another stage in Collins's apprenticeship in his chosen profession. Writing about the life of his father gave Collins the opportunity to reflect upon his own history and formation, and he used the occasion as a means of distancing himself from his father and defining himself and his own beliefs in relation to—and sometimes in opposition to—those of William Collins. Moreover, writing about a father who was a successful painter also gave the aspiring fiction writer an opportunity to reflect upon the formation of a professional artist. The publication of the *Memoirs* in 1848 also served to place Collins in a useful position from which to launch his career as a professional writer of fiction when he completed *Antonina*. Certainly the *Memoirs* focused public attention on its author as well as its subject. It had good reviews in such leading periodicals as the *Athenaeum*, the *Westminster Review*, and *Blackwood's*, receiving praise for its style, judgement, and insight.

William Collins's death changed the dynamics of the Collins family in ways which proved quite liberating for his wife and sons. The prudence which had marked his professional and parental life left William's family well provided for, but the conditions of his will also left his sons dependent on their mother, during her lifetime, for any money that they did not earn for themselves. However, no longer bound by her husband's extreme prudence in financial matters, nor by his extreme rectitude in matters of social conduct, Harriet Collins became a much more entertaining companion, and provided a very congenial setting for the social life of her sons, who were to remain with her for the next decade (Collins did not finally move out of his mother's home until about 1859). First in Blandford Square, where she moved shortly after her husband's death, and then in Hanover Terrace, Regent's Park, Harriet seems to have recovered some of the spirit of the youthful actress that she was before her conversion to evangelicalism. She kept open house for her sons and their friends. The young Pre-Raphaelite painters Augustus Egg, William Holman Hunt, and John Everett Millais were frequent visitors; indeed,

Millais more or less lived in the Collins household at Hanover Terrace at one point. Other friends included Charles Ward (the Collins family's bank manager at Coutts and Wilkie's sometime companion on his French trips), Charles's brother Edward, and their mutual friend Edward Pigott, who was called to the Bar at the same time as Collins. One episode involving this group, which was to inform a number of Collins's novels, was his involvement in arranging the clandestine marriage of Edward Ward and his 16-year-old former pupil Henrietta Ward. Collins made use of his rudimentary legal 'training' and his legal contacts to unravel the marriage laws, and he employed some of his developing plotting skills to bring the Wards together in the characters of bride and groom in May 1848.

With his mother's active encouragement, Collins also began to indulge the theatrical tastes which he had developed on his French trips, by producing and acting in Sheridan's *The Rivals* and Goldsmith's *The Good-Natur'd Man*, which he staged in the 'Theatre Royal Back Drawing Room' in his mother's house. He also wrote a pastiche eighteenth-century prologue for the Goldsmith play, which he substituted for Samuel Johnson's original. Collins also tried his hand at playwriting, adapting a French melodrama which was staged as *A Court Duel* at Miss Kelly's Theatre, Dean Street, in late February 1850. He also acted in this charity performance (in aid of the Female Emigration Fund[14]), which took place just a few days before Richard Bentley and Son published his first novel, *Antonina*. By mid-March *Antonina* had been favourably reviewed in (among others) the *Spectator* and the *Athenaeum*, although the reviewers in both of these magazines felt it necessary to warn the young author against his tendency to resort to 'strong effects',[15] and 'the needless accumulation of revolting details'.[16] Naturally enough, *Bentley's Miscellany*, which was owned by the publisher of *Antonina*, welcomed the arrival of an author who 'in his first work, has stepped into the first rank of romance writers'.[17] *Bentley's Miscellany* not only provided a 'puffing' review to propel Collins into the public eye, but it was also, in the next few years, to provide a useful outlet for his stories, essays, and reviews, and thus played an important part in launching his career as a professional writer. Bentley also published Collins's next book, *Rambles Beyond Railways* (published in January 1851), an illustrated collection of travel sketches describing a journey around Cornwall which he had taken in the summer of

1850 with his friend, the artist Henry Brandling (who provided the illustrations).

The Dickens Years

By early 1851 Collins was the author of a biography, a novel, and a travel book, all of which had received good notices and had sold quite well. His unofficial writer's apprenticeship in the 'prison on the Strand' was beginning to bear fruit. Eighteen fifty-one was also a milestone of another kind, since it was in this year that Collins began a friendship that was to be as important for English fiction and magazine writing in the mid-nineteenth century as it was for the two individuals involved. It was through their mutual interest in the theatre that Wilkie Collins and Charles Dickens met early in 1851, when Dickens, by then the leading novelist of the day, was putting on a production of Sir Edward Bulwer Lytton's *Not So Bad As We Seem*. The staging of this specially commissioned play was intended to raise money for the newly formed Guild of Literature, a benevolent association which Dickens saw as a way of enhancing the status of writers; Bulwer Lytton was its President and Dickens its Vice President. When Dickens needed an extra actor he asked Augustus Egg—who had been part of Dickens's theatrical group for about three years—to approach Collins. *Not So Bad As We Seem* was first staged at Devonshire House (Dickens's home at that time) on 16 May 1851, before an audience which included Queen Victoria and Prince Albert as well as Collins's mother and brother. Collins's part was a small one, and his acting talents were not of the first rank, but his involvement in this extremely enjoyable and successful theatrical venture—the first of many theatrical collaborations with Dickens—cemented what was to be a lifelong interest in the theatre. The company later went on a 'wonderful theatrical campaign' (*Letters*, i. 82), taking the play to theatres in Bristol, Manchester, Birmingham, Newcastle, Shrewsbury, and Liverpool. Collins revelled in the enthusiasm of the audiences in the provinces, declaring in a letter to Edward Pigott, '*King Public* is a good king for Literature and Art!' (*Letters*, i. 82).

As well as developing his interest in plays and the theatre, *Not So Bad As We Seem* also provided Collins with a stimulating companion and a professional ally. For the next fifteen years or so he and

Dickens regularly dined together, visited theatres, and rambled the streets of London and Paris together, wrote and acted together, and worked closely together when Collins became a member of the staff of Dickens's magazine *Household Words* in October 1856 (see Chapter 3). Collins frequently stayed with or near the Dickens family on their summer holidays in France or on the Kentish coast, and he was regarded as an honorary uncle by Dickens's children. When not plagued by the various illnesses which were to bedevil his life as he grew older, Collins was an excellent companion for the married man seeking an escape from his family or diversion within it. He was a bon viveur, with a passion for fine wines, dry champagne, and French food. Like Dickens he adored Paris, and even with his illnesses he was an easygoing travelling companion. Dickens was drawn to Collins's unconventionality, and the social ease which came, in part, from his complete lack of interest in social advancement and living as a 'gentleman'. Collins's tolerance in sexual matters made him a congenial fellow traveller on what Dickens described as their 'Haroun Alraschid' expeditions (Pilgrim, viii. 623) in search of female company. The younger man's own domestic arrangements, when he made them, had no place for marriage (see below), and although Dickens did not entirely approve of all aspects of his friend's domestic establishments, Collins's unconventionality was no doubt a source of support when Dickens's marriage came increasingly under strain—and finally collapsed—when he became involved with the actress Ellen Ternan in the late 1850s.

As well as discovering a congenial companion in Collins, Dickens also recognized him as a serious fellow professional and a talented writer. He later recalled that he had, 'from the *Basil* days', regarded Collins as 'the writer who would come ahead of all the field—being the only one who combined invention and power, both humorous and pathetic, with that invincible determination to work, and that profound conviction that nothing of worth is to be done without work, of which triflers and foreigners have no concept' (Pilgrim, x. 128). Dickens would have had ample opportunity to have observed Collins's industry at close quarters in the *Basil* days, since the young writer was working on this novel while he was also touring in *Not So Bad As We Seem*, and he completed it while he was staying with the Dickens family in Dover in September 1852 (and while Dickens was writing *Bleak House*). In fact, the completion of Collins's first novel of modern life was delayed in part by his industrious and pleasurable application to Dickens's theatricals and in part by his regular writing of art reviews and stories for *Bentley's Miscellany*, an activity which served to keep him in the public eye as well as generating an income. The stories for *Bentley's* included 'The Twin Sisters' (March 1851), 'A Passage in the Life of Mr Perugino Potts' (February 1852) and 'Nine o'Clock' (August 1852). During the writing of *Basil* Collins was also writing reviews of plays, exhibitions, and books and contributing to the 'Portfolio' section of the *Leader*, a weekly paper espousing radical views, in which his friend Edward Pigott purchased a controlling interest in 1851. Following Dickens's example (although not his financial success), Collins also interrupted his work on *Basil* to write a Christmas book, *Mr Wray's Cash-Box; or The Mask and the Mystery: A Christmas Sketch*, published by Bentley (with a frontispiece by Millais) for Christmas 1851. He also wrote 'A Terribly Strange Bed', a story about an unpleasant night in a Paris gambling house, which was his first contribution to Dickens's *Household Words* (24 April 1852).

Praised by Dickens for the 'admirable writing, and many clear evidences of a very delicate discrimination of character' (Pilgrim, vi. 823), *Basil* attracted mixed reviews when it was published by Bentley in November 1852. Several reviewers shared Dickens's opinion that Collins had too little respect for 'the probabilities' (Pilgrim, vi. 49), and some thought he had too little respect for the proprieties. Collins, however, was content to refer to the judgement of 'King Public', and later claimed in his 1862 'Letter of Dedication' to *Basil* that his story slowly but surely 'forced its way through all adverse criticism, to a place in the public favour which it has never lost since'. Meanwhile Collins continued to write for the *Leader*, wrote 'Mad Monkton' a story about the curse of hereditary insanity, which Dickens declined on the grounds that it might upset the readers of *Household Words*, and 'Gabriel's Marriage'—a story of crime, family estrangement, and forgiveness set in Brittany at the time of the French Revolution—which appeared in *Household Words* for 16–23 April 1853. In the same week Collins began work on *Hide and Seek*, which he continued—with some interruptions by illness in the early summer months—during an extended stay at the Dickenses' summer base, the Château des Molineaux in Boulogne. In early October Collins, Dickens, and Egg returned to Boulogne to begin an extended pleasure expedition that would take them to Paris, which Collins found 'overflowing with English travellers, and altered . . . past all recognition by the commencement of a magnificent new Street . . . [which] will be the broadest, longest and grandest in the world when it is finished' (*Letters*, i. 98). From Paris they travelled to Venice, via Strasbourg, Basle, Berne, Lausanne, Milan, Genoa, Naples, Rome, and Florence.

Collins's letters to his mother, brother, and friends give vivid accounts of the people, places, and landscapes that they encountered on their travels, including their sometimes unconventional travelling arrangements: for example, Collins and Egg slept in the storeroom on one of the boats they took, while Dickens 'had share of a friend's cabin' (*Letters*, i. 111). Collins and Egg were very much the junior partners on this trip, travelling slightly in the shadow of the wealthier and more successful man: Collins remarks on the 'prodigious sensation in the English colony at Lausanne' caused by the arrival in its midst of the eminent writer. In his letters to Harriet and his brother Charles, Collins frequently recalls their Italian sojourn of 1836–8 (and Dickens's letters to his wife on this trip indicate that he found Collins's constant harking back to his adventures as a cosmopolitan 13-year-old rather irritating). Collins found Naples and Genoa much changed, but Rome and Florence were exactly as he remembered them in his childhood. Only the dramatis personae of their Italian visit had changed, as he notes with pleasure in a letter to Charles which throws light on Collins's view of life at this time. He describes a gloomy meeting with William Iggulden (a banker whom the Collins family had known during their stay in Rome sixteen years earlier) and his son, a 'tall young gentleman with a ghastly face, immense whiskers, and an expression of the profoundest melancholy'. 'Do you remember little "*Lorenzo*" who was the lively young "Pickle" of the family in our time?' asks Collins with amazed amusement, 'Well! This was Lorenzo!!!!' (*Letters*, i. 114). He is even more delighted to recount that Lorenzo's brother, 'the pattern goodboy who used to be quoted as an example to me', has 'married a pretty girl *without* his parent's consent—is out of the banking business in consequence—and has gone to Australia to make his fortune as well as he can'. Collins reports himself 'rather glad to hear this, as I don't like "well-conducted" young men! I know it is wrong! But I always feel relieved and happy when I hear that they have got into a scrape' (*Letters*, i. 114–15). In Venice, the trio led 'the most luxurious, dandy-dilettante sort of life . . . among pictures and palaces . . . operas, Ballets and Cafés' (*Letters*, i. 118). Fresh from the galleries of Rome and Florence, Collins was struck once more by the 'glorious pictures', and by the 'superiority of the Venetian painters', especially Tintoretto. He writes to his mother that 'Charley and Millais and Hunt, ought to come here if they go nowhere else' as the Venetians, 'employed as they almost always were, to represent conventional subjects, are the most original race of painters that the world has yet seen' (*Letters*, i. 118).

It is clear that Collins intended his letters to be passed around among his friends, and that he also regarded them as notes to stimulate 'reflection and remembrance' (*Letters*, i. 119) on his return, so that he might work them up into travel sketches for publication. If Collins had entertained hopes of defraying some of the expenses of his journey in this way he was to be disappointed, as Bentley declined to publish them on the grounds that the *Miscellany* had recently run a series of essays on Italy and Italian art. Once back in England, Collins returned to work on *Hide and Seek*, which was published in three volumes on 5 June 1854, some ten weeks after the outbreak of the Crimean War, an unfortunate timing which Collins felt adversely affected the sales of this novel. *Hide and Seek* was dedicated to Dickens, and it was with Dickens that Collins took his relaxation following the novel's completion. First he took up Dickens's invitation to be his 'vicious associate' in 'a career of amiable dissipation and unbounded license in the metropolis' (Pilgrim, vii. 366), and then he accompanied him to Boulogne for the summer.

The years following the publication of *Hide and Seek* were crowded with activity, as Collins pursued the busy journalistic career and literary collaborations that were part of his working friendship with Dickens. He completed a novella, *A Rogue's Life* (serialized in *Household Words* in 1856), and *The Dead Secret*, a novel about a woman with a secret which foreshadowed the sensation novels of the 1860s (serialized in *Household Words* in 1857). He worked on the manuscript of the autobiographical narrative which his mother had written in 1853, and which she hoped that he might publish under his own name; in the end he did not publish it, but used some of the material from it in the narrative which linked together his first collection of short stories, *After Dark* (1856), and he also borrowed some details for later novels. Collins also continued to write plays: *The Frozen Deep* and *The Lighthouse* (based on his own story 'Gabriel's Marriage') were staged by Dickens in 1857, and *The Red Vial* was put on at the Olympic Theatre in 1858 (and duly flopped). In between—and sometimes during—this furious literary production, there were regular trips to Paris with Dickens. On one such trip in 1856 Collins, browsing the Paris bookstalls, picked up Maurice Méjan's *Recueil des causes célèbres* which he was to use in plotting *The Woman in White*. Despite being caught up in the Dickens whirlwind, Collins did not neglect his other friends, and it was in this period that he developed what was to become a lifelong passion for sailing, after a trip with Edward Pigott. 'The Cruise of the Tomtit' was the first literary outcome of this new interest, and it also made an appearance in his novel *Armadale*. Without doubt, however, the major event of the Dickens years was Collins's response to Dickens's invitation to provide an exciting serial novel (to follow his own *A Tale of Two Cities*) for his new periodical *All the Year Round*. This novel, *The Woman in White*, which is usually credited with inaugurating the fictional sub-genre known as the 'sensation novel', certainly inaugurated the most successful decade of Collins's career as a novelist.

Family Secrets and Secret Families

The plots of sensation novels typically involve marital irregularities of various kinds, and frequently focus on a woman with a secret. By the time *The Woman in White* appeared both Collins and Dickens were involved in their own 'marital' irregularities and each of them was the cause of a woman becoming a woman with a secret. In May 1858 Dickens separated from his wife, made a public declaration that no other person was involved and continued with his clandestine relationship with Ellen Ternan, a young actress he had met while acting in Collins's *The Frozen Deep* in 1857. Collins, meanwhile, with somewhat less secrecy (and in Dickens's opinion, with considerably less discretion), had formed a relationship with Caroline Graves, a young widow whom he had met in the early 1850s, and with whom he lived from about 1858 until his death—apart from one break in 1868–9 when Caroline unaccountably married someone else. Caroline Graves (née Elizabeth Compton), was born in

Toddington in Gloucestershire in about 1830—the exact date is not known, and Caroline appears to have been in the habit of mis-representing her age. She was the daughter of a carpenter named John Compton and his wife, but her tendency towards socially aggrandizing fantasies led her to describe herself as the daughter of a gentleman named Courtenay. In 1850, when she was living in Bath, she married George Robert Graves, a shorthand writer and son of a stonemason. Caroline and George Graves subsequently lived in Clerkenwell in London, and it was there that their daughter (and Caroline's only child) was born. George Graves died in January 1852.

It is not clear precisely when and how Collins first met Caroline, although in his biography of his father, J. G. Millais suggested that their first meeting inspired Collins's depiction of Walter Hartright's first encounter with Anne Catherick in *The Woman in White*. It is now thought most likely that they first met when Collins was staying temporarily in lodgings in Howland Street (off the Tottenham Court Road) in 1856. Certainly Caroline and her mother-in-law were living in that neighbourhood at the time. By the end of 1858 Collins seems to have been living with Caroline at 124 Albany Street; she was the registered ratepayer at this address, and Collins wrote several letters from there in 1858/9. They moved from Albany Street to 2a New Cavendish Street, and eighteen months later to Harley Street, where they rented rooms from a dentist. At this last address Caroline was known as Collins's wife, and her daughter was passed off as a young servant. At the Harley Street address Collins completed a census return as a married lodger, recording his profession as barrister and author of works of fiction. Collins did not long trouble to maintain the fiction of their marital status. To his male friends he openly acknowledged Caroline's place in his life, and she began to act as hostess at informal and convivial dinners for them, and, later, to accompany him on trips in England and on the Continent. Some of Collins's female friends would have known of his domestic set-up, but, in accordance with the customs of the double standard, they would not have accompanied their husbands to the dinners that Collins hosted with Caroline. The fictional identity of Caroline's daughter, who was known as Carrie, was also quickly dropped. He described Carrie as his godchild, treated her as an adopted child, and paid for her education. Carrie lived with Collins until her own marriage to Henry Powell Bartley, a 'respectable' solicitor who turned out to be much more extravagant and reckless than her 'bohemian' adoptive father, and whose profligacy was later to undo the careful plans which Collins had made to secure her financial future.

Collins's unconventional domestic establishment was one which had many obvious advantages for the male partner, as it combined the freedom of a bachelor existence with the security and comfort of married life. His setting up of this establishment marked the end of his apprenticeship in life and in letters. For the first time Collins became quite independent of his mother, although he continued to have a close and loving relationship with her. His arrangement with Caroline provided him with a secure base from which to pursue his increasingly successful career as a novelist. Caroline was Collins's constant companion during the planning and writing of *The Woman in White*, staying with him—and ministering to his various health complaints—on an extended visit to Broadstairs in the summer of 1859, when he was engaged in 'slowly and painfully launching my new serial novel' (*Letters*, i. 176). She also helped him to enjoy the fruits of its success, as Dickens noted in March 1861:

Wilkie is in a popular and potential state . . . He has made his rooms in Harley Street very handsome and comfortable. We never speak of the (female) skeleton in that house, and I therefore have not the least idea of the state of his mind on that subject. I hope it does not run in any matrimonial groove. I *cannot* imagine any good coming of such an end in this instance. (Pilgrim, ix. 388)

Dickens's sensitivities about Wilkie's household skeletons were no doubt heightened by his worries about his own female skeletons and also by fears that he himself would be compromised by any scandal that attached to the Collins family, as Wilkie's brother Charles had married Katie Dickens—against her father's will—in the summer of 1860.

Dickens need not have worried about Collins's mind running 'in any matrimonial groove' as far as Caroline, or indeed anyone else was concerned. However, before too long Collins's domestic affairs were to become even more complicated and scandalous than Dickens envisaged when he wrote the words quoted above. During the most productive years of his career, when he wrote most of what are generally acknowledged to be his best novels Collins doubled the

Wilkie Collins, 1850, by
J. E. Millais

Caroline Graves in the early 1870s

Martha Rudd

irregularity of his domestic life by beginning another relationship that was to lead to the establishment of a second Collins household outside of the matrimonial groove. The beginnings of Collins's relationship with Martha Rudd, who was to be the mother of his three illegitimate children, are as shrouded in mystery as are the beginnings of his relationship with Caroline Graves. However, it is probable that the 40-year-old Collins met the 19-year-old Martha when he was staying in Great Yarmouth researching the Norfolk scenes of *Armadale* in 1864. Martha and her elder sister, the daughters of a Norfolk shepherd, were certainly working as servants for an innkeeper at Great Yarmouth in the early 1860s. It is not clear exactly when Martha moved from Yarmouth to London, but by 1868 she was living at 33 Bolsover Street in a house rented by Collins. It is possible that this move was one of the circumstances that precipitated Caroline's rather surprising marriage to Joseph Clow, a much younger man, in October 1868.

Collins's mother's death on 19 March 1868 may have led Caroline to try to force the issue of matrimony: Collins could no longer claim that Harriet's objections were an obstacle to his marriage. Whether in frustration at Collins's refusal to marry her, or in pique at the discovery of his relationship with Martha, or for some other reason entirely, Caroline suddenly married Joseph Clow on 29 October 1868, in a ceremony witnessed by Collins and his doctor Frank Beard. Martha gave birth to Collins's first child, Marian, at Bolsover Street in July 1869, and a second daughter, Harriet, was born in May 1871. Three and a half years later Martha gave birth to a son, William Charles on Christmas Day 1874. This third child was the only one of the Collins children whose birth he formally registered (by 1874 this was a legal requirement), but Collins recognized all the children as his own, and provided for them with much the same care with which his own prudent father had provided for his legitimate family. Collins endowed his 'morganatic family' (as he described them to his friends the Lehmans) with a modicum of respectability by assuming the fictional identity of 'Mr William Dawson' at the addresses at which they lived, and by describing Martha as 'Mrs Dawson' and giving all of the children the surname of Dawson. Collins continued to support Martha financially throughout the rest of his life, and he made careful financial provision for her and all of their children in his will.

After Caroline's marriage to Clow, her daughter Carrie (by then aged 17) remained with Collins in his main household, and she stayed with him until her own marriage in 1878. Caroline left Clow after only two years of marriage and returned to live with Collins and her daughter. Thereafter Collins maintained two separate households, with Caroline acting as his housekeeper and continuing to entertain his friends at his 'official' irregular residence. He made regular visits to his other home which contained Martha and his children, but he did not entertain his friends there. As far as is known, Caroline and Martha did not meet, but the 'Dawson' children made frequent visits to the house Collins shared with Caroline, and they sometimes accompanied Caroline and Collins on holidays. Collins also took separate seaside holidays with his Dawson family.

One odd episode in the life of this multiply unmarried man, was the fictional marriage which he constructed in letters, written towards the end of his life, to Anne Elizabeth le Poer Wynne, or 'Nannie' Wynne as he called her. Nannie was the daughter of a member of the Indian Civil Service who had died of cholera when he was only 35 (and before his daughter's birth). Catherine Peters surmises that Collins probably met Nannie and her widowed mother in 1885 through his doctor Frank Beard, who was also doctor to the Wynnes. Collins's friendship with Nannie was conducted at luncheon parties and afternoon visits with the mother and daughter, and through a regular correspondence with Nannie. From June 1885, when she was only 12 years old, until February 1888 Collins wrote a series of letters to Nannie, addressing her as 'Dear and admirable Mrs Collins', 'Mrs Wilkie Collins', 'dearest Mrs', and 'carrissima sposa mea', and referring to her mother as 'my mother-in-law'. The letters are consistently playful in tone and on one occasion Collins makes encouraging comments about Nannie's own writing: 'I am proud of my wife. Her account of the earthquake is the best that I have read yet' (*Letters*, ii. 508). Some twenty-first-century readers of these letters might be perturbed by the thought of a 63-year-old man imagining a 14-year-old girl rushing into the street during the earthquake in question 'in the costume of a late queen of the Sandwich Islands—a hat and feathers and nothing else' (*Letters*, ii. 508), but on the whole the correspondence seems odd and whimsical rather than perverse. However, one cannot help but feel that Collins the iconoclast, the man who resolutely did not marry either of the women whom in the eyes of society he should have married, took great pleasure in constructing the fiction of a marriage with a girl (some fifty years his junior) whom it would have been entirely inappropriate for him to have married. For the most part, the letters seemed to serve as a means by which Collins could displace some of the anxieties about his work and health which troubled his later years, by parodying them and joking about them. Thus, he welcomes Nannie and her mother back from the holiday on which they have experienced the earthquake: 'Here we have had neuralgia in place of earthquake terrors—I have been taking forced holidays with my excellent friends Opium and Quinine until all my literary work has fallen into arrear—and now I am obliged to perform the detestable penance called "making up for lost time" ' (*Letters*, ii. 509).

The Pains of Literary Labour

Although he seems to have been a reasonably healthy child, Collins was plagued by illness and experienced increasing bodily discomfort throughout his adult years. From his late twenties he suffered from the painful symptoms of what he called 'rheumatic gout' and neuralgia, and he also suffered from increasingly acute inflammation of the eyes (which he wrongly attributed to gout). Some of Collins's health problems were possibly hereditary; Collins certainly thought that he had inherited some of his afflictions from his father, whose sufferings from violent rheumatic pains and inflammation of the eyes he described in the *Memoirs*. Others of Collins's problems were undoubtedly self-inflicted; he was a gourmand who over-indulged his appetite for rich food and good wine both at home and on his frequent trips to France. Quite often the excesses of his trips to France would incapacitate him; for example, in both 1855 and 1856 he was laid up with rheumatic pain when in Paris with Dickens. It has also been suggested that some of Collins's painful symptoms might be attributable to a venereal disease, perhaps contracted on one of his Haroun Alraschid expeditions with Dickens. Some of Collins's health problems were probably what we would now call stress-related. It is surely not entirely coincidental that his symptoms and sufferings should have worsened during the 1860s under the pressure of constantly writing to deadlines, nor that they should have been further aggravated by the need to keep the literary pot boiling in the 1870s and 1880s. Collins's working habits, like Dickens's, put a great strain on his health. His habit was to research and ruminate on a novel for a lengthy period, constructing a kind of mental scaffolding, before writing at some speed and under great pressure of the deadlines for serial publication. The physical and nervous symptoms produced by this process included palpitations, trembling, and depression as well as gout, neuralgia, and eye problems. These symptoms sometimes impeded the progress of a work. For example, the writing of *The Moonstone* was severely impeded by 'suffering . . . so great . . . that I could not control myself and keep quiet', he told William Winter. 'My cries and groans so distressed my amanuensis, to whom I was dictating, that he could not continue his work, and had to leave me . . . I was blind with pain, and I lay on the couch writhing and groaning'.[18] Carrie Graves often assisted Collins by acting as his amanuensis when his health deteriorated during the writing of a book. In later years, as his health deteriorated further, the completion of a book would sometimes lead to a total collapse. Thus in February 1883, after finishing *Heart and Science*, he informed Nina Lehman: 'For six months—while I was writing furiously, without cessation, one part sane and three parts mad—I had no gout. I finished my story, discovered one day that I was half dead with fatigue—and the next day the gout was in my right eye' (*Letters*, ii. 455).

During the 1860s, when Collins's health really began to plague him, he tried all manner of cures, including herbal remedies, visits to Continental health spas, Turkish baths, and electric baths. Another 'remedy' that he was prescribed in the early 1860s was to make Collins into a lifelong 'opium eater' through his addiction to laudanum. His friend and doctor, Frank Beard, first prescribed laudanum to relieve the painful symptoms of Collins's rheumatic gout in 1861. Laudanum was freely available (until 1868) and was the main ingredient of numerous patent medicines, such as 'Battley's Drops' which his father had taken during the illnesses of his final years. At first the laudanum prescribed by Beard relieved Collins's symptoms. However, he became increasingly dependent on it, needing larger and more frequent doses, until he was taking it in a dose large enough to have killed several ordinary people who had not developed Collins's tolerance for opium. In the early years of his dependency Collins tried to wean himself off the drug. In 1863 he tried to control

Wilkie Collins photographed for *Men of Mark*

the pain of his gout by substituting laudanum with a course of hypnosis with John Elliotson (described as 'one of the greatest of English physiologists' by another laudanum user, Ezra Jennings, in *The Moonstone*; see Chapter 6 below). In 1869 he tried replacing the laudanum with morphine injections, but again to no avail. No doubt some of Collins's palpitations and depressions of the 1870s and 1880s were due to his opium dependency. He also experienced hallucinations, and a sense of being haunted, and on some occasions he did not recognize as his own work the writing which he had done while in an opium trance. Several critics have attributed what they see as a decline in the quality of Collins's writing in the 1870s and 1880s to the effects of his opium addiction.

In 1868 Wilkie Collins was too ill to attend his mother's funeral, and from this point on his letters suggest that he was increasingly preoccupied with his own health and with mortality, as he records his physical and nervous afflictions and the deaths of friends. Dickens's very sudden death from a brain haemorrhage was one of the first of these losses, as Collins reported rather tersely in a letter to William Tindell: 'I finished "Man and Wife" yesterday—fell asleep from sheer fatigue—and was awakened to hear the news of Dickens's death' (*Letters*, ii. 341). By 1870 the two men were not as close as they had once been, separated, perhaps, by their divergent 'domestic' paths and perhaps also by the literary success which had taken Collins out of Dickens's shadow; nevertheless the loss to Collins was significant. Dickens's death was followed a couple of years later by the death of his son-in-law, Collins's younger brother Charles, on 9 April 1873. Edward Ward, whose secret marriage Collins had helped to arrange in the 1840s, committed suicide in 1879 during one of the depressions to which he was prone. Edward's brother Charles, Collins's companion on some of his early Paris trips and later on sailing holidays, died in 1883. Responding to yet another death in 1886 (that of his Australian representative Biers), Collins reported on his own health with a not entirely characteristic stoicism: 'As for my health, considering that I was 62 years old last birthday—that I have worked very hard as a writer—and that gout has tried to blind me first and kill me afterwards, on more than one occasion—I must not complain. Neuralgia, and nervous exhaustion generally, have sent me to the sea to be patched up' (*Letters*, ii. 523).

Debilitating though his health problems were, one must not exaggerate the gloominess of the last two decades of Collins's life. He continued to travel, emulating Dickens by undertaking an extensive reading tour of the United States in 1873–4 (although this was curtailed by health problems and by a domestic emergency at his 'family' home). He continued to enjoy sailing trips with his friends, to take seaside holidays with his various family groups, and to travel on the Continent (although such visits were often represented to his correspondents as primarily restorative). He continued to be very productive in terms of literary output, and to try new forms of publication, such as syndication with Tillotson's Fiction Bureau (see p. 78). He also enjoyed watching his children grow up, acting as 'grandfather' to Carrie's children, and making new friends, such as Nannie Wynne and her mother, the journalist Harry Quilter, and the novelist Hall Caine. Quilter, who started the *Universal Review* in 1888, persuaded Collins to write one of his few autobiographical pieces, 'Reminiscences of a Story-Teller' mentioned earlier.

Despite his illnesses, Collins retained his conviviality until the end of his life. It was when he was returning from a dinner given by Sebastian Schlesinger, an American whom he had met during his American tour in the early 1870s, that Collins had a lucky escape from death, when he was injured in a carriage accident. This accident occurred in January 1889, and 'gave . . . [him] a shake and stirred up the gout' (*Letters*, ii. 562). By March he was suffering from bronchitis and neuralgia, and envying the 'happy lot of the African savage, who lives under a nice warm sun' and has never heard of these conditions (*Letters*, ii. 562). He continued to work at his current serial, *Blind Love*, but in July he suffered a stroke, and despite the fact that at first he seemed to be making a good recovery from it, he arranged for Walter Besant—a fellow novelist and former colleague at *All the Year Round*—to complete it. A further attack of bronchitis followed the stroke and Collins died on 23 September 1889. He was buried at Kensal Green Cemetery, where at least a hundred mourners, some of them carrying copies of their favourite Collins novels, thronged round the steps of the church.[19] The chief mourners included Harriet Graves and Carrie. Martha Rudd and Collins's children did not attend the funeral, but the 'Dawson' family sent a large wreath.

CHAPTER 2

THE SOCIAL CONTEXT

WILKIE COLLINS was born in the fourth year of the reign of George IV (who had served as Prince Regent 1811–20), and he died two years after Queen Victoria's Golden Jubilee. He was born twelve years into Lord Liverpool's lengthy period as Tory Prime Minister, two years into Sir Robert Peel's period as Home Secretary, and five years after the disturbances at St Peter's Fields in Manchester (the Peterloo Massacre, 1819), when the Manchester Yeomanry and a regiment of the Hussars violently broke up a large gathering which had assembled to demand electoral reform. By Collins's fourth year the Duke of Wellington had become Tory Prime Minister and his government had succumbed to pressure from the opposition to repeal the Test and Corporation Acts which had prevented Catholics and Nonconformists from holding public office and serving on corporations, though it was many years before the Anglican monopoly on the Cabinet was broken. By Collins's fifth year Robert Peel and the Duke of Wellington had steered the Catholic Emancipation Act through both Houses of Parliament and Peel had established the Metropolitan Police Force (1829). Collins was 8 when the first Reform Act was passed in 1832; by the time he died the Third Reform Act (1884) had been passed, Gladstone had ended his second period as Liberal Prime Minister (1880–5), having resigned following the defeat of the 1885 Budget, the Irish Home Rule Bill had been introduced and defeated (1886), and organized Socialism was becoming an increasingly important part of the political scene (both the Social Democratic Foundation and the Fabian society were founded in 1884).

Collins's early years coincided with a period of political agitation and social reform (and resistance to reform), a period still haunted by the spectre of the French Revolution. They also coincided with revolutions of a different kind: the Industrial Revolution, the machine age, and the transformation of Britain (and especially England) from a predominantly rural, mercantile society to an entrepreneurial industrial society that was mainly urban in character. When Collins was born in 1824 (and even when Victoria ascended the throne in 1837), 'only a handful of British workers had ever seen the inside of a "dark satanic mill", the most numerous occupational groups were agricultural labourers and domestic servants', and 50 per cent of the British population lived in rural conditions.[1] By 1885 over one million people were employed in factories, compared with the approximately 355,000 thus employed in 1835, and the population of the great towns and cities of Britain had multiplied several times over: the population of London (then the largest city in the western world) grew from 1,600,000 in 1821 to 4,770,000 in 1881, while in the same period Birmingham grew from 102,000 to 546,000, Bradford from 26,000 to 183,000, Cardiff from 4,000 to 83,000, Glasgow from 147,000 to 653,000, and Manchester from 135,000 to 502,000.

Another revolution which occurred in Collins's lifetime was the revolution in transport. Collins was born at the dawn of the railway age, the age of the 'iron horse' and of the coming-of-age of steam power. Although railways had existed in England since the seventeenth century they had been horse-drawn or, more latterly, cable railways powered by static track-side engines. The real railway revolution came with the advent of steam traction, and the transporting of people as well as coal and goods. In the year after Collins's birth the Stockton–Darlington Railway, the first railway line to carry passengers, was opened (September 1825). This was followed by the Manchester–Liverpool line in 1830. By the time Collins died, in 1889, Britain had a comprehensive railway system (indeed, the main railway lines of England were all completed or planned by 1852), and London had the beginnings of the modern tube system (the Inner Circle Underground Line had been completed in 1884). The railways transformed the landscape and townscape of Britain, with cuttings, embankments, viaducts, and bridges, signal boxes, linesmen's huts, and stations—from the rural halt to the magnificent Gothic edifices of the great metropolitan and city termini. Railways made the island of Britain seem a smaller place, by shrinking journey times and speeding up communications (as letters passed at great speed along railway lines from one end of the land to the other). Railways thus transformed the pace of life and the pursuit of work and leisure. They enabled the better-off to put a greater distance between their place of work and their home (opening up new and successive phases of suburbanization). Rail links to seaports brought Continental Europe ever closer for the businessman, or for those, like Collins, who liked to make regular pleasure trips to the French coast or to Paris. Cheap railway travel also increased the mobility of the less-well-off sections of the community, enabling working people from all over England to travel to the Great Exhibition held in London in 1851, the London International Exhibition of 1862, and other exhibitions in London and elsewhere. Cheap railway travel also enabled the inhabitants of industrial towns and cities to take pleasure excursions to the seaside or countryside—at first simply for the day, but as prosperity increased for longer periods.

What kind of world did Wilkie Collins live in and write about? What kind of society formed this writer and the fiction that he wrote? An incantation uttered by Solomon Gills in Dickens's novel *Dombey and Son* (1846–8) gives us one perspective on the early Victorian years in which Collins came of age: 'competition, competition—new invention, new invention—alteration, alteration' (*Dombey and Son*, Chapter 4). Alteration, invention, and competition: these are indeed Victorian keywords, and they convey a sense of the excitement and energy, as well as the uncertainty and sense of instability experienced by those who lived through this period of rapid social, political, and intellectual change. Change was the order of the day: changes in geography and demography as the landscape and townscape of Britain were transformed by the building of railways, changing patterns of agriculture, the building or enlarging of factories and warehouses, and the development of towns and cities in which to house, feed, clothe, and entertain the 'hands' who worked in them. There were changes, too, in the composition of the social groups or classes that made up British society and changes in the relations between these groups and classes. If there were changes in the nature of the social family there were also changes in the family as a social unit, and in particular in the roles of its male and female members and in the relations between men and women more generally.

Alteration, for good and ill, was one of the themes of Thomas Carlyle's essay, 'Signs of the Times', published in 1829, just five years after Collins's birth:

What wonderful accessions have thus been made, and are still making, to the physical power of mankind; how much better fed, clothed, lodged and, in all outward respects, accommodated men now are, or might be, by a given quantity of labour, is a grateful reflection which forces itself on everyone. What changes too, this addition of power is introducing into the social system; how wealth has more and more increased, and at the same time gathered itself more and more into masses, strangely altering the old relations, and increasing the distance between rich and poor.[2]

In addition to the widening of the gulf between the rich and the poor, the most profound changes noted by Carlyle in this essay are the increasing mechanization of society. He writes vividly of the way in which steam power and machinery and a mechanistic conception of economics worked together to reduce workers into mere 'hands', he laments the growing tendency for the hearts and minds of human beings to become mechanical, and he deplores the rise of materialism, the loss of spirituality, and the erosion of traditional shared beliefs about the meaning of life.

Edward Bulwer Lytton, writing seven years after Collins's birth, in the wake of the First Reform Act and some four years before Victoria succeeded to the throne, focused on the discomforting disorientation of living in an age of fundamental change, or, as he put it, 'visible transition':

We live in an age of *visible transition*—an age of *disquietude and doubt*—of the removal of timeworn landmarks, and the *breaking up of the hereditary elements of society*—old opinions, feelings—*ancestral customs and institutions are crumbling away*, and both the spiritual and temporal worlds are darkened by the shadows of change. The commencement of one of these epochs—periodical in the history of mankind—is hailed by the sanguine as the coming of a new Millennium—a great iconoclastic reformation, by which all false gods shall be overthrown. To me such epochs appear but as the *dark passages in the appointed progress of mankind*—the times of greatest unhappiness to our species—passages into which we have no reason to rejoice at our entrance, save from the hope of being sooner landed on the opposite side.[3]

A quarter of a century after the above passage was published, Dickens began *A Tale of Two Cities* (1859) with this sketch of the 'times':

It was the best of times, it was the worst of times, it was the age of wisdom, it was the age of foolishness, it was the epoch of belief, it was the epoch of incredulity, it was the season of Light, it was the season of Darkness, it was the spring of hope, it was the winter of despair, we had everything before us, we had nothing before us, we were all going direct to Heaven, we were all going direct the other way—in short, the period was so far like the present period, that some of its noisiest authorities insisted on its being received, for good or for evil, in the superlative degree of comparison only. (*A Tale of Two Cities*, Book the First, Chapter I)

Of course, the best and worst of times about which Dickens is writing here are the years leading up to and including the French Revolution. However, as the reference to 'the present period' indicates, this wonderful evocation of the heady mixture of optimism and terror which characterized the revolutionary period at the turn of the eighteenth and nineteenth centuries serves equally well as a characterization of the contrasts and contradictions of nineteenth-century—and especially of Victorian—Britain. It also serves to remind us of the continuing power of the French Revolution and the spectre of revolution generally in the nineteenth-century cultural imagination.

The years in which Collins grew up and began his writing career were years of great prosperity, in which Britain became the workshop of the world. However, they were also years of fluctuating economic conditions, of boom and depression, years which saw great rural and urban poverty as well as lengthy periods of high wages and social improvement. These were years when, according to many commentators, Britain was not one, but two nations—the rich and the poor. Collins lived his adult life in the age of the great Victorian cities. Manchester, Birmingham, Leeds, Liverpool, and, of course Collins's home city London, all expanded rapidly during the author's lifetime, and in the 1860s, 1870s, and 1880s their improved sanitation and housing and their splendid Greek, Gothic, or Italianate town halls, banks, art galleries, and libraries and their public parks and gardens were evidence of—and became monuments to— industrial and entrepreneurial wealth and civic pride. The Victorian age was an age of progress and reform, an age of improvement which was also experienced as the 'crumbling away', or violent destruction of ancient customs and institutions. It was an age of science and materialism, which also saw a growth of interest in mysticism and the occult. It was the age of piety and public professions of faith, and a flurry of church and chapel building, but it was also the age of Darwin, doubt, and falling church and chapel attendance. It was an age of 'self-help', of societies for the propagation of useful knowledge (Samuel Smiles's *Self-Help* was published in 1859), but it was also an age of self-destructive competitive individualism. It was the great age of the family, but one in which both individual families and the institution of the family became sites of conflict and contestation.

Protest and Reform

Has anybody told you that 'The Jubilee' was an outburst of Loyalty? I tell you that it was an outburst of Fear and Cant. In my neighbourhood, there was a report that we should have our windows broken if we did not illuminate. In the year 1832, when I was eight years old, my poor father was informed that he would have *his* windows broken if he failed to illuminate in honour of the passing of the First Reform Bill . . . Before we went to bed the tramp of the people was heard in the street. They were marching six abreast (the people were in earnest in those days) provided with stones, and with their officers in command. They broke every pane of glass in an *un*illuminated house, nearly opposite our house, in less than a minute. I ran out to see the fun, and when the sovereign people cheered for the Reform Bill, I cheered too. Fifty five years later, I heard of the windows being in danger again, and illuminated again (on a cheap scale which accurately represented the shabby nature of my loyalty). This time, the people had no interest in the affair. . . . everywhere the people behaved well—and that was the one creditable circumstance in connection with the Jubilee. (*Letters*, ii. 541)

Collins lived in an age of protest and reform, an age of increasing democracy in which 'the people' (referred to in this letter), were becoming more visible and vociferous. He published his first book—the *Memoirs of the Life of William Collins, Esq., RA*—in 1848, the year of revolutions in Europe. By the 1870s he was questioning whether 'in these times of fierce political contention, and absorbing political anxiety', his efforts could be considered 'important enough to waken the attention, or even to amuse the leisure of others' (*Letters*, ii. 337). In the section of the *Memoirs* which refers to the early 1830s, Collins notes the effect of the outbreak of the cholera and 'the Reform Bill agitation' on the patrons of the arts:

those momentous public occurrences . . . produced that long and serious depression in the patronage and appreciation of Art which social and political convulsions must necessarily exercise on the intellectual luxuries of the age. The noble and the wealthy . . . believing that their possessions were threatened by a popular revolution, which was to sink the rights of station and property in a general deluge of republican equality, had little time, while engrossed in watching the perilous events of the day, to attend to the remoter importance of the progress of national Art. . . . there were not wanting many to predict, from the aspect of the times, the downfall of all honourable and useful pursuits, the end of the aristocracy, and even the end of the world . . . (*Letters*, i. 345)

The process of electoral reform which was to find legislative expression in the Reform Acts of 1832, 1867, and 1884 had been debated since the mid-eighteenth-century. It had begun (slowly) in the 1820s with attempts to rectify some of the worst excesses of electoral corruption (where the outcomes of elections for over-represented 'rotten boroughs' or 'pocket boroughs' were determined by bribery or controlled by an aristocratic patron), and it became an important focus of social and parliamentary debate and various forms of extra-parliamentary activism in response to the growing outrage at both the continued exclusion of the majority of the population from the electoral process and the inequitable distribution of parliamentary seats. The composition of the electorate, like the distribution of parliamentary seats, had remained more or less unchanged since the eighteenth century. However, the social composition of Britain and the distribution of its population had changed considerably since this time, and was in the process of further rapid change in the years of Collins's boyhood and youth (as, indeed, it was throughout his life). In 1830 Birmingham, Manchester, and Leeds had no separate parliamentary representation, and the only influence that these rapidly expanding towns could exert on the composition on the House of Commons was through the role played by some of their citizens as County Electors, or by getting themselves represented for closed or rotten boroughs—a process known as virtual representation. Agitation for change by the new industrialists and middle-class radicals throughout the 1820s, and by the rural population (the so-called Swing riots) in the early 1830s were met by an increasing willingness by the Whig government to effect a measure of parliamentary reform—on both philosophical and pragmatic grounds.

Achieved after much debate, much marching and demonstrating (some of which was witnessed by an excited 8-year-old Collins, as he recalled in the letter quoted at the head of this section), and a general election in which reform was the central issue, the First Reform Act redistributed 143 parliamentary seats from relatively unpopulated rural areas of the south and west of England to the increasingly populous and urban areas of the midlands and north. After the 1832 Act, Birmingham, Leeds, Manchester, Sheffield, Bolton, and Oldham all had an MP for the first time. Nevertheless, over fifty 'pocket boroughs' survived the redistribution exercise, leaving a particular member of the local gentry with the power to nominate the MP. The 1832 Act widened the electorate from about 515,000 to 813,000 from a total population of about 24 million. However, this was far from being democratic: women were still excluded from the electorate (and remained so until the 1918 Representation of the People Acts gave the vote to women over 30), and the right to vote was still dependent on a property qualification (for example, the ownership or occupancy of property of a certain rental value, or the leasing of a particular piece of land for several generations). One important change sought by reformers, the introduction of a secret ballot, was not included in the 1832 Act, and consequently the electoral process remained subject to open bribery and corruption as well as the more subtle forms of influence and pressure that the powerful could bring to bear on voters in their constituencies (see Dickens's chapters on the Eatanswill election in *Pickwick Papers*).

Successive Reform Acts in 1867, 1884, and 1885 led to further redistribution of seats (1867 and 1885) and to changes in the size and composition of the electorate. The electoral reform movement gained fresh impetus in the early 1860s from the activities of trade unions, middle-class radicals advocating the democratic systems of the United States, Canada, and Australia, and the example of European democratic and socialist movements—some of whose adherents had been living as exiles and émigrés in London since 1848, the year of a series of attempted revolutions throughout Europe. The 1867 Act virtually doubled the electorate from 1.36 million to 2.46 million, most of the new voters being town-dwelling industrial workers: an electoral leap in the dark which Thomas Carlyle likened to 'shooting Niagara'. In the boroughs there was something approaching dem-ocracy (at least for men), but in the counties the property or tenancy requirements prevented most agricultural workers and miners in rural pit villages from obtaining a vote. Moreover, the 1867 elections remained 'the pre-engaged servant of the long purse', like the law in *The Woman in White*, as the lack of a secret ballot meant that voters remained open to bribery and the newly enfranchised industrial workers in the boroughs were susceptible to the influence (or pressure) of their bosses or landlords. The parliamentary map and the composition of the polity were further modified in Collins's declining years: the Parliamentary Reform Act of 1884 again doubled the electorate, although even as late as 1917 about 50 per cent of the male population still could not vote (for example, adult sons living in the parental home did not qualify for the vote).

The modest measure of electoral reform achieved in 1832 did not deliver a new polity or a new political class. The Whig government that emerged from the parliament elected by the reformed system in December 1832 was still made up of wealthy aristocrats, most of whom felt that they had done enough for the reform movement by passing the 1832 Act. Nevertheless the post-Reform Act parliament responded to pressure for social reforms from Benthamite Radicals, evangelicals, and progressive factory owners and made the 1830s a reforming decade, and the harbinger of a reforming era (or age of 'improvement'). In 1833, after much opposition from the owners of West Indian sugar plantations and those involved in the sugar trade (whose number included many MPs), the Whigs passed an Act to abolish slavery in the British Empire. In the same year, again after much opposition, parliament passed a Factory Act which sought to regulate and improve the conditions of employment in textile mills. A Factory Inspectorate was established to monitor compliance with the Act, which banned the employment of children under 9, restricted the hours of employment of children and young people, and introduced an element of compulsory education for factory children (two hours per day for those between 9 and 13). The improvement and regulation of working conditions in factories and mines continued to occupy trade unions, humanitarian and evangelical reformers (including some factory owners and MPs) throughout Collins's lifetime—such improvements also continued to be resisted by others who saw nothing wrong with the way things were, and were afraid that improvements in the conditions of the labouring classes would mean a reduction of their own power and comforts. Further Factory Acts in 1844, 1847 (introducing the ten-hour day), 1850, 1874, and 1878 sought to regulate (and restrict) the employment of children and women, and to reduce the working hours of all factory workers. The Mines Act of 1842 extended to the mining industry the ethos of the early Factory Acts concerning the employment of women and children, and subsequent Acts in 1850, 1860, and 1887 sought to improve safety and regulate and monitor working conditions through a Mines Inspectorate.

Another reforming act from the 1830s which paved the way for subsequent social and health reforms was the Municipal Corporations Act of 1835, which began the process of making local government more democratic by establishing borough councils whose members were elected for three-year periods by male ratepayers. The Act also began the professionalization of local government by requiring all councils to have a paid town clerk and treasurer, to form a police force, and to have properly audited accounts. It also permitted (though it did not require) councils to undertake social improvements such as improved drainage and street-cleaning. A common theme of the reforms of the 1830s, which was to reverberate throughout Collins's lifetime, was social improvement through investigation, regulation, and monitoring. Collins lived in an age of Parliamentary Blue Books, Royal Commissions, and a proliferation of inspectorates (for factories, mines, education, public health, etc.). The age of reform was also an age of measuring and recording. In 1836 the Births and Deaths Registration Act made the civil registration of births and deaths compulsory, a development which at once contributed to Collins's preoccupation with modern legal identities and provided him with many narrative opportunities.

One 'reform' of the 1830s that brought about a very dubious improvement was the Poor Law Amendment Act of 1834. The existing Poor Law (as it had been operated since 1795) was extremely unpopular, because the system of 'outdoor relief' (known as the Speenhamland system after the place in which it had first been used) had the effect of encouraging farmers to reduce the wages of their labourers in the knowledge that they would be supplemented by 'poor relief' which was a charge on an increasingly resentful community of ratepayers. In February 1832 a Commission was appointed to look into the system of providing poor relief. The resulting legislation was extremely successful in providing relief for ratepayers, as the new system was much cheaper. However, it did not relieve poverty, indeed it increased poverty among the rural poor and it increased social tension in the industrial north in the trade recession of the late 1830s. The failings of the Poor Law Amendment Act of 1834 and of the Reform Act of 1832 were instrumental in providing support for popular protest movements in the 1830s, particularly the Chartist movement.

Chartism belongs to the period which Collins retrospectively labelled as the days in which 'the people were in earnest', and, as I have already indicated, it was at the forefront of public attention in 1848, the year in which Collins published his first book. This was not only the year of the climax of Chartist activities, but it was also the year of revolutions in Europe, and the year in which the pivotal events of *The Moonstone* occur. Thomas Carlyle, who belonged to an older generation of writers although he died only four years before Collins, described Chartism as 'the bitter discontent grown fierce and mad, the wrong condition therefore or the wrong disposition of the Working Classes of England'.[4] The 'bitter discontent' of the working classes grew fiercer and madder as a result of poor economic conditions (which were exacerbated by the 1834 Poor Law and by the depression of trade in the late 1830s), difficult working conditions, poor living conditions, and a lack of political power. From this mass of frustrations the London Working Men's Association was formed in 1837 and its leaders drew up the 'Charter' which gave the movement its name. By 1838 there were over a hundred branches campaigning for the 'six points' contained in the Charter. The six points aimed at a radical change in the social order via a parliamentary democracy in which (to adapt the words of Chartist activist, Bronterre O'Brien), working men would be at the top instead of at the bottom of society, or else there would be a new kind of society in which there would be no top or bottom. The six points demanded by the Chartists were: a vote for every man over 21; a secret ballot; the abolition of the property qualification for parliamentary candidates; equal electoral districts (i.e. all MPs should represent approximately the same number of voters); the payment of MPs; annual elections. Various branches made their own additions to the six points, for example, the abolition of the tax on newspapers, the repeal of the new Poor Law Act, an eight-hour day for factory workers, the abolition of child labour, and 'the establishment of general happiness'.

In February 1839 a National Chartist Convention drew up a petition containing some one and a quarter million signatures which was taken to the House of Commons and presented to parliament, where it was rejected by a huge majority. Strikes, protest meetings, and rioting followed this rebuff, and several Chartist leaders were imprisoned and in two cases transported. Three years later (1842) another National Convention met and collected three and a quarter million signatures for a second petition. This petition was escorted to parliament by a hundred thousand people and presented by sympathetic MPs, and again it was rejected by a huge majority. Once more there were strikes and rioting—this time accompanied by looting and the death of several policemen in Manchester. In 1848, spurred on by the news of the successful uprising in Paris, another National Convention was organized and a third Charter was drawn up, to be presented to parliament following a rally on Kennington Common. There was talk of revolutionary consequences if the Charter were to be rejected, and, perhaps mindful of recent events in France, the Whig government banned the march on parliament and large numbers of troops and special constables were posted around London. A mere handful of violent incidents—not the revolution which had been threatened—followed the rejection of the Charter.

The Chartist movement had begun to dissipate by the time Collins reached his mid-twenties, but the Chartist agenda did not disappear. Political unrest and the threat (perhaps more than the reality) of political violence were key features of the period between Collins's eighth and twenty-fourth years, and they continued to resurface throughout his lifetime. Although Collins inhabited a different world from the one in which industrial disturbances and election riots of the 1850s and 1860s occurred, political unrest and the power of the 'mob' did make an impact on well-to-do Londoners, even bohemian Londoners such as Collins and his circle. Collins was already working with Dickens at *Household Words* when the older writer visited Preston to report on the conditions and activities of striking workers in February 1854. In the following year the peace of Hyde Park (in the heart of fashionable London) was disturbed by rioters protesting against the ban on Sunday trading. There were further Hyde Park riots in 1862 and again in 1866 in support of the Second Reform Bill. Whether in the streets, around dinner tables, or in the pages of the newspaper and periodical press, debates about power—its use and abuse, where it resides and who should exercise it—were waged throughout Collins's life. Throughout this period, too, the press was full of articles engaging in or reporting the investigation and exposure of social evils of various kinds, making suggestions for their reform, or, conversely, denying their existence.

Collins himself was associated with reforming journalism through his work for the liberal weekly paper, the *Leader*, in the early 1850s and subsequently for Dickens's *Household Words* and, in the early 1860s, for *All the Year Round*. The *Leader* was founded by Thornton Hunt and George Henry Lewes in 1850, and its main interests were politics and economics (domestic and international) and the metropolitan literary and artistic world. It stood, in the main, for political and social reform (especially labour reform) and championed the causes of the lower and middle classes. Collins became involved with the paper in late 1851 when his friend Edward Pigott purchased the paper and took over its general editorial policy. In 1852 Hunt reassured readers that the new owner would not change the paper's politics and that he and Lewes would continue to argue for 'national franchise' and 'the right of labour to reproductive employment'.[5] Collins's main contributions to the *Leader* were reviews of books, plays, and exhibitions, but he also contributed to the 'Portfolio' section, which consisted of essays, poems, and serialized stories. One of his first 'Portfolio' pieces was 'A Plea for Sunday Reform', which argued against the restrictions of the English Sunday about which the Hyde Park demonstrators were to protest in 1855 (27 September 1851). Certainly in his twenties Collins shared the *Leader*'s reforming agenda, declaring himself in agreement with the paper's 'confession of political faith', and a supporter of its 'Red Republicanism'.[6]

Women, the Law, and Law Reform

In January 1852 Collins wrote to his friend Edward Pigott offering advice on the content and organization of the *Leader*. One subject which Collins was particularly anxious for the *Leader* to engage with was the law:

I should like to see Law [doubly underlined] made another division, and more attended to in the Leader. Abstracts of the results of the week's 'cases', both civil and criminal, are wanted—They might be the merest abstracts, and still be of use . . . And *legal anomalies and corruptions might be thoroughly* [*lashed*] from time to time, in leading articles—*Legal abuse* is a subject on which even your mild Protestant 'Church and State' man, can

feel and talk furiously. King Public would go with us with all his heart and
soul, quote us, praise us, learn us by heart, on such a subject as *Law
Reform*, I find no articles in the Times and the Examiner so highly praised
by all parties, and so constantly reproduced second hand in conversation
as the Law articles. Let us then . . . as opportunity offers, politely d——m
Magistrates, and spit in the face of Juries. A birch-rod for the backside of
old Mother 'Justice', is a weapon for which people are beginning to feel
a household sympathy. Lay it on, Mr Editor! Lay it on thick! (*Letters*, i.
79–80, emphasis added)

The 'antiquated and chaotic'[7] state of English law was the cause of
much debate and reforming activity throughout the nineteenth century, and, as readers of Collins soon discover, the unreformed legal
system provided a broad target for the novelist's satiric arrow, and
rich pickings for the fiction writer in search of plot situations and
complications. *The Woman in White* and *No Name* are excellent
examples of this, as are the later, more self-consciously reforming
novels-with-a purpose, *The Law and the Lady* and *Man and Wife*.
During the course of Collins's lifetime, legal reforms made the criminal law more humane, simplified the law of real property, laid the
foundations of modern company law, and, in the great Judicature
Act of 1873, simplified the chaotic system of courts each with its
own separate procedures and bodies of law, into one Supreme Court
of Judicature.[8]

The legal abuses and law reforms which are particularly important
for the reader of Collins's fiction are those concerned with the family,
marriage, and relations between the sexes. This area of the law,
particularly the laws relating to the property rights of married
women and broader issues relating to women's legal position
within marriage—including their freedom to end an unsatisfactory
marriage—was also the subject of close scrutiny and reforming activism by feminist campaigners. One landmark in the history of feminist campaigns was Barbara Leigh Smith's (later Bodichon) *A Brief
Summary, in Plain Language, of the Most Important Laws Concerning
Women, Together With a Few Observations Thereon* (1854). The single
most important aspect of the laws concerning women was the
distinction in the legal status of the married woman as opposed to
her unmarried counterpart. A single woman had the same rights to
property and to the same legal protection as a man, and she could
also act as a trustee, be an executrix for a will, or an administratrix of

the personal property of her deceased next of kin. However, in common law a married woman had no legal identity separate from her husband, and for much of the nineteenth century the married woman's legal situation remained much as it was when it was memorably summarized by Leigh Smith: 'A man and wife are one person in law: the wife loses all her rights as a single woman, and her existence is entirely absorbed in that of her husband. He is civilly responsible for her acts; she lives under his protection or cover, and her condition is called coverture.'[9] As far as property was concerned the practice of coverture meant that, upon marriage, the legal possession or control of any property owned by a woman, or inherited by her during her marriage, passed to her husband. The exact nature and degree of the husband's control depended on the nature of his wife's property. Common law distinguished between 'real' and 'personal' property: real property—property in freehold land and any income arising from it—was controlled by the husband during marriage, but he could not dispose of his wife's real property (during her lifetime) without her consent which had to be recorded in court. A woman's personal property—that is property in leasehold land, or goods and chattels—passed into the absolute control of her husband upon marriage for him to use and dispose of as he wished during his lifetime and (through his will) after his death. The Caroline Norton case, which resulted in the Infant Custody Bill of 1849, gave a divorced or separated wife limited rights to the custody of infants and children under 7 years of age, but until the passing of the 1886 Custody of Infants Act a husband was considered in law to be the sole parent of his legitimate children.

By the nineteenth century the custom and practice of equity, which had grown up alongside the common law, recognized the separate legal existence or identity of a wife, and her right to own property independently of her husband. Equity operated on the principle that although a wife could not, in common law, control property, it could be controlled on her behalf by a trustee. Hence the system of marriage settlements or pre-nuptial agreements according to which a woman's family or friends, or even the woman herself, could designate certain property as her 'separate property', free from her husband's common law rights. However, if no trustee was appointed to carry out the terms of the settlement, the Courts of Equity named the husband as trustee. Equity law gave a woman rights over her property but, like the common law, it gave her no responsibilities: A wife with a 'separate property' in equity (exactly as in common law) was not liable for her own debts, nor was she legally liable to provide any support for her children or husband. In short, the law disempowered and infantilized women, placing them in the same category as criminals, idiots, and minors, to use the phrase employed by Frances Power Cobbe in her *Fraser's Magazine* article in 1868 on the need for the reform of the law affecting women's property rights: 'Criminals, Idiots, Women and Minors: Is the Classification Sound?'

The campaigning activities of Caroline Norton in the 1830s and 1840s, Barbara Leigh Smith in the 1850s, Frances Power Cobbe in the 1850s, and others throughout the period, led to a number of improvements in the law affecting the property rights of married women, their rights over their own bodies, and their ability to divorce, and to have custody of their children. Such improvements included the Custody of Infants Acts already referred to, the Married Women's Property Acts of 1870 and 1882, and the Divorce Act of 1857, the Matrimonial Causes Amendment Act of 1859, and the Matrimonial Causes Acts of 1878 and 1884. Before 1857 the only way in which a wife could extricate herself from a marriage was by an annulment in the ecclesiastical courts or by private Act of Parliament. The 1857 Divorce Act enabled a woman to divorce her husband through the civil courts, but only on the grounds of aggravated adultery—that is if he were physically cruel or guilty of incest or bestiality as well as being adulterous. The Matrimonial Causes Acts of 1878 and 1884 were designed to restrict a husband's ability to treat his wife's body as his legal property which he was free to incarcerate, beat, or exercise his 'conjugal rights' on as he wished.

The sexual subordination of women and their rights to resist the invasive appropriation or examination of their bodies was also an important feature of the vociferous campaign to repeal the Contagious Diseases Acts which were passed in 1864, 1866, and 1869 in an attempt to reduce the number of prostitutes (by rescuing them from their trade) and to curtail the spread of venereal diseases among soldiers and sailors. These Acts permitted the authorities to submit any woman suspected of being a prostitute to an invasive medical examination, and, if she were found to have a sexually transmitted disease, to commit her to a 'Lock Hospital' for the duration of her treatment and cure—preferably from both the disease and the condition into which she had fallen.

The legal rights and restrictions of women were kept in the public consciousness or—perhaps more accurately—deeply embedded in its political unconscious, in press debates about the reform campaigns mentioned above, and in newspaper reports of the proceedings of the divorce courts set up as a result of the Act of 1857. Fiction, too, played its part in this process. The legal vulnerability of women, and their position as objects of exchange between men were already staples of the Gothic plot when Collins began writing, and partly as a result of his efforts they became central to the plots of sensation novels in the 1860s. Moreover, the laws of inheritance, the economic and legal complexities of marriage, and women's status as marriageable objects were the founding conditions of domestic fiction from the late eighteenth century onwards.

The feminist-inspired focus on women's legal position not only had the effect of removing some of their legal disabilities, but it also put male conduct under the spotlight. From the 1840s onwards male domestic violence was added to the raft of social problems which was preoccupying social reformers and campaigning journalists. John Stuart Mill and Harriet Taylor wrote a series of letters to the *Morning Chronicle* in 1850 and 1851 deploring the light sentences given to wife-beaters and castigating parliament for its unwillingness to address the matter by drafting new laws. By the 1860s, as Martin J. Wiener has noted, 'this new sensitivity to domestic violence had clearly penetrated the criminal justice system' and 'the professional men who increasingly made up the judicial bench . . . began to press juries to crack down on violent husbands'.[10] However, juries proved resistant to the pressure of the judiciary, and continued to be sympathetic to male defendants accused of domestic violence. In 1878, after reading in the newspaper 'a whole series of frightful cases of this kind',[11] Frances Power Cobbe took up the cause and wrote an article for the *Contemporary Review* on 'Wife-torture in England', which helped in the enactment of the 1878 Matrimonial Causes Bill.

Crime, Criminality, and Policing

In several of his novels Collins was concerned with the chaotic state of the law and its barbarousness (see Chapter 4). However, in the first half of the nineteenth century most members of the middle and upper classes were more concerned with the barbarity of criminals and the threat of social chaos that they posed. Collins grew up at a time when there was a growing alarm about a perceived rise in crime, particularly of violent crime, which was seen as a sign of both moral decay and social disorder. The growth of the industrial towns with their factories in which men and women worked promiscuously together, and their growing street and pub cultures led to a concern with disorderly conduct, drunkenness, and prostitution. Added to this, the fear of working-class violence, as seen in strikes, Swing riots, and Chartist activism, combined to produce a spectre of savagery to haunt the middle and upper classes, many of whom feared that the barbarians were at the gates of society, and that the social order was threatened by the dangerous and criminal classes. For much of the first half of the nineteenth century criminality was associated with the unleashing of unrestrained passions; it was considered to be a form of moral insanity. The domestic ideal and contemporary ideas about gender (see below) played an important part in the construction of criminality: lower-class women were thought to be more vulnerable than their male counterparts to the degrading and demoralizing effects of modern urban conditions.

The discourse on criminality, and debates about how to eliminate it or mitigate its effects, were informed by the concepts of self-management and self-discipline. However, the pervasive fear of the absence of self-management was one of the factors that led to the rise of policing during the second quarter of the century. Peel's Metropolitan Police Act (1829) established a professional police force for London, and the Municipal Corporations Act (1835) required the Corporations to establish their own police forces, each controlled by a watch committee. The Rural Constabulary Act (1839) and the County and Borough Police Act (1856) extended the creation of local police forces and the latter established an inspectorate to oversee their activities. Attempts to discipline the criminal population by a growing network of police forces were matched by attempts to build a more disciplined and professional police force. Both the conceptualization of criminality and the policing of it were based on ideas of 'public character building'.[12] The police were to be made more professional and respectable in order to enforce middle-class standards of respectability on the lower, criminal classes. On the other hand both the police and the criminal classes were to be brought within middle-class conceptions of self-discipline. By the 1860s, as Martin Wiener points out, the law 'was being employed with increasing consistency as an instrument for developing self-disciplining and gratification-deferring personalities in the population at large. To counter the crime wave and immorality wave of the first half of the century stood a newly character-building law.'[13]

By the 1860s the fear of the mob and of violent crime and casual crime began to diminish, as more effective policing enforced self-restraint if 'character building' was failing to do its work. Improved economic conditions may also have contributed to an actual reduction of crime. At mid-century, attention began to shift from working-class to middle-class conduct and crime. A whole new category of 'white-collar' crime arose from infringements of the new laws relating to employment and to health and safety at work (see above). Railway mania and other frenzied episodes of financial speculation in the 1840s and 1850s had turned the spotlight on fraud and financial misconduct. The law was increasingly being used to regulate private as well as public financial dealings through new forms of contracts and wills. The private lives of the middle and upper classes were also subjected to public and legal scrutiny through the divorce courts, which established standards of marital conduct. All of these factors meant that from the 1860s the attention of the middle classes turned away 'from the streets to the home, from the public house to the counting house, and in general from the unruly populace to persons of apparent respectability'.[14] Indeed, whereas in the first half of the century criminality was regarded as antithetical to respectability, some of the new crimes which seized public attention in the 1860s— such as fraud, embezzlement, poisoning, blackmail—actually depended on the appearance of respectability. The sensation novel of the 1860s was one expression of and response to this development.

Crime became increasingly associated with professional criminality in all sorts of ways in the second half of the nineteenth century. Not only were the professional classes becoming implicated in criminality through a whole new series of laws, but there was also a widespread perception that felons were becoming more professional. This professionalization of crime was accompanied by (indeed, perhaps, to some extent produced by) the increasing professionalization of policing. By the time that Collins created his own professional policeman, Sergeant Cuff in *The Moonstone*, his friend Dickens had already brought the new detective force to public attention in a series of articles in *Household Words* in 1850 and 1851. In the first of these essays 'Detective Police' (*Household Words*, 27 July 1850), Dickens draws a comparison between the policeman of the bad old days of the Bow Street Runners (who were allowed to stay outside Peel's new unified Metropolitan Police force in 1829) and the new detective force which had been established in London in 1842:

We are not by any means devout believers in the old Bow Street Police. To say the truth, we think there was a vast amount of humbug about those worthies. Apart from many of them being men of very indifferent character, and far too much in the habit of consorting with thieves and the like, they never lost a public occasion of jobbing and trading in mystery and making the most of themselves. . . . [A]s a Preventive Police they were utterly ineffective, and as a Detective Police were very loose and uncertain in their operations . . .

On the other hand, the detective Force organised since the establishment of the existing Police, is so well chosen and trained, proceeds so systematically and quietly, does its business in such a workmanlike manner, and is always so calmly and steadily engaged in the service of the public, that the public really do not know enough of it, to know a tithe of its usefulness.[15]

In order to make the public better acquainted with the usefulness of the Detective Force Dickens introduces his readers to some of their number and reports on their exploits. Two things stand out. The first is Dickens's insistence on the respectable appearance of the officers; at least one of them might have been taken for a schoolteacher, and all of them are 'respectable-looking men; of perfectly good deportment and unusual intelligence'.[16] The second point of note is the way in which the officers explain their craft: they are professionals who have to outwit fellow professionals—the criminals who all have their own particular specialisms and whose activities they recount with a detail 'exact and statistical'.[17]

Another aspect of the professionalization of crime was the rise of a scientific discourse on crime and criminality. In the first half of the century the new science of statistics was used to map and measure criminal behaviour. At the same time, phrenology, a science which sought to understand the mental make-up of a human being through a study of the shape of the skull, was used to account for it physiologically. Criminal behaviour was also being explained in terms of economic conditions and social environment. 'Natural' (non-moral) explanations of criminality became more prominent in the second half of the century, as criminality became increasingly medicalized and psychologized. It was during the second half of the century that the notion of the physically or mentally degenerate and hereditary criminal type developed; the criminal was increasingly seen as someone who inherits a faulty mental or physical constitution and criminal propensities.

Gender and Sexuality

The campaigns about the legal disabilities of women, and the interventions of the law in the regulation of family life, discussed in the section on the law and reform above, were part of a wider response to women's demands for changes in their social and familial roles, demands which grew more forceful as the century wore on. They were also both symptomatic of and instrumental in the redefinition of gender roles that was occurring throughout Collins's lifetime. Many contemporary commentators saw women's desire for improvements in their civil rights, for increased educational and employment opportunities, and for a life that was not entirely defined in terms of obedient daughterhood or marriage, or wifehood and self-sacrificial motherhood, as a 'masculinization' of women. Paradoxically this so-called 'masculinization' occurred in a period seen by both nineteenth-century commentators and subsequent historians as one in which there was a widespread 'feminization' of middle-class society and culture.

By the 1850s, when a number of middle-class women had already begun their campaigns to change women's domestic roles and expand their opportunities, and when a growing number of working-class women had, for some years, been working outside the home in factories and workshops of various kinds, the feminized 'domestic ideal' was becoming increasingly firmly established in a range of social and cultural discourses and practices. At the heart of the domestic ideal was a moralized version of the home as a sacrosanct privatized space, as opposed to the public sphere of work, economics, and politics. The home of the domestic ideal was the repository of moral and spiritual values which were nurtured and, to some extent, policed by a particular version of feminine gentility embodied in the middle-class wife and mother, or the angel in the house.[18] One of the most forceful contemporary articulations of this ideal is found in John Ruskin's essay 'Of Queens' Gardens' in *Sesame and Lilies* (1865):

This is the true nature of home—it is the place of peace; the shelter, not only from all injury, but from all terror, doubt and division. In so far as it is not this, it is not home; so far as the anxieties of the outer life penetrate into it and the inconsistently-minded, unknown, unloved, or hostile society of the outer world is allowed by either husband or wife to cross the threshold it ceases to be a home; it is then only a part of the outer world which you have roofed over and lighted fire in. But so far as it is a sacred place, a vestal temple, a temple of the hearth watched over by household gods . . . so far it vindicates the name and fulfills the praise of home.

And wherever a true wife comes, this home is always round her . . . home is wherever she is; and for a noble woman it stretches far round her . . .[19]

The Ruskinian domestic ideal depends upon a theory of gender difference in which men and women are complementary opposites. According to this view, men and women 'are in nothing alike, and the happiness and perfection of both depends on each asking and receiving from the other what the other only can give'. Ruskin goes on to delineate the 'separate characters' of men and women:

The man's power is active, progressive, defensive. He is eminently the doer, the creator, the discoverer, the defender. His intellect is for speculation and invention; his energy for adventure, for war, for conquest. . . . But the woman's power is for rule, not for battle and her intellect is not for invention or recreation, but sweet ordering, arrangement and decision. She sees the qualities of things . . . Her great function is to praise. . . . By her office and place, she is protected from all danger and temptation. The man, in his rough work in the open world, must encounter all peril and trial—to him therefore must be the failure, the offence, the inevitable error; often he must be wounded or subdued, often misled, and always hardened.[20]

Both Collins's life and his fiction (in common with quite a lot of Victorian fiction) suggest that the Victorian home, family, and gender roles were rather more fluid and complex in practice than they were in this ideological inscription (and, to be fair, Ruskin does go on to complicate this version of the home, and to point out some of its limitations). In practice, real historical men and women lived their lives in a variety of ways. Nevertheless, the domestic ideal was a very powerful force in shaping nineteenth-century thinking about gender roles.

The concept of femininity at the heart of the domestic ideal was used as a way of keeping women in their place (see, for example, Collins's representation of Laura Fairlie in *The Woman in White*), but it was also a means of disciplining men and of shaping the culture more generally. Martin Wiener regards some of the developments in the civil and criminal law outlined in my earlier section on the law and law reform (and more particularly the contest between judges and juries on the sentences for crimes of domestic violence) as examples of the disciplining of men by the 'domestic ideal', and as part of a 'broader "feminization" of social standards': 'at the same time that women were being increasingly pressed to remain within the boundaries of the home,' he notes, 'men were more and more pressed to take on hitherto "feminine" characteristics.'[21] The same was true for women. They too were being increasingly pressed to take on the 'feminine' characteristics of the middle-class domestic ideal—through etiquette and conduct books and manuals of instruction, such as Sarah Stickney Ellis's *The Women of England*, *The Wives of England*, and *The Daughters of England* in the 1840s or Isabella Beeton's *Book of Household Management* (1867), and through novels and magazines, as well as through familial training. This middle-class version of femininity also exerted its influence on women in the classes above and below the class in which it was formed.

Advice books also played their part in the construction of Victorian masculinity. The 'domestic affections and domestic authority' pervaded the advice literature aimed at men for much of the Victorian period, and domesticity was regarded as 'central to masculinity' in an unprecedented way.[22] If the dominant image of respectable femininity (or the womanly woman) was that of the wife and mother, then the dominant image of respectable bourgeois masculinity was that of the husband and father, the head of the family and household. The cult of the home arose at a time when, for most men, the workplace and the home were becoming physically separate, and when the experience of work was becoming increasingly alienating as a result of industrial and economic developments—the growth of technology and increasing commercial competitiveness. The domestic sphere thus became not simply a place of mental and physical rest and recreation, but also a space whose creation justified men's efforts in the world of work and which restored them to themselves and made them fully human. As John Tosh has demonstrated, there was always a tension between domestic masculinity and two other important aspects of masculinity. The first of these was 'homosociality—or regular association with other men',[23] a form of male bonding which reinforced male power and privilege through the pursuit of extra-domestic pleasures or through networking and intervening in society by means of associations and committees. The second was 'heroism and adventure' which required quite different qualities from those needed 'to sustain the routines of production and reproduction'.[24]

One of the most important of the qualities needed to sustain the domestic ideal and the routines of production and reproduction was the ordering and regulation of emotion and passion, especially sexual passion. Self-control and self-restraint were the watchwords of both domestic man and woman. Victorian men and women were not universally the sexual prudes that they have sometimes been supposed to be. There is a great deal of documentary evidence to suggest that many Victorians lived very fulfilled sexual and emotional lives, though many aspects of contemporary religion and medical thought conspired to make some of their sexual pleasures guilty ones. Nevertheless, for most of the nineteenth century the only socially sanctioned form of sexuality was heterosexuality within marriage. Of course there were a great many other forms of sexual activity, and a great many private and collective fears and fantasies about sexuality. Many of these came together around the figure of the prostitute and the fallen woman.

If the maternal angel in the house was at the heart of the domestic ideal, paradoxically, so too was her opposite, the prostitute. In the imagination of respectable society the prostitute represented both female degradation (the antithesis of a femininity and womanliness defined in terms of middle-class respectability) and illicit and unbridled sexuality. A creature of the streets, who functioned (often precariously) outside the regulated sexual economy of marriage, the degraded prostitute was both a vindication of the domestic ideal and a threat to it. The prostitute was also a product of the domestic ideal. There is some evidence to suggest that in the 1850s and 1860s (when there was a great deal of campaigning against the 'social evil' of prostitution) men were postponing marriage in order to acquire the income and social position necessary to sustain the kind of establishment increasingly required by middle-class marriage. This phenomenon was referred to by W. R. Greg as the 'growing and morbid luxury' of genteel marriage in an essay on 'redundant woman' that he wrote for the *National Review* in 1862.[25] In the mean time they visited prostitutes, or, like Godfrey Ablewhite in *The Moonstone*, they kept mistresses.

Although not socially sanctioned, this latter practice was tacitly accepted, even by some of those who campaigned against prostitution and were involved in ventures to rescue 'unfortunates' or 'fallen women', as prostitutes were euphemistically known. Charles Dickens gave both time and money to such ventures, but it is quite likely that the 'Haroun Alraschid' expeditions that he undertook with Collins in the 1850s involved entertaining and being entertained by 'ladies of the night'. All this is evidence of the 'double standard' which viewed male licentiousness as an acceptable part of the experience of respectable men, but regarded illicit sexual activity on the part of women as placing them completely beyond the pale of respectability. Of course, such licentiousness was one of the defining characteristics of the bohemian world of the male artist.

Class

It is undoubtedly the case that for most—perhaps all—of the nineteenth century, Britain was a hierarchical society ruled by a landed elite. However, this broad generalization masks the lengthy and uneven processes of change and challenge at work in this period. One of the most important processes of change was the transformation of the social structure of England from one based on rank to one based on class. By the late 1860s (in the essays that made up *Culture and Anarchy*) Matthew Arnold was describing England as a society based on just three classes: the Barbarians (aristocracy), the Philistines (middle classes), and the Populace (working class), each with its own distinct character and interests. Ten years later T. H. S. Escott divided English society into 'the higher classes, the middle classes, the lower middle classes, and that vast multitude [in fact some 75 per cent of the total population], which for the sake of convenience may be described as the proletariate [*sic*]'.[26] Of course the picture was more complex than either Arnold or Escott indicate, and contemporary literary texts and the work of later social historians demonstrate the extent to which the Victorians remained obsessed (as perhaps the English still are) with subtle distinctions of class and rank.

Important changes in the social structure came as a result of the challenges to the power of the landed elite posed by the increasing economic and social power of the middle classes, and by the development of a large urban working class. Changes to the social structure also came from the ability of the aristocracy to adapt to and make accommodations with these challenges. If England continued to be ruled by a landed elite, it remained—as it had long been—a relatively open (or at least permeable) one. Indeed, perhaps one of the most interesting aspects of the social structure of nineteenth-century England, and certainly one that was a subject of endless fascination for the novelists of the day, was social mobility and the (admittedly differential) permeability of the social classes. Here is Escott writing on *England: Her People, Polity, and Pursuits* in 1879:

In the constitution of English society at the present day, the three rival elements—The aristocratic, the democratic, and the plutocratic—are closely blended. The aristocratic principle is still paramount, forms the foundation of our social structure, and has been strengthened and extended in its operation by the plutocratic, while the democratic instinct of the race has all the opportunities of assertion and gratification which it can find in a career conditionally open to all the talents.[27]

From the late eighteenth century onwards, the aristocracy had involved itself in commerce and banking. Since they owned most of the land, members of the aristocracy (and the landed 'gentry') were also owners of coal mines, and the mining of other minerals which fuelled successive industrial revolutions. In many cases they owned the land on which railways and factories were built. The 'middling classes' who grew prosperous on the proceeds of industry and commerce in their turn became landowners, and made alliances with the aristocracy through marriages which conferred social status on the middle-class family and bolstered the sometimes ailing family fortunes of the aristocratic family involved in such a cross-class marriage. Historians dispute just how permeable and open the ruling elite was. However, if the open elite was a myth it was a very powerful one, which arose from numerous actual and fictional examples of wealthy individuals who, having made their money in industry and commerce, entered the aristocracy or lived in aristocratic or gentry style. Certainly, after 1840 it became increasingly common for successful manufacturers and retailers to make their way into the landed elite and to enhance the social position of their sons by sending them to public schools. Here is (the somewhat Panglossian) Escott again:

> Our territorial nobles, our squires, our rural landlords great and small, have become commercial potentates; our merchant-princes have become country gentlemen. The possession of land is the guarantee of respectability, and the love of respectability and land is inveterate in our race.
>
> The great merchant or banker of to-day is an English gentleman of a finished type. . . . He is a man of extensive culture, an authority upon paintings, or china, or black-letter books; upon some branch of natural science; upon the politics of Europe; upon the affairs of the world. Does he then neglect his business? By no means. He has, indeed, trustworthy servants and deputies; but he consults personally with his partners, gentlemen in culture and taste scarcely inferior, it may be, to himself.[28]

Respectability, self-cultivation, and self-improvement (often through the imitation of one's social superiors) were goals pursued by members of all social classes in the nineteenth century. They also lie at the heart of the nineteenth-century novel's preoccupation with social mobility and with manners and conduct.

The grandfather of the model merchant-prince referred to in the last-quoted passage 'would have lived with his family above the counting-house', but he himself would have had a town house in Belgravia or Mayfair and a place in the country. According to the complaisant Escott, one of the keys to this social harmony was the law and custom of primogeniture, whereby the property of a family passes to the eldest son, and as a result of which landed estates were kept intact and younger sons were motivated to make their way in the world (sometimes by marrying into the class beneath them). Patterns of inheritance, the wills and codicils by which they are secured, as well as the adventures of the younger sons and daughters (of whatever position in the family) are, of course, the stuff of nineteenth-century novels, not least those by Wilkie Collins.

Escott dates the 'enlargement of English society' ('society' here means those with social status and power) from the enactment of the Reform Bill of 1832. He describes the process of enlargement as one which 'has substituted, in a very large degree, the prestige of achievement for the prestige of position'.[29] Another feature of this movement towards a more meritocratic society is the rise of the professions:

The degrees of esteem allotted to the different English professions are exactly what might be expected in a society organized upon such a basis and conscious of such aims. Roughly it may be said professions in England are valued according to their stability, their remunerativeness, their influence, and their recognition by the State.[30]

The increasing complexity of the social and economic organization of England, the growth of local government and state bureaucracies, and the development of science and technology all led to a growing demand for specialists of various kinds. Such specialists increasingly organized themselves into professional groups to oversee the training of new entrants, to regulate entry into the profession (through examinations), and to disseminate knowledge and good practice through professional journals. From mid-century onwards, architects, engineers, doctors, pharmacists, and teachers all organized themselves in this way.

There were, as always, subtleties of gradation. Escott, for example, suggests that those professions whose members had 'immediate pecuniary dealings' with their clients were likely to be regarded as being lower in the social pecking order than those whose remuneration came via a less direct route. In this respect, attorneys, surgeons, dentists, and physicians are said to be socially indistinguishable from tailors, wine merchants, and grocers.

Another socially ambiguous calling or profession is that of the artist. Escott (irrespective of the accuracy or otherwise of his delineation) throws interesting light on Collins's own social position and his fictional portrayal of artists and other professionals.

We live in an age whose boast is that it can appreciate merit or capacity of any kind. Artists and actors, poets and painters, are the much-courted guests of the wealthiest and the noblest in the land . . . To all appearance, the fusion between the aristocracy of birth, wealth, and intellect is complete . . . Still the notion prevails that the admission, let us say, of the painter into society is an act of condescension on society's part, none the less real because the condescension is ostentatiously concealed.[31]

In Escott's view, the painter, despite the nobility of his calling, is more likely than the adherent of any other branch of the artistic professions to carry the taint of a rather louche bohemianism. As Dickens was eager to show in his depiction of David Copperfield, the professional writer can be both respectable and methodical. Indeed, methodicalness may even be essential to the writer's success. However, the painter is different, at least in the estimation of the great British public:

The keen-scented, eminently decorous British public perceives a certain aroma of social and moral laxity in the atmosphere of the studio, a kind of blended perfume of periodical impecuniosity and much tobacco smoke. . . . the popular view of the painter—speaking now . . . of the guild, not the individual member of it—is that the calling which he elects to follow lacks definitiveness of status, and that it is not calculated to promote those serious, methodical habits which form an integral part of the foundation of English society.[32]

Interestingly, serious methodical habits are precisely what the painter Walter Hartright develops as he writes down the story of his transition from professional painter and drawing master to Victorian paterfamilias and membership of the landed elite through his wife's ownership of Limmeridge House. However, for much of the duration of *The Woman in White*, Hartright is represented as a liminal figure, with no clear social place or gender role. Hartight is a 'cultural intellectual', and like many Victorian writers Collins seems to have been extremely preoccupied with the status of this figure. As John Kucich has persuasively argued, Collins's novels repeatedly pit 'cultural intellectuals'—artists, writers, dilettantes, proto-bohemians, 'who live on the margins of intellectual and social life, and who combine the methods of scientific deduction with creative imagination' (such as Fosco and Hartright in *The Woman in White*, Ozias Midwinter in *Armadale*, or Franklin Blake or Ezra Jennings in *The Moonstone*)—against 'pretentious scientific intellectuals', such as professional detectives or doctors.[33]

Education

Education played an important part in the production and reproduction of class identities and roles as it did in the construction and maintenance of gender identities and gender roles. Until 1833 education was entirely in the hands of private individuals, religious groups, or ancient foundations, and as far as the middle and upper classes were concerned this remained the situation for most of Collins's lifetime. Collins's own period of formal schooling was much briefer than it would normally have been the case for a boy of his class, but otherwise it was what might have been expected of a son of the relatively well-to-do middle class: he attended private schools—the Maida Hill Academy and Highbury school. The sons of wealthier men (and those with a more clearly defined social station than Collins's artist father) would have boarded at the so-called 'public' schools (Eton, Harrow, Winchester, Rugby, and a number of less-well-known establishments), following a classical curriculum and acquiring the homosocial friendship networks that would assist them in their later lives and careers and in running the country in their roles as members of the House of Commons or Lords, judges, or senior Civil Servants. As noted in the previous section, during Collins's lifetime the sons of landowners and aristocrats would have increasingly been joined at their public schools by the sons of the wealthier merchants and factory owners. Like the public schools, the grammar schools also taught a curriculum based on Latin and Greek but their fees were more modest than the public schools—they even provided free places for some poorer pupils. During Collins's lifetime these schools also came to play an increasingly important part in the education and formation of the growing middle class and those who were to fill the new professions (see above).

The education of middle- and upper-class boys was a much-debated topic during Collins's own schooldays and beyond. In part, the debate was fuelled by tensions arising from the domestication of masculinity referred to earlier in this chapter: on the one hand, the home was regarded as too feminine a space for the formation of the male child into proper adult masculinity, but on the other, the traditional public school was too barbarous for the formation of disciplined male subject of the domestic ideal. As John Tosh points out, from the 1850s the job of the public schools became that of instilling 'manly self-reliance in boys who had been raised in comfortable conditions of domesticity'.[34] From 1828, when Thomas Arnold became the headmaster of Rugby School, the English public schools were engaged in an extensive (and extended) process of reform. The influence of Arnold and of his disciples led to the transformation of the culture and the curriculum of public schools. Modern languages were added to the classical curriculum, and the inculcation of discipline, honesty, commitment to the school community and its ethos, and athleticism developed a culture of Christian manliness or muscular Christianity (which was satirized by Collins in *Man and Wife*). The education of middle-class girls was no less hotly debated. During the period of his childhood, girls of Collins's class would usually have been educated at home—often in a rather rudimentary fashion—but the mid-century campaigns of feminists led to demands for higher education for women and, with more immediate success, for the foundation of schools for girls which would be on a par with the public schools.

However, perhaps the most important developments in this period were the increasing involvement of the state in the funding, provision, and regulation of education, and the widespread extension of education beyond the privileged classes. As a result of Althorp's Factory Act of 1833, government accepted, for the first time, some responsibility for educating the poor (or, indeed, for educating anyone) by making a grant to the National Society (Anglican) and the British and Foreign Schools Society (Nonconformist) to provide the two hours' schooling per day for factory children stipulated in the Act. Thus began the process of state involvement in education, through the provision of financial support which was eventually to lead to Forster's Education Act of 1870, and to produce the mass readership which was exerting new pressures on the literary marketplace by the end of Collins's writing career. During Collins's boyhood and youth, the vast majority of the population received very little education. To be sure, there were 'voluntary' schools of various kinds—Sunday Schools, dame schools (like the one which Dickens's Pip attends in *Great Expectations*, 1861), or charity schools. A number of factory schools were established as a result of Althorp's Act, and another factory reformer, Anthony Ashley Cooper (Lord Shaftesbury) was president of the Ragged Schools Union which established numerous ragged schools in very poor areas in the 1840s. In the 1840s government began to provide financial support for the teacher training colleges established by the religious societies, and the Department of Education was established in 1856 to administer the increasing government expenditure on education (by now some £500,000 a year). When the Newcastle Commission reported in 1861, one in seven children was said to be receiving some kind of education. The Newcastle Report led to the 'payment by results' system, and the regular testing of children and 'cramming' methods of teaching (attacked by Dickens in his depiction of the schools run by Bradley Headstone and Miss Peacher in *Our Mutual Friend*, 1865). Fresh impetus for extending education to the poorer sections of the population, and for increasing the involvement of the state in its provision, came in part from the extension of the franchise in the 1867 Reform Act, and the growing economic power of industrial workers. As the Liberal politician Robert Lowe noted as soon as the Second Reform Bill was passed, it was now essential 'to compel our future masters to learn their letters'.[35]

Religion

Religion was a very contentious matter for Collins's contemporaries, and the nature, extent, impact, and meanings of Victorian religion have been the subject of intense debate by subsequent historians. Collins's contemporaries habitually referred to England as a Christian country. What did they mean by describing their country in this way? Was it a statement of fact or of faith? Was it merely a pious hope or a denial of the creeping tide of secularism that some historians have traced in the nineteenth century? The picture is complex. However, if we begin by noting that there were important class and regional variations of religious belief and practice, it is possible to hazard the generalization that throughout Collins's lifetime the majority of the population (although historians disagree about the exact size and composition of this majority) would have accepted Protestant Christianity, even if in many cases their acceptance was tacit and passive. This broad acceptance would have included, as Hugh McLeod has suggested, 'acceptance of the Bible as the highest religious authority, and of moral principles derived from Protestant Christianity, practice of the Christian rites of passage, and observance of Sunday'.[36]

The 'observance of Sunday' included attendance at church or chapel. However, the religious census of 1851 (as interpreted by later social historians) reveals that on Sunday, 30 March 1851 not less than 47 per cent but no more than 54 per cent of the total population of England and Wales over 10 years old attended a religious service. Of those present on census Sunday, 51 per cent attended Anglican churches, 44 per cent attended Nonconformist churches or chapels, and 4 per cent were at Roman Catholic churches. Clearly, therefore, for quite a large proportion of the population Sunday observance did not involve attendance at a religious service, and the observance of Sunday certainly became a source of tension during Collins's lifetime. For most working people Sunday was the one day of the week which they had free for rest and recreation, but custom, social pressure, and the law all conspired to ensure that it was also the one day of the week in which they could not pursue most recreations: 'theatres, pleasure grounds, and all other places of entertainment charging for admission remained . . . closed, and London's pubs and shops would have been . . . had not Parliament been intimidated by popular demonstrations in their favour in 1855.'[37]

Collins hated the English Sunday, but one of the best descriptions of the awfulness of the urban Victorian Sunday is to be found in Dickens's *Little Dorrit*:

It was a Sunday evening in London, gloomy, close and stale. Maddening church bells of all degrees of dissonance, sharp and flat, cracked and clear, fast and slow, made the brick and mortar echoes hideous. Melancholy streets in a penitential garb of soot, steeped the souls of the people who were condemned to look at them out of windows, in dire despondency. . . . Everything was bolted and barred that could by possibility furnish relief to an overworked people. No picture, no unfamiliar animals, no rare plants or flowers, no natural or artificial wonders of the ancient world—all *taboo* with that enlightened strictness, that the ugly South sea gods in the British Museum might have supposed themselves at home again. . . . Nothing to change the brooding mind, or raise it up. Nothing for the spent toiler to do, but to compare the monotony of the seventh day with the monotony of his six days, think what a weary life he led, and make the best of it—or the worst, according to the probabilities. (Book the First, Chapter III)

The joylessness of the Victorian Sunday, and of much else, was often associated with evangelicalism both within the Anglican Church and in the Nonconformist community of dissenters who had broken away from the hierarchically organized and 'established' Church of England. The evangelical movement within the Anglican communion became both fashionable and influential in high society and the upper middle classes in the early nineteenth century, and, throughout most of Collins's lifetime, 'claimed the high ground of moral and social reform'.[38] Its adherents organized themselves into philanthropic societies and societies for the improvement and regulation of individual behaviour and social conditions. Nonconformity, too, gained in influence as the economic and political power of the industrial middle classes increased and some of the prohibitions on their involvement in local and central government were removed. With its history of exclusion and dissent and its distrust of state control, the culture of Nonconformity was in many ways an instinctively reforming culture. In fact, Nonconformists and Anglican evangelicals both played an extremely important part in campaigning for many of the social reforms discussed in an earlier section of this chapter.

Evangelicalism, whether Anglican or Nonconformist, was closely based on the Gospel of the New Testament, and placed a great deal of emphasis on individual conscience, personal conduct, and self scrutiny. At the heart of evangelical religion was a very personal recognition of the truth of the Gospel, a conversion experience by which the individual achieved salvation by consciously (and repeatedly) acknowledging the depravity of humankind and giving him- or herself up to God's mercy as embodied in the atoning sacrifice of Christ. Those who take their impressions of evangelicalism and Nonconformity from nineteenth-century fiction are likely to have a very negative view. From the Reverend Stiggins in Dickens's *Pickwick Papers*, through Brocklehurst in Charlotte Brontë's *Jane Eyre*, and the Reverend Chadband in *Bleak House*, evangelicals are represented as self-serving hypocrites (and sometimes as downright cruel). For a more sympathetic picture we must turn to the portrait of the female itinerant Wesleyan preacher, Dinah Morris, in George Eliot's *Adam Bede* (although, interestingly, this novel is set at the end of the eighteenth century).

Frances Power Cobbe, an avowed atheist who corresponded with Collins on the subject of vivisection (against which they both campaigned in the 1880s), offers an interesting perspective on an evangelical upbringing in her autobiography, *The Life of Frances Power Cobbe, As Told By Herself* (1894). Cobbe writes affectionately of a childhood lived 'morally . . . in a room full of sunlight', noting that no one but a fanatic could 'regret having been brought up as an Evangelical Christian . . . of the mild, devout, philanthropic Arminianism of the Clapham School, which prevailed amongst pious people in England and Ireland from the beginning of the century till the rise of the Oxford Movement, and of which William Wilberforce and Lord Shaftesbury were successively representative'. However, Cobbe also indicates some of the damaging effects of the 'evangelical training' which depends on a concept of God as 'the All-seeing Judge'. Chief among these is the 'excessive introspection and self-consciousness'[39] which also (de)formed Miss Clack in *The Moonstone*.

The 'Clapham School' (sometimes known as the Clapham Sect) was the name given by Sydney Smith (one of the founders of the *Edinburgh Review*) to a group of middle-class evangelical and anti-slave-trade philanthropists who were based in Clapham. The Clapham Sect exerted a moral, political, and social influence disproportionate to its size, as did the group associated with Unitarianism. Heirs of the rational dissenters of an earlier age, Unitarians were Christians who believed in the unity of God as a single being, and rejected the idea of the Trinity and the divinity of Christ. Like the Clapham Sect, they owed their influence in part to their wealth and their prestige in their local communities, and partly to their intellectual impact through their publications and organiza-tion of discussion groups. Families such as the Hennells in Coventry (who influenced the thinking of the young Marian Evans, who became the novelist George Eliot) and the Unitarian minister William Gaskell and his wife, the novelist Elizabeth Gaskell, in Manchester were at the centre of philanthropic and intellectual communities which formed a powerful opposition to establishment thinking in both religious and secular life throughout the first half of the nineteenth century. Unitarians were involved in many of the new developments in science and medicine, they led the opposition to 'do-nothing', laissez-faire, economic policies and spearheaded movements for social reform.[40]

This section began by citing Hugh McLeod's claim that for most (perhaps all) of the Victorian period the majority of the population of Britain would have accepted Protestant Christianity. However, as the 1851 church and chapel attendance survey revealed, this did not necessarily mean that the majority of the population would have been regular church- or chapel-goers. Indeed, there was a great deal of concern in some quarters about the failure of the new urban working class to engage in such activity. Moreover, there were also many exceptions to McLeod's general rule of acceptance of Protestant

Christianity. First, there were those who embraced the Roman Catholic faith: on mainland Britain, some of these would have belonged to old Catholic families whose Roman Catholicism had survived the sectarian religious turmoils of the sixteenth and seventeenth centuries, but many would have been of Irish or other immigrant descent. Second, there were the Anglo-Catholics or High Anglicans, those members of the Church of England who believed in the authority of the Church and a priesthood based on the Apostolic Succession, and in the importance of ritual and sacramental worship: the Oxford Movement (or Tractarians) of the 1830s and 1840s followed the methods (if not the message) of the evangelicals, by preaching fervently from the pulpit and in a series of tracts against the heretical 'liberalism' of the modern Anglican Church. Then there were those who were beyond the reach of Christianity. These included British Jews who were descended from eighteenth-century immigrants (mainly from Germany), and new immigrants who continued to settle in London and the larger cities throughout the nineteenth century; there were about 35,000 Jews in Britain in 1850, and about 60,000 by 1881. However, for the social and cultural historian of nineteenth-century Britain, perhaps the most important group of non-Christians were the agnostics and atheists whose inability, or unwillingness, to believe in the existence of God or in the divinity of Christ, or to accept the Bible as revealed truth, were symptoms or causes of the so-called 'Crisis of Faith'.

From the 1840s letters, diaries, poems, novels, periodical articles, and philosophical treatises testify to the religious doubt and sometimes intellectual and emotional turmoil of middle-class intellectuals and artists born (like Collins) in the first quarter of the nineteenth century. At the same time 'thousands of working-class men and women . . . joined secular societies and in doing so exposed themselves to economic discrimination much sharper than anything a doubting Oxbridge don had to suffer'.[41] The causes of this great unsettling of religious faith were numerous: two important destabilizers of religious orthodoxy were the developments in geology in the 1830s—such as Charles Lyell's *Principles of Geology* (1830) and Robert Chambers's anonymously published *Vestiges of the Natural History of Creation* (1844)—which undermined the biblical account of the creation of the earth, and the new historical studies of the Bible which further undermined scriptural authority. As well as these scientific objections there were also moral objections to the evangelicals' punitive conceptions of original sin and everlasting punishment imposed by an all-seeing God. Indeed, many historians now think that the moral revulsion against evangelicalism played a more significant part in undermining religious belief than either the developments in science or biblical criticism. However, as the century went on the increasing influence of new scientific, materialist explanations of the world, as seen for example in the impact of works such as Darwin's *On the Origin of Species by Means of Natural Selection* (1859) continued to undermine the authority of Scripture, and also, by further eroding the boundaries between humankind and nature, undermined (for some Victorians) the sense of man's divinely ordained place at the centre of God's universe. In addition, the growing prestige of scientists and the secular professions tended to displace the clergy as repositories of wisdom and social authority.

Where did Collins stand on religious questions? Most of Collins's biographers up until the late twentieth century have concluded that it is difficult to make definitive statements about Collins's religious and spiritual beliefs, or to infer them from his fiction. They have tended to imply that he did not have any religious beliefs, or (as in the case of Nuel Pharr Davis), that he actively rebelled against 'his father's piety' and developed an 'aversion to religion' which became more profound as he got older. Davis even goes so far as to describe Collins as 'an atheist who was debarred from all that aspect of the human drama even remotely connected with sin and salvation'.[42]

The situation is more complex, as both Sue Lonoff and Keith Lawrence have shown. Lawrence agrees with the widely held view that although 'men of the cloth—some of them renegades, some of them more or less admirable—figure importantly' in Collins's fiction, his novels are, on the whole, 'strangely silent' on the 'subject of religion'. However, he suggests that if Collins 'consistently veils his personal beliefs' in his fiction, an important correspondence between the author and his friend Edward Pigott reveals a great deal about his beliefs in the 1850s.[43] Sue Lonoff suggests that there is both biographical and fictional evidence to undermine the common supposition that Collins was 'an agnostic and a man who had no use for religion', a supposition which has arisen because he did not appear to 'believe in an afterlife . . . attended church rarely and largely to please others, lived in "sin" with not one but two women, and openly censured Catholics and Dissenters'.[44] The biographical evidence is to be found in the letters which Collins wrote to Pigott; the fictional evidence comes from *The Moonstone*, which, as Lonoff points out, repeatedly 'alludes to the state of religion in mid-nine-teenth-century England',[45] and from *The Fallen Leaves* (1879). Amelius Goldenheart, the hero of this late novel, is initially sent to America to be brought up by the members of a religious community because his father believed that 'the Christian religion, as Christ taught it, has long ceased to be the religion of the Christian world. A selfish and cruel Pretence is set up in its place' (Book the First, Chapter II). Amelius is brought up to live his life according to the Christianity of the Sermon on the Mount rather than to follow doctrine.

We find our Christianity in the spirit of the New Testament—not in the letter. . . . To reverence God: and to love our neighbour as ourselves: if we had only those two commandments to guide us, we should have enough. The whole collection of Doctrines (as they are called) we reject at once, without even stopping to discuss them. We apply to them the test sug-gested by Christ himself: by their fruits ye shall know them. The fruits of Doctrines, in the past . . . have been the Spanish Inquisition, the Massacre of St. Bartholomew, and the Thirty Years' War—and the fruits, in the present, are dissension, bigotry, and opposition to useful reforms. Away with Doctrines! In the interests of Christianity, away with them! We are to love our enemies: we are to forgive injuries: we are to help the needy; we are to be pitiful and courteous, slow to judge others, ashamed to exalt ourselves. That teaching doesn't lead to tortures, massacres, and wars; to envy, hatred, and malice . . .

Of course we must be careful not to equate the words of this fictional creation with the beliefs of their author. However, this advocacy of a pure, ethical Christianity does seem to fit in with the repeated attacks on doctrinal cant and the cant of religious ideologues which we find in Collins's novels: Miss Clack and Godfrey Ablewhite in *The Moonstone* are perhaps the best examples.

The most direct expression of Collins's personal views on religious matters are to be found in his letters to Pigott. As noted in the section on 'Protest and Reform' above, Pigott became the owner of the freethinking weekly paper, the *Leader*, at the end of 1851. In two letters written in February 1852 Collins wrote at some length (and in a manner which suggests that he was continuing an argument begun and to be continued in conversations with Pigott) about his disagreements with, and distaste for, the paper's approach to religious matters. In the second of these letters, dated 20 February 1852, Collins declared himself in agreement with the *Leader*'s line on literature, politics, and—on the whole—social matters. However, he took serious issue with the paper's policy of giving religion 'equal freedom of utterance' with other matters. Collins objected to the mixing of private spiritual belief and matters of public policy, the sacred and the secular. On 16 February 1852 he wrote:

As to what is 'irreligious' or what is 'heterodoxy', or what is the 'immensity' of the distance between them, you and I differ; and it is useless to broach the subject. Nothing will ever persuade me that a system which permits the introduction of the private religious, or irreligious, or heterodoxical opinions of contributors to a newspaper into the articles on politics or general news which they write for it, is a wise or a good system . . . It is for this reason *only* that I don't desire to be 'one of you'—simply because a common respect for my own religious convictions prevents me from wishing to. (*Letters*, i. 82)

Four days later Collins made it clear that he objected to the 'anomalous coupling of the sacred and the profane'. He found it perfectly acceptable for a newspaper to run opinion pieces on religious politics, but not on religious belief:

It is not your freedom of religious thought that I wish to object to; but your license of religious expression—a license which is, to *me*, utterly abhorrent. I have never seen any religious *thought* in the paper. . . . If you are to take a leading position in religion as well as in Politics, let us know what your religion is, just as you have let us know what your politics are—What does the Leader believe in, and what does it disbelieve in?—Readers have a right to ask that question of a Journal which starts for the discussion of *religious* subjects, as well as political. Surely your mission is to *teach*, as well as to *inquire*. Surely you ought to teach something definite in religion, just as you teach something in politics, if you *must* have this 'freedom of religious thought'. Why not let Mr Holyoake [George Jacob Holyoake, founder of the Secularist movement who was imprisoned for atheism in 1841] write a series of articles on the advantages of atheism as a creed?—his convictions have been honestly arrived at, miserable and melancholy as they are to think of.

But I repeat, *religion* itself is not a subject for the columns of a newspaper—*religious politics* . . . are fair game if you please . . .

I go with you in politics . . . in social matters . . . in Literature—but, in regard to your mixing up the name of Jesus Christ with the current politics of the day, I am against you—against you with all my heart and soul. (*Letters*, i. 84–5)

A few paragraphs later Collins states unequivocally: 'I do not desire to discuss this or that particular creed; but I believe Jesus Christ to be the Son of God . . .'

Collins himself may have believed in the divinity of Christ and in certain of the Christian doctrines and the ethical framework that derived from Christ's divinity. However, as a further note to Pigott suggests, he had little time for the Roman Catholic Church (or for institutionalized religion more generally), or for the religious temper of his times. The note to Pigott refers to the proclamation by Pope Pius IX in 1854 which made the immaculate conception an official Catholic doctrine. Collins dismissed the proclamation itself as a piece of 'sacred Tom Foolery', but expressed surprise that his Protestant fellow countrymen felt that such irrational Tom Foolery would damage the Catholic Church: 'Dunderheaded humanity when it falls to being religious, wants anything you please in a religion—*except* common sense. In an age where thousands of people join the Mormons, I cannot see, for one, why the Immaculate conception should stand in the Papists' way in making new converts' (*Letters*, i. 85). As Lawrence notes, the correspondence with Pigott reveals three important aspects of Collins's 'religion': his 'distrust of established churches', which, as we can also see from his fiction, 'he viewed as hypocritical and manipulative'; his broad acceptance—at least during his early and middle years—of certain fundamental Christian doctrines, centred in the divinity of Christ, and his absolute insistence on 'reticence and confidentiality in matters of personal worship and religious conviction'.[46] Collins's later letters suggest that these religious views persisted throughout his life.[47]

Empire and Race

The above discussion of the social, political, and economic contexts of Collins's life and work has focused mainly on the British mainland, and particularly, given Collins's experience and interests, on England. I have tried to be quite careful in my use of the words 'British' and 'English', using the former only when referring to aspects of social life that could be said to apply in all parts of mainland Britain. In this last section I return to the concept of a wider Britain by looking at the British Empire as one of Collins's social, economic, and imaginative contexts. Again, the language is tricky, since in the context of empire the concept of Britishness is often rather Anglo–centric.

England's history as a colonial power goes back to the Elizabethan age. By the nineteenth century she had lost one major colony (America), but otherwise continued to expand her territories and influence, and became a self-proclaimed imperial power when Victoria was made Empress of India in 1876, by means of an Act passed in the Westminster Parliament. The idea of British imperialism was not a Victorian invention, but it certainly gained a new force and a distinctive character during Victoria's reign. Britain's unequal relations with her 'dependencies' were essential to her economic power in the nineteenth century, and the colonies and dependent territories also provided her with a 'dumping ground' in which to dispose of convicts until 1868 (various of the Australian colonies), 'surplus women' who couldn't find husbands, unemployed workers, and the problematic, impecunious younger sons of upper-class families. The Empire provided the raw materials for the newly emerging workshop of the world, and also provided an expanding market for its products, and, as P. J. Cain and A. G. Hopkins have shown, the growth of commercial, financial, and service sectors of the British economy were all deeply involved with the development of empire.[48]

If the British way of life in the nineteenth century was increasingly dependent on the Empire, then the Empire was increasingly justified in terms of the superiority of Britons and the British way of life (for Briton we must usually read Englishman). British imperialism in the nineteenth century was fuelled by a 'civilizing mission'. Convinced of both their innate and their cultural superiority the British sought to bring Christianity and civilization (that is to say their view of what constituted civilization) to the 'primitive' peoples whose lands they took. Why did the British consider themselves innately superior to the indigenous peoples of the lands which they appropriated? One answer, which became of increasing importance throughout the course of the century, is race. As Christine Bolt has argued, British racial attitudes changed and hardened during the Victorian period, not least because the general Victorian rage for classification and categorization extended itself to the question of race.[49] In the first half of the century there was a general belief (derived from a mixture of evangelical and utilitarian ideas) that mankind was a single type or genus, and that the perceived backwardness of the non-white peoples was due to a lack of development. By the 1860s, however, there was broad agreement that race was a key determinant of physical, intellectual, and moral character, and that the white races were superior to the dark ones. 'Who are the dark races?' Robert Knox asked in *Races of Men; A Fragment* in 1850; 'Are the Jews a dark race? The Gypsies? The Chinese, &c.? Dark they all are to a certain extent; so are all the Mongol tribes— the American Indian and Esquimaux—the inhabitants of nearly all Africa—of the East—of Australia'.[50]

The 'dark', 'primitive', or 'savage' races were seen as children of nature—at best innocent, at worst infantile, creatures merely of instinct and passion. The theory (or superstition) of the superiority of the white races was given further impetus after 1859 by interpretations of Darwin's *Origin of Species*. Although Darwin himself was wary of such applications of his findings, others were quick to suggest that his model of the evolution of higher from lower forms could also be traced within the human species: in short, that the white European male was the most highly evolved form of *Homo sapiens* and that beneath him, occupying the different gradations in the evolutionary scale, were other human forms from women to 'savages'. Moreover, the version of the theory of natural selection, as the survival of the fittest, that was popularized by some of Darwin's followers seemed to validate the casual treatment of the lives and livelihoods of the less highly evolved, 'primitive', 'dark' races.

Although during Collins's lifetime most Britons probably never saw a black person, and relatively few of them lived in or visited any of its far-flung outposts, the Empire was at the heart of the cultural imaginary in a variety of ways. The 'Great Exhibition of the Industry of All Nations' in 1851 was, in one sense, a great imperial display— the British and Colonial section occupied one-half of the space. The people and places of the Empire were the subject of numerous articles in the periodical press, pictorial images of empire were to be found in illustrated magazines, and many novels and stories had imperial settings. From time to time colonized peoples drew themselves to the attention of the metropole, as the Bengal sepoys did in 1857 by staging a mutiny, and as the Jamaicans did in 1865 when they rebelled against their British masters, only to be violently suppressed by Governor Eyre.

The relationships between colony and metropole were extremely complex on both a practical and a cultural and imaginative level. Indeed the practical functioning of empire depended to a large extent upon culture. Although military force played a major part in both acquiring and keeping colonial territories, it was not the only means of securing imperial rule. Other important strategies of domination included the development of elaborate bureaucracies (many of them staffed by the new professionals mentioned in the section on class), and the colonization of the minds of the subjected peoples through Christianity and, later, through an Anglo-centric form of education. If the native peoples were to survive, in Darwinian terms, then the only way they could do so (or so some thought) was to become more like the white man. Thus began the task of domesticating the savage and disciplining him or her to the same routines of production and reproduction as the English man and woman at 'home'.

Some of the problematic aspects of the relationship between colony and home surface in *The Moonstone*, whose plot turns on the theft of a diamond originally plundered in an imperial adventure in India, and whose characters include a group of mysterious Indians, who terrify the natives (i.e. the English people) and can only be understood by Murthwaite the 'expert' in things Oriental. Collins's main narrator, Gabriel Betteredge, whose 'bible' is *Robinson Crusoe* (whose hero colonizes the island on which he is shipwrecked and makes a servant of the 'native' he encounters), brings into sharp relief the relationship between colony and home when he laments the invasion of 'our quiet English house' by 'a devilish Indian Diamond', and confesses his surprise that such a thing could occur 'in an age of progress, and in a country which rejoices in the blessings of the British constitution' (*The Moonstone*, First Period, Chapter V; discussed further on pp. 158 ff. and 170 ff.).

Like many of his contemporaries, Collins self-consciously anatomized and satirized the 'age of progress' and modernity in which he lived and raised questions about the blessings of the British constitution and legal system. At the same time he also celebrated and exploited the social changes that occurred during the course of his lifetime, eagerly embracing the new reading public that emerged in an increasingly prosperous and democratic society and in an age of mechanized printing and cheap paper. Collins may have satirized the materialism of the age of commerce and industry, but he also created a role for himself as a productive and entrepreneurial professional writer with an understanding of the demands of the consumer and an eye for new markets. In his own private life, in which he contrived to combine the role of a bohemian bachelor with the guise of a middle-class paterfamilias, Collins enacted some of the complexities and contradictions of contemporary sexual mores as well as the shifting class, gender, and familial roles which were a prominent feature of both the society in which he lived and of the fiction that he wrote about it.

CHAPTER 3

THE LITERARY CONTEXT

COLLINS's first novel, *Antonina*, was published in 1850. His last, *Blind Love*, appeared posthumously in 1890. When he began to publish fiction Charles Dickens and William Makepeace Thackeray were the leading novelists of the day, Anthony Trollope, Elizabeth Gaskell, and Charles Kingsley had just begun their novel-writing careers, and George Eliot was still to publish her first work of fiction. By the last decade of Collins's career, all these novelists were dead and the literary landscape had been occupied by new realists such as Thomas Hardy, George Moore, and George Gissing, and new romancers such as Robert Louis Stevenson, Rider Haggard, and Rudyard Kipling, none of whom had been born when Collins first began to publish. Collins was thus the 'lonely survivor of the mid-century generation, still prolific and . . . still receiving his share of attention from both readers and reviewers' as the nineteenth century drew to its close.[1]

Collins lived through a period of profound change in novel-writing and publishing. When he was born the novel was still regarded as a morally suspect form of amusement rather than a serious literary form, by the time he died it had become the dominant form of literature. In the early nineteenth century Utilitarians, evangelicals, and dissenters had tended to dismiss novels as frivolous or impious, but by 1848 it was not unusual to find the novel referred to as a reviewer in *Blackwood's* did in 'A Few Words About Novels— A Dialogue': 'the novel now really represents the mind of a country in all its phases, and, if not the only, is nearly the best of its literature.'[2] In 1859 David Masson, a particularly perceptive commentator on the mid-nineteenth-century novel, reported that his studies of the form led him to conclude that it was 'becoming more real and determinate, in so far as it can convey matter of fact, more earnest, in so far as it can be made a vehicle for matter of speculation, and more conscious, at the same time, of its ability in all matter of phantasy'.[3] By 1870, in a lecture entitled 'On English Prose Fiction as a Rational

Amusement', Trollope was announcing the triumph of the novel: 'We have become a novel-reading people,' he asserted,

[n]ovels are in the hands of us all: from the Prime Minister down to the last-appointed scullery maid. We have them in our library, our drawing-rooms, our bed-rooms, our kitchens,—and in our nurseries. Our memories are laden with the stories which we read . . . Poetry also we read and history, biography and the social and political news of the day. But all our other reading put together hardly amounts to what we read in novels.[4]

Of course, as a professional novelist Trollope had a vested interest in affirming the importance and popularity of his chosen literary form, but it is undoubtedly the case that throughout Collins's lifetime the audience for fiction was growing and diversifying, and the novel was gaining in literary prestige. From the middle of the nineteenth century the work of individual novelists and the novel as a genre were the subject of serious critical discussion and debate in the heavyweight periodical press.

Novel Reading and Novel Readers

Who were the readers of fiction in the nineteenth century? What kind of fiction did they read? Where and how did they obtain it? Questions about the nature and size of the nineteenth-century audience for fiction are notoriously difficult to answer, and they take us to further questions about literacy, gender, and class, as we shall see below. Collins himself was extremely interested in readers, or 'King Public', as he called them in letters to Pigott in January 1852 (*Letters*, i. 79, 82), and some ten years into his own career as a published writer he wrote an essay in which he offered his own analysis of a reading public that was clearly demarcated along class lines. In 'The Unknown Public', first published in *Household Words*, 21 August 1858, Collins announced his 'startling discovery' that his previous assumptions about the composition of the reading public were entirely mistaken, and that there were, in fact, two reading publics which inhabited different social worlds, and obtained their reading material in quite different forms and from entirely different kinds of outlets. The 'known' public, that is, the readers with whom Collins and his *Household Words* readers were familiar—'the customers at publishing-houses, the members of book clubs and circulating libraries, and the purchasers and borrowers of newspapers and reviews'—in fact represent 'nothing but a minority' of English readers. This 'known' public was largely middle class, and made up of sometimes overlapping sub-groups: the religious public with its own literature; the public that reads for information and instruction, 'and devotes itself to Histories, Biographies, Essays, Treatises, Voyages and Travels'; the public that reads for amusement, 'and patronizes the Circulating libraries and the railway-bookstalls'; and the public that read only newspapers. However, below the tip of this iceberg of readers was the vast mass of the 'unknown public', 'the lost literary tribes' (*My Miscellanies*, p. 252), the 'monster audience' (*My Miscellanies*, p. 262) whose existence Collins became aware of (or, at least for rhetorical purposes, presents himself as becoming aware of) when looking at the publications displayed in the windows of small stationers' or small tobacconists' shops in the course of his walks around the 'second and third rate neighbourhoods' of London; publications which could be found replicated in every town in England, 'in oyster shops, in cigar shops, in lozenge shops'.

The 'new species of literary production' which the middle-class author had discovered was the literature of the millions, 'the unfathomable, the universal public' (*My Miscellanies*, p. 251), who read the penny weeklies which had emerged in the 1830s and 1840s, and which offered soap-opera-like extended narratives, often with a Gothic flavour, that went on interminably, or which came to an end only when the public became bored with them. Collins's essay offers an early form of market research and content-analysis. From his quizzing of the shopkeepers and his examination of the stories published in the penny papers, Collins concludes that 'the Unknown Public reads for amusement, and that it looks to quantity in its reading, rather than to quality'. From his examination of the 'Answers to Correspondents' pages of the penny journals he makes further deductions about 'the social position, the habits, the tastes, and the average intelligence' of their readers (*My Miscellanies*, p. 253), and 'the general amount of education they have acquired' (*My Miscellanies*, p. 256). Collins assumes a working-class readership for the penny weeklies, but by the late 1850s their readers also included many lower-middle-class families. Whatever class it belonged to, the unknown public which Collins constructs from his own reading of the penny journals is one which is 'in a literary sense, hardly beginning, as yet, to learn to read'; its members are, 'from no fault of theirs, still ignorant of almost everything which is generally known and understood among readers whom circumstances have placed, socially and intellectually, in the rank above them'. Collins's interest in the unknown public is, in large part, an interest in expanding the audience for his own fiction, which he regards as having a literary sophistication and merit which require 'discriminating' readers: the unknown public must be taught to read 'in a literary sense' (*My Miscellanies*, p. 263).

In 'The Unknown Public' Collins assumed a widespread basic literacy, which, by 1858, had created a substantial market for the penny journals. In fact, historians have disagreed widely about who could and did read in the nineteenth century. There are no definitive statistics on literacy, and those that are available are notoriously difficult to interpret. Some historians of reading use the ability to sign the marriage register (rather than merely to make one's mark with a cross) as evidence of standards of literacy, as people usually acquired the ability to write after they had learned to read. By this measure about 67 per cent of men and 51 per cent of women were literate in 1841. These figures had risen to 81 per cent and 73 per cent respectively in 1871, and 97.2 per cent and 96.8 per cent by 1901. So the ability to read was progressively increasing throughout the century, but what about opportunity? Increased prosperity and increased leisure time gave more opportunities for reading at most levels in society. Successive Acts regulating the working day and the working week (noted in Chapter 2) created leisure time for those employed in factories and mines, and not all of this increased leisure time was spent in gin shops and public houses (as some temperance campaigners feared). Among the middle classes the increased separation of work and the home led to the growth of commuting for men and increased leisure time for women, each of which gave separate opportunities for reading for amusement, and some of the shared family leisure time was also given over to such reading. The middle-class fiction market was thus both expanding and stratifying into distinctive (but overlapping) niche markets: women's reading, men's reading, and family reading.

The growth and democratization of the reading public, and particularly the growth in fiction reading, led to protracted and often heated debates throughout the century on the dangers of reading, the power of fiction to corrupt, the vulnerability of women readers and adolescent readers of both sexes, and the vulnerability or depravity of working-class readers. These debates, and the practice of family reading among the middle classes, exerted their influence on what subjects were permitted in novels, and how they could be treated. The tone and temper of fiction reviewing and the mechanics of the literary marketplace (see below) encouraged novelists to avoid 'sensitive' subjects (particularly sex) which were likely to inflame the passions or bring a blush to the cheek of a young person. Similarly, novels were scrutinized from the perspective of domestic discipline: there was at least a tacit consensus among fiction reviewers that fiction should not make its readers discontented with 'the routines of production and reproduction', and, preferably, that it should prepare them for and reconcile them to such routines and reinforce moral norms. Some middle-class reviewers tended to feel that the reinforcement of domestic discipline and moral norms was particularly important in fiction intended for the working classes. Thus an article on 'Penny Novels' which appeared in *Macmillan's Magazine* in 1866 refers back to an earlier anxiety that 'our lower classes were being entertained with tales of seduction, adultery, forgery, and murder'.[5]

Collins was often taken to task for his treatment of sensitive subjects, such as illegitimacy (particularly in *No Name*), adultery (*Basil*), forgery and fraud (*The Woman in White*, *No Name*, *Armadale*), and prostitution (*The New Magdalen* and *The Fallen Leaves*). In turn, he was equally ready to castigate what he thought of as middle-class cant on fiction, such as the reply of the disreputable Dr Downward (in *Armadale*) to a mother who asks whether his patients are allowed novels:

Nothing painful, ma'am! There may be plenty that is painful in real life— but for that very reason, we don't want it in books. The English novelist who enters my house (no foreign novelist will be admitted) must understand his art as the healthy-minded English reader understands it in our time. He must know that our purer modern taste, our higher modern morality, limits him to doing exactly two things for us, when he writes us a book. All we want of him is—occasionally to make us laugh; and invariably to make us comfortable. (*Armadale*, Book the Last, Chapter III)

The Production and Distribution of the Novel

How did 'healthy minded English reader[s]' obtain their fiction in the nineteenth century? Most of Collins's readers would not have purchased his (or anyone else's) novels hot off the press in volume form. For most of the nineteenth century books were expensive to buy, and most readers would either have borrowed fiction from a circulating library (if they could afford the subscription) or purchased it in individual paper-covered parts, or in weekly or monthly instalments in a magazine. Whereas in our own day a novel first appears in hardback (or large-format trade paperback) and then, some little while later, in a cheaper paperback edition, for most of Collins's lifetime it was the other way round: the hardback version, usually in three volumes (the 'three-decker'), followed by a cheaper one-volume edition, would appear after the novel had appeared serially in a cheap paper-covered form. Fiction written explicitly for the working classes (Collins's 'Unknown Public') would have been published only in the cheap paper-covered version.

While Collins himself was still a schoolboy, Charles Dickens, among others, adapted the serial fiction of the penny and twopenny weeklies and took it upmarket, publishing his novels in twenty one shilling monthly parts over a period of nineteen months (the last number was a double issue). Dickens also played an important part in creating a new market for serialized magazine fiction. He published *Oliver Twist* in *Bentley's Miscellany*, a monthly magazine which sold for a shilling a copy, before establishing his own weekly magazines, *Household Words* (1850–9) and *All the Year Round* (1860–95). Both of Dickens's magazines sold for twopence a copy and contained stories and serialized novels alongside entertaining and/or instructive essays on a wide range of subjects. *All the Year Round*, in which *The Woman in White* and *The Moonstone* were first serialized, was launched at the beginning of a decade which saw an enormous growth in the number of fiction and general interest magazines for the middle classes, following the abolition of the Stamp Duty (a tax on publications carrying news items) in 1855, and the removal of the tax on paper in 1861.

Collins first began to publish in serial form in 1857 when *The Dead Secret* appeared weekly in Dickens's *Household Words* (it also ran in the United States, with a few weeks' time lag, in *Harper's*

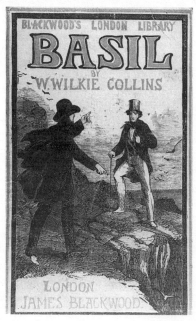

The opening of *Armadale*, serialized in
the *Cornhill Magazine*, 1864

James Blackwood's 1856 edition
of *Basil*

Library label for W. H. Smith's circulating library

Weekly and *Littell's Living Age*). From this point on until the late 1860s, all Collins's novels made their first appearance in serial form in Dickens's weeklies, the only exception being *Armadale*, which appeared in the *Cornhill*, a monthly magazine owned by George Smith, and edited until March 1862 by Thackeray. In the 1870s, when his popularity began to wane, Collins's novels were serialized in monthly miscellanies such as *Temple Bar* and *Belgravia* and weeklies such as the *Graphic* and the *World*. In the last decade of his career, Collins's serial fiction reached a new audience in the pages of newspapers. In 1873 William Tillotson, proprietor of the *Bolton Weekly Journal* and several other Lancashire newspapers, established his 'Fiction Bureau'. For a fixed fee Tillotson's bought the rights to serialize the novels of popular authors in his syndicate of English newspapers. Mary Elizabeth Braddon, Charles Reade, and Anthony Trollope all became Tillotson's authors. Collins saw this form of publication as a way of maximizing the earnings from his fiction and reaching some of that 'unknown public' which he had written about in 1858. He first signed up with Tillotson's in 1879, and *Jezebel's Daughter* appeared in the *Bolton Weekly Journal* and several other northern newspapers from September 1879 until January 1880. Partly because of his uneasiness about his changing status as a 'commercial' rather than a 'gentlemanly' author,[6] Collins's dealings with Tillotson's were not easy, and subsequently (in another innovation) he used the services of A. P. Watt, one of the first of the new literary agents, to arrange the syndication of *The Evil Genius* (1885–6) and *The Legacy of Cain* (1888).

Whether it appeared in separate paperback numbers, in magazines, or in newspapers, the serial mode of the publication of fiction clearly exerted an influence on the form of the nineteenth-century novel. Each instalment had to keep to a set length, and had to end in a way that would make the reader look forward eagerly to reading (and buying) the next one. In addition, each instalment had to work as a free-standing unit as well as functioning in a longer narrative. As a writer in the *London Morning Herald* for 10 January 1843 put it, in 'publishing periodically, the author has no time to be idle . . . he must always be lively, pathetic, amusing, or instructive; his pen must never flag—his imagination never tire'. Because the reading process of a serial novel was interrupted by the days or weeks between the publication of the various parts, writers often gave their characters striking verbal tics or other mannerisms which helped readers to recognize them or keep them in mind. Although some authors simply published in instalments a book that they had already written, others actually wrote their novels in parts, delivering their weekly or monthly copy to the printer's boy with the ink still wet. Writing in instalments could be a precarious business, and it sometimes led to unevenness and inconsistencies, as an author who wrote serially could not revise the earlier part of the novel in the light of later developments (although some authors, including Collins, did revise their work in the course of its transition from part or serial publication to volume form). The serial production (rather than merely the serial distribution) of fiction also meant that occasionally the progress of a story was delayed by the author's ill-health, or, like Dickens's *The Mystery of Edwin Drood*, was brought to a (literal) dead end as a result of the author's death. Collins gives a vivid account of the pains of serial writing in his 1871 Preface to *The Moonstone*, in which he recalls that he had written parts of the novel 'under the weight of [the] double calamity' of his mother's final illness and the crippling torture of his own rheumatic gout.

I had my duty to the public still to bear in mind. My good readers in England and in America, whom I had never yet disappointed, were expecting their regular weekly instalments of the new story. I held to the story— for my own sake, as well as for theirs. In the intervals of grief, in the occasional remissions of pain, I dictated from my bed that portion of *The Moonstone* which has since proved most successful in amusing the public—the 'Narrative of Miss Clack.'

Collins found the rigours of serial writing increasingly difficult as his health deteriorated in his later years, and in August 1889, realizing that he was too ill to finish *Blind Love* which was then being serialized in the *Illustrated London News*, he engaged his friend Walter Besant (a popular novelist in the 1880s and 90s) to complete the novel from the author's working notes.

As serials were often reviewed during the course of their serial run, an author who wrote in instalments was susceptible to the influence of reviewers, and also to pressure from readers. In many cases a special relationship developed between authors and their serial-reading public. Dickens famously resisted public pressure not to kill off little Nell in *The Old Curiosity Shop* in 1841, but succumbed to the persuasion of his friend John Forster in changing his intended ending for *Great Expectations* in 1861. In his Preface to the first three-volume edition (1860) of *The Woman in White*, Collins pronounced himself compelled to note the 'warm welcome which my story has met with, in its periodical form, among English and American readers' and thanks his 'many correspondents (to whom I am personally unknown) for the hearty encouragement I received from them while my work was in progress'. The Preface indicates that the serial author had received advice and exhortations as well as encouragement:

I remember very gratefully that 'Marian' and 'Laura' made such warm friends in many quarters, that I was peremptorily cautioned at a serious crisis in the story, to be careful how I treated them—that Mr Fairlie found sympathetic fellow-sufferers, who remonstrated with me for not making Christian allowance for the state of his nerves—that Sir Perceval's 'secret' became sufficiently exasperating, in course of time, to be made the subject of bets . . . and that Count Fosco suggested metaphysical considerations to the learned in such matters.

If serial publication helped shape the form of the novel in the nineteenth century, magazine publication helped shaped the ways in which it was read. Many of the best-known nineteenth-century novels (including most of Collins's novels) were first read in magazines or newspapers, alongside items of news, articles on contemporary events, and polemical or campaigning pieces on issues of the day. The first readers of nineteenth-century novels would thus have been constantly moving between the fictional world and the real world, and authors would often incorporate references to the events that were reported or referred to elsewhere in the newspaper or magazine in which the novel was appearing. Sometimes the relationship between the serial novel and the material which surrounded it was orchestrated in quite a self-conscious manner. Dickens, for example, described his own editorial role as that of the 'Conductor' of his magazines, and, as Deborah Wynne has demonstrated, in common with other editors in the 1860s, he invited his readers 'to adopt an intertextual approach to magazines',[7] actively encouraging them to read the various items in each issue in relation to each other and to make connections between the serial novel and the other features. Another way in which magazine editors shaped Victorian novels was through their active intervention in form and content. Dickens was a notoriously interventionist editor who sought to 'improve' upon the style or structure of the novelists published in his magazines—often in late proof stage, when it was too late for the author to rescue their work from his efforts. The interventions of some other editors were directed towards sparing the blush on the cheek of the young person and avoiding offending against the official morality of the middle classes. Such editorial interventions were sometimes made at the instigation of publishers, and sometimes as a consequence of an editor's assumptions about what would be acceptable to his publishers. For example, the publishers of *Cassell's Magazine* objected to some of the expletives used in *Man and Wife* which they serialized in 1869–70. Collins agreed to remove an offending 'Damn it', but noted that:

Readers who object to expletives in books, are—as to my experience— readers who object to a great many other things in books, which they are too stupid to understand. It is quite possible that your peculiar constituency may take an exception to things to come in my story, which are essential to the development of character, or which are connected with a much higher and larger moral point of view than they are capable of taking themselves. In these cases, I am afraid that you will find me deaf to all remonstrances—in those best interests of the independence of literature which are *your* interests (properly understood) as well as mine.[8]

In 1875 Collins required the *Graphic* to print a statement acknowledging that the editor had suppressed part of a passage of *The Law and the Lady*, on the grounds that the original was 'objectionable', and also to print the references to burning lips and physical grappling which the editor had cut.[9]

It is easy to see how editorial and authorial assumptions about what will and will not be acceptable to publishers and readers can operate as a form of censorship just as much as the direct suppression of material in my last example. A similar form of self-censorship, as well as actual censorship, can be seen at work in the relationship between writers and the owners of circulating libraries, the other major players in the production and distribution of fiction in the nineteenth century. As noted earlier, nineteenth-century novels for a middle-class audience appeared either as a three-volume publication followed (often much later) by a cheaper two-volume or one-volume edition, or they appeared first in part form or as a serial in a magazine and then in three-volume (again sometimes followed by one-volume form). In the early part of the century the cheap one-volume edition of a novel might not have been produced until some years after the issue of the three-decker, and when it appeared it often did so as part of a reprint series that might have included 'standard' or 'classic' in its title—such as Colborn and Bentley's 'Standard Novels' which began in 1831 and included one-volume editions of works by Jane Austen and Bulwer Lytton among others. The main purchasers of the three-decker novel were the circulating libraries, who hired novels out by the volume to readers paying a yearly subscription. Circulating libraries had been in existence since the eighteenth century, but they became even more important with the expansion of the reading public and the growth of novel reading in the nineteenth century. The most famous and powerful of the nineteenth-century circulating libraries was Mudie's, owned by Charles Edward Mudie, who opened his first 'Select Library' in Southampton Row in London in 1842. By the time of Mudie's death in 1890 his library had some 25,000 subscribers. An annual subscription of one guinea entitled a reader to borrow one volume at a time, so in order to read a complete novel each one-guinea subscription holder would have to complete three transactions with Mudie's. In the early 1860s W. H. Smith and Son also entered the circulating library business (Smith's also ran railway bookstalls), and although they outlived Mudie's they did not challenge its dominance in the nineteenth century: Smith's membership was about 15,000 by 1894. Between them, Mudie's and Smith's were the major purchasers of hardback fiction and were able to negotiate purchasing deals with the main publishers of fiction. Mudie's decision to buy or reject a particular novel and the exact size of his order could determine its success or failure.

Mudie's and W. H. Smith were 'the twin tyrants of literature'.[10] Their own tastes and their assumptions (or prescriptions) about the tastes of their readers were extremely influential in determining what was published. For example, in 1873 Mudie suggested that Collins should change the title of *The New Magdalen*, lest it should give offence. Collins stood his ground, but wrote anxiously and angrily to his publisher: 'this ignorant fanatic holds my circulation in his pious hands. Suppose he determines to check my circulation— what remedy have *we*? What remedy have his subscribers?'[11] In the last decade of Collins's life a number of authors began to challenge the tyranny of Mudie's taste and the dictatorship of the circulating library. In 1884 George Moore published (in the *Pall Mall Gazette*) an essay, entitled 'A New Censorship of Literature', in which he objected to the fact that a 'mere tradesman' such as Mudie should set himself up 'to decide the most delicate artistic question that may be raised'.[12] Moore's essay was prompted by the failure of his novel, *A Modern Lover* (1883), which had attracted extremely good reviews but had been sunk by Mudie's decision to order only fifty copies on the grounds that it was 'immoral'. Moore retaliated by seeking to cut the circulating librarian out of the distribution chain and to attract buyers rather than borrowers. To this end he published his next novel, *A Mummer's Wife* (1885) in a one-volume edition priced at six shillings. Others followed his example, and by 1894 the three-volume novel was all but dead. The demise of the three-decker was almost certainly what Collins had in mind when he wrote to his publisher, George Smith, in 1871 about a proposal (which he abandoned) to take *The Woman in White* to the 'unknown public' by reissuing it in penny numbers: 'My own impression is that a *very few* years more will see a revolution in the publishing trade for which most of the publishers are unprepared . . . I don't believe in the gigantic monopolies, which cripple *free* trade, lasting much longer. The Mudie monopoly and the W. H. Smith monopoly are anomalies in a commercial country' (*Letters*, ii. 349). In fact, the revolution in the publishing trade which was to be completed with the demise of the three-decker in 1894 had begun some years before Collins wrote this letter. The move towards the single-volume novel began with the phenomenon of 'railway novels' or 'yellowbacks'. In December 1848 George Routledge issued the first volume in the Routledge's 'Railway Library' series—a one-volume reissue of James Fenimore Cooper's *The Red Rover* produced in a small format that was suitable for carrying in a pocket or a handbag, bound in boards with an illustration on the front cover, and priced at one shilling. This series was much imitated in the 1850s and 1860s, as several publishers adopted the small format (approximately 17.5 by 12.2 centimetres), and the distinctive yellow-glazed boards with a racy illustration on the front and advertisements on the back. The growth of 'railway reading' was also associated with the rise of the sensation novel in the 1860s (discussed below) and other 'fast' novels, sold on railway bookstalls, which offered 'something hot and strong' to grab the attention of 'the hurried passenger' and relieve the dullness of the train journey.[13] The mid-nineteenth century also saw the first paperback revolution, as Blackwood, Bradbury and Evans, and others in the 1850s produced one-volume paper-covered reissues of 'classic' novels, translations, and abridgements. The availability of cheap reprints also created a demand for cheap one-volume editions of current fiction, which most publishers continued to resist until after Collins's death.

The Forms of the Novel

The novel was the dominant literary form of the nineteenth century, but as always the novel took many forms. For his first novel, *Antonina*, Collins chose a genre, the historical romance, which had been perfected at the beginning of the nineteenth century by 'the glorious Walter Scott (King, Emperor, President, and God Almighty of novelists)',[14] and popularized by Bulwer Lytton in the 1820s and 1830s and by Harrison Ainsworth in the 1830s and 1840s. However, by the time Collins began his novel-writing career the historical romance had begun to go out of fashion. Collins's second novel, *Basil*, announced itself as a 'story of modern life', and this was more in keeping with the growing tendency of nineteenth-century novelists, at least those who wrote primarily for a middle-class audience, to set their narratives in the present or the very recent past, and to replace romance with realism. By the 1850s, the realistic, or 'faithful' treatment of ordinary, everyday life, advocated by George Eliot in reviews and essays in periodicals and in the famous intervention by the narrator in Chapter 17 of *Adam Bede* (1859; see below), was replacing both the '*mind-and-millinery* species' of novel which she accused 'lady novelists' of producing in her 1856 essay on 'Silly Novels by Lady Novelists',[15] and the novels of high life ('silver fork' novels) or low life (often criminal low life, as in the so-called 'Newgate' novels) produced by their male equivalents.

Although he did not publish his first novel until 1850, Collins began writing fiction in the 1840s, a decade dominated by Dickens: *The Old Curiosity Shop* appeared between 1840 and 1841, *Barnaby Rudge*, a historical novel set at the time of the Gordon Riots, in 1841, *Martin Chuzzlewit* in 1843–4, *Dombey and Son*, the first of his great social novels, in 1846–8, and *David Copperfield*, his autobiographical novel about the making of a nineteenth-century novelist, in 1849–50.

The year 1850 also saw the completion of William Makepeace Thackeray's novel about (among other things) the making of a nineteenth-century novelist, *Pendennis* (which appeared in monthly parts between 1848 and 1850). *Vanity Fair*, Thackeray's vast social panorama set in the years around the battle of Waterloo, had appeared in 1847–8. Whether they were set in the present, or in the recent or the more distant past, the novels that Dickens wrote in the 1840s were very much concerned to represent, explore, and critique what Thomas Carlyle called the 'condition of England'. Other novelists of the 1840s who concerned themselves with contemporary social problems included Benjamin Disraeli, whose 1845 novel *Sybil* described England as consisting of 'two nations' (the rich and the poor), Charles Kingsley, whose Christian Socialist novel *Yeast* appeared in 1848, and Elizabeth Gaskell, whose 1848 novel *Mary Barton* was set in industrial Manchester at the time of strikes and Chartist activism. Gaskell returned to the issue of industrial relations and relations between the rich and poor in *North and South* (1854–5). Industrial unrest in the north of England is also one of the contexts for Charlotte Brontë's *Shirley* (1849), although in this case the unrest belongs to the Luddite protests of 1811–12. On the other hand, *Jane Eyre*, the other novel which Charlotte Brontë published in the 1840s (in 1847), was a mixture of realism and romance, which combined a *Bildungsroman* (a novel about the development of the central protagonist to maturity) with a 'governess novel', and rewrote the Cinderella and Bluebeard stories. The novels of the other Brontë sisters also belong to this decade: Emily's *Wuthering Heights* and Anne's *Agnes Grey* (another 'governess novel') both appeared in 1847, and in 1848 Anne Brontë published *The Tenant of Wildfell Hall*, an early example of the sensation novel, a genre which, according to many commentators, Collins invented in *The Woman in White* (1860). The 1840s also saw the beginning of Trollope's prolific career as a novelist with the publication of his Irish novels, *The Macdermots of Ballycloran* (1847) and *The Kellys and the O'Kellys* (1848).

Thus, by the time Collins published his first full-length novel in 1850 the fiction market was extremely varied. In the 1850s Dickens continued to be a major figure, striking out in new directions with his sharp social satire *Bleak House* (1852–3), a condition-of-England novel, *Hard Times* (1854), *Little Dorrit* (1855–7), a dark novel of modern life, and his second historical novel, *A Tale of Two Cities* (1859). However, in the 1850s Dickens's supremacy was challenged by newcomers such as Collins himself, and by their friend Charles Reade, whose theatrical and melodramatic novels *Peg Woffington* and *Christie Johnstone* appeared in 1853, followed by his 'novel with a purpose', *It Is Never Too Late to Mend*, in 1856. Another new voice appeared towards the end of the decade, when George Eliot published her well-received *Scenes of Clerical Life* (1858) and the extremely successful *Adam Bede* (1859). Having been a prominent advocate of realism in art in her essays of the mid-1850s, Eliot now became its chief exponent, seeking to put into practice what she had earlier criticized Dickens for failing to do, by offering (what she saw as) a truthful representation of the life of the people, of 'their conceptions of life and their emotions', rather than simply of their 'external traits' (as, in her view, Dickens did).[16] Eliot was responsible for bringing a new seriousness and a new prominence to the domestic novel in realist mode, which became a (perhaps *the*) dominant sub-genre of fiction in the 1850s and 1860s. Like the Dutch painters whom she admired, Eliot created and celebrated 'faithful pictures of a monotonous homely existence, which has been the fate of so many more among my fellow-mortals than a life of pomp or of absolute indigence, of tragic suffering or of world-stirring actions' (*Adam Bede*, Chapter 17). Sometimes referred to as 'sentimental fiction', domestic fiction was particularly (although by no means exclusively) popular with women readers and writers during the middle of the nineteenth century. Histories of provincial life such as Eliot's *The Mill on the Floss* (1860), Anthony Trollope's Barsetshire novels, and Margaret Oliphant's Chronicles of Carlingford were extremely popular during the middle years of the century. Eliot's *Middlemarch* (1872) is perhaps the high point of domestic realism, which, as Henry James argued 'set a limit' to the genre.[17]

If the domestic novel in realist mode focused on the dramas of everyday life, here now and in England, so too did the sensation novel, a fictional sub-genre which came to the forefront of popular and critical attention in the 1860s, and with which the name of Wilkie Collins was closely associated. Although sharing some of its characteristics, the sensation novel was defined in opposition to the domestic novel and for a brief period in the 1860s it seemed to have displaced it as the dominant fictional sub-genre. Thomas Hardy gives us something of the flavour of the sensation novel in his Preface to *Desperate Remedies* (1871), when he describes this novel, his own anonymously published contribution to the sensation genre, as a 'long and intricately inwrought chain of circumstance', involving 'murder, blackmail, illegitimacy, impersonation, eavesdropping, multiple secrets, a suggestion of bigamy, amateur and professional detectives'. According to the anonymous reviewer of 'The Popular Novels of the Year' in *Fraser's Magazine* in August 1863, sensationalism had so completely taken over the fiction market, that a 'book without a murder, a divorce, a seduction, or a bigamy, is not apparently considered either worth writing or reading; and a mystery and a secret are the chief qualifications of the modern novel'.[18] With their sometimes racy characters and complicated plots, sensation novels were accused of focusing on unpleasant subjects and unsettling their readers, 'destroying conventional moralities, and generally unfitting the public for the prosaic avocations of life'.[19] Sensation novels, according to their critics, were aimed directly at the bodies and nervous systems of their readers, providing shocks, thrills, and even sexual arousal. The sensation 'product', as advertised in a parodic prospectus for an invented newspaper called the *Sensation Times* which appeared in *Punch*, was devoted to 'Harrowing the Mind, making the Flesh Creep . . . [and] Giving Shocks to the Nervous System'.[20]

Sensation novels drew on the Gothic novels of the turn of the eighteenth and nineteenth centuries (such as Ann Radcliffe's *The Mysteries of Udolpho*, 1794, and *The Italian*, 1797), which employed a variety of devices (including the supernatural) to instil fear and terror into their readers, and whose plots often involved dynastic ambition and intrigue, and the persecution and imprisonment of women. They also owed something to the 'Newgate' novels of the early nineteenth century. These novels took their name from the London prison to which notorious felons were sent before transportation or hanging, and drew on real-life crime stories from the *Newgate Calendar* to create criminal protagonists and heroes who were often represented sympathetically as being the victims of an unjust and outmoded legal and penal system. Many sensation novels derived their plot situations from newspapers, especially from the police reports and the reports of the new divorce courts, and they sometimes borrowed the techniques, character types, and plot situations of lower-class literary forms such as popular melodrama and penny dreadfuls. Indeed, one of the many criticisms which reviewers for middle-class magazines levelled at sensation novelists was that they had blurred the boundaries between lower-class and middle-class reading and readers by 'making the literature of the kitchen the favourite reading of the Drawing room'.[21]

Whatever their ancestry and antecedents, sensation novels were tales of modern life. As one writer in the *Quarterly Review* put it:

> The sensation novel, be it mere trash or something worse, is usually a tale of our own times. Proximity is, indeed, one great element of sensation. It is necessary to be near a mine to be blown up by its explosion; and a tale which aims at electrifying the nerves of the reader is never thoroughly effective unless the scene be laid in our own day and among the people we are in the habit of meeting.[22]

A generic hybrid, the sensation novel mixed romance with realism, the fantastic with the journalistic and, as Dickens observed of *The Moonstone*, the 'wild' with the 'domestic' (Pilgrim, xi. 385).

Sensation novels were often concerned with family secrets. Indeed, as Elaine Showalter has suggested, sensation novels focused on secrecy as 'the fundamental enabling condition' of the middle-class family in the nineteenth century.[23] Unlike Gothic novels, which usually involved the machinations of aristocratic characters in castles or monasteries in exotic foreign settings, or Newgate novels which centred on the urban dens, dives, and streets in which low-life criminals carried out their trade, sensation novels involved middle-class families (or the relations between middle-class and aristocratic families) in domestic settings in the English countryside, the suburbs, or the 'respectable' areas of towns. As Henry James noted, Mary Elizabeth Braddon 'created the sensation novel' with *Lady Audley's Secret*, but she 'had been preceded in the same path by Collins who must take the credit for

> introducing into fiction those most mysterious of mysteries, the mysteries that are at our own doors. This innovation gave a new impetus to the literature of horrors . . . Instead of the terrors of Udolpho we were treated to the terrors of the cheerful country house, or the London lodgings. And there is no doubt that these were infinitely the more terrible.[24]

In many sensation novels, the middle-class home, which in the domestic novel (and in the cultural imaginary) was a haven of tranquillity and a refuge from the harsh world of commerce and the unruly world of the urban streets, was more likely to be the source and scene of violence, intrigue, and crime. In *The Woman in White*, the home is the scene of Sir Percival Glyde's effective imprisonment of his wife and her half-sister before abducting them and imprisoning them elsewhere, and his actions are motivated by a family secret (the secret of his birth). In *The Moonstone*, 'our quiet country house' is disrupted by the theft of the diamond from the cabinet in Rachel Verinder's bedroom (a crime which has its origins in the domestic secrets of its perpetrator). The narratives of both *Armadale* and *No Name* originate in family secrets, and the development of the plots of both novels involves the role of female impostors (Lydia Gwilt and Magdalen Vanstone) who marry under a false identity in an effort to gain, or, in Magdalen's case, regain, their fortune. Mary Elizabeth Braddon's Lady Audley similarly marries under an assumed identity and this lower-middle-class schemer disrupts the calm of an English country house with her increasingly desperate efforts to maintain her secret. In Ellen (Mrs Henry) Wood's best-seller *East Lynne*, the household of an upwardly mobile country lawyer is revealed as a place of secrecy and jealousy even before it is disrupted by the adultery of Isabel Vane, his aristocratic wife.

Braddon's Lady Audley (and her later heroines such as Aurora Floyd) and Wood's, Isabel Vane, as well as in Collins's Lydia Gwilt and Magdalen Vanstone, were a new kind of female protagonist: the 'angel in the house' of the domestic novel had been re-created as the devil in the house. Much of the critical debate on sensation fiction focused on its creation of a new kind of heroine: a woman whose conduct transgressed the norms of middle-class femininity, but who nevertheless engaged the reader's interest and sympathy. Collins's sensation heroines from Marian Halcombe, through Magdalen Vanstone, to Lydia Gwilt and Rachel Verinder are all, in their different ways, examples of this new kind of female protagonist. In fact, women—as characters, writers, and readers—were at the centre of the sensation novel phenomenon. As E. S. Dallas observed in his *Times* review of *Lady Audley's Secret*, the mid-nineteenth century was 'the age of the lady novelists, and lady novelists naturally give first place to the heroine' who is 'pictured as high-strung . . . full of passion, purpose, and movement—very liable to error'.[25] The Reverend Francis E. Paget, author of a satire on the novels of Braddon and Wood, was less sanguine about the age of the lady novelists:

No *man* would have dared to write and publish such books . . . no *man could* have written such delineations of female passion . . . No! They are women, who by their writings have been doing the work of the enemy of souls, glossing over vice, making profligacy attractive, detailing with minuteness the workings of unbridled passions, encouraging vanity, extravagance, willfulness, selfishness . . . Women have done this,—have thus abused their power and prostituted their gifts,—who might have been bright and shining lights in their generation.[26]

One lady novelist, Margaret Oliphant, repeatedly castigated women writers for their sensational representation of female characters and for focusing on their physical (and especially sexual) sensations, and she also attacked female readers for flocking to buy such books: 'It is a shame for women so to write; and it is a shame to the women who read and accept as a true representation of themselves and their ways the equivocal talk and fleshly inclinations herein attributed to them.'[27] As a novelist who was reviewed as a sensationalist, Collins was thus associated both with female writers (and readers) and with a form of fiction that was perceived to be feminine, a fact which Tamar Heller has argued gave him an 'ambiguous place in Victorian literary culture'.[28]

Collins's *The Woman in White* has often been singled out as the first sensation novel. It was the subject of one of the earliest influential reviews of sensation fiction, in which Margaret Oliphant reviewed Collins's novel alongside Dickens's *Great Expectations* and Ellen Wood's *East Lynne* (1861).[29] Did Collins or any of his contemporaries actually see themselves as sensation novelists? Or was sensation merely a new label which reviewers in the 1860s began to apply to novels concerned with passions, crime, or madness? Mary Elizabeth Braddon, who sometimes felt herself trapped by the sensationalist tag, created a fictional sensation novelist, Sigismund Smith, who demonstrated that sensationalism was both a label and a fact of literary life: 'Mr Sigismund Smith was a sensation author. That bitter term of reproach, "sensation," had not been invented for the terror of romancers in the fifty-second year of this present century; but the thing existed nevertheless in divers forms, and people wrote sensation novels as unconsciously as Monsieur Jourdain talked prose.'[30] 'Sensation' may not have existed as 'a bitter term of reproach' in 1852, but in that year Collins published a novel, *Basil*, which had many of the characteristics that were later labelled as sensational: a tale of modern life which begins on an omnibus, it revolves around a secret cross-class marriage, an adultery plot, and an inter-generational revenge plot in which the deeds of the fathers continue to reverberate in the lives of their sons. Four years earlier Anne Brontë's *The Tenant of Wildfell Hall* included many of the ingredients of the sensation novel, especially as later developed by Collins: a dispersed narrative (made up of letters, a journal, and an editorializing commentary from its hero); a woman with a secret; and a preoccupation with the sufferings that women undergo as the result of the peculiarities and inequalities of the marriage laws and the laws governing the custody of children. Moreover, long before Oliphant labelled *Great Expectations* as a sensation novel in 1862, Dickens had been writing sensation fiction in novels which focused on family secrets and on crime and criminals. *Dombey and Son* has a kind of adultery plot (when Edith Dombey 'elopes' with Carker), and *Bleak House* has a woman with a secret (Lady Dedlock), a cross-class marriage and a detective plot, all of which were to become staples of the sensation novel of the 1860s.

Sensation novels often had a detective plot, and the growth of detective fiction is another important part of the literary context in which Collins wrote. Indeed, Collins has sometimes been credited with either inventing or perfecting the English detective novel with *The Moonstone*. From Dickens's Inspector Bucket in *Bleak House* through Collins's Inspector Cuff in *The Moonstone* to Arthur Conan Doyle's Sherlock Holmes stories in the 1880s, the professional detective became an important figure in English literature. Just as important was what Collins termed 'the Confidential Spy of modern times . . . the necessary Detective attendant on the progress of our national civilization' (*Armadale*, Book the Third, Chapter xv). Such figures include private detectives such as Dickens's Nadgett in *Martin Chuzzlewit*, Collins's Bashwood (the younger) in *Armadale* (1864–6), and Holmes himself. Other 'confidential spies' include amateurs who get drawn into detection, such as Mary Elizabeth Braddon's Robert Audley (*Lady Audley's Secret*, 1862) and Eleanor Vane (*Eleanor's Victory*, 1863), Collins's Walter Hartright in *The Woman in White*, and Franklin Blake and the others who fall prey to the 'detective fever' that breaks out in *The Moonstone*. As Ronald

Thomas has observed: 'almost every Victorian novel has at its heart some crime that must be uncovered, some false identity that must be unmasked, some secret that must be revealed, or some clandestine plot that must be exposed.'[31]

Thomas attributes the rise and pervasiveness of detection in the nineteenth-century novel to 'the creation of the modern bureaucratic state' and the disciplined, self-policing subjectivity which it required. Others have seen it as a symptom of a specifically urban (even metropolitan) modernity. Walter Benjamin, for example, has traced the origins of the nineteenth-century detective story to the anonymity of modern city life—the 'obliteration of the individual's traces in the big-city crowd'[32]—and to the universal suspicion with which the inhabitants of the modern city regard each other. In the mid-nineteenth century, detective novels, like sensation novels, were criticized for putting plot rather than character at their centre. Perhaps both this criticism and the literary practice which prompted it were produced by an anxiety that character is a function of plot, just as, in the modern bureaucratic state and the modern town or city, human identity is a function or product of the tangled social plots which human beings inhabit.

Sensation novels were often, like many domestic novels, also 'marriage problem novels' and 'novels-with-a-purpose', concerned to expose social and moral ills of various kinds. Such novels were to become even more prominent in the 1880s and 1890s as women (and some of their male supporters) campaigned against the iniquities and inequities of the laws and customs of marriage. In the first decade of his career Collins ranked entertaining his readers more highly than instructing them, taking as his dictum, 'make 'em laugh, make 'em cry', make 'em wait', and putting these words into the mouth of Jessie Yelverton, a character in 'The Queen of Hearts':

I'm sick to death of novels with an earnest purpose . . . of outbursts of eloquence, and large-minded philanthropy, and graphic descriptions, and unsparing anatomy of the human heart . . . [W]hat I want is something that seizes hold of my interest, and makes me forget when it is time to dress for dinner—something that keeps me reading, reading, reading, in a breathless state, to find out the end. ('The Queen of Hearts', Chapter 4)

At his best Collins was able to keep his readers reading 'in a breathless state, to find out the end' and at the same time to engage them with characters, plots, and situations which were designed to make them think seriously about themselves and their society, and about his own particular preoccupations—such as the state of the family and marriage. Later on, he seems to have forgotten the words he gave to Jessie Yelverton, and wrote more self-consciously didactic novels-with-a-purpose, such as *Man and Wife* (his 1870 attack on 'the present scandalous condition of the Marriage Laws of the united Kingdom', Chapter I), *The New Magdalen* (1873) and *The Fallen Leaves* which took up the cause of Christian Socialism and 'fallen women', and *Heart and Science* (1882–3) which took up the cause of antivivisectionism. Many critics, then and now, have felt that Collins's novels-with-a-purpose represented a falling off of his literary powers, and have generally agreed with Swinburne's oft quoted lines:

> What brought good Wilkie's genius nigh perdition?
> Some demon whispered—'Wilkie! have a mission!'[33]

However, even when he was pursuing a mission, Collins never forgot how to tell a tale.

Some of the later novels—*The Fallen Leaves* and *The Legacy of Cain* (1889), for example—explore questions of heredity, environment, and destiny. These questions had been taken up by the French Naturalist novelist, Émile Zola in his Rougon-Macquart series of novels which had begun to appear in 1871, and by his English imitators such as George Moore. However, Collins was not in sympathy with either the French or English Naturalist novel of the 1870s and 1880s, describing the 'realistic rubbish' of modern French novels as 'Dull and Dirty' (*Letters*, ii. 409). By the last decade of his career he felt that he was living in 'a period of "decline and fall" in the art of writing fiction' (*Letters*, ii. 467).

The Novel and the Theatre

As noted in the first chapter, Collins was extremely interested in plays and the theatre. He took part in private theatricals from the late 1830s onwards, and was an enthusiastic playgoer both in England and on his travels abroad (especially in his trips to Paris with Dickens and others). He was in many ways a very dramatic novelist. Indeed, as he noted in the Letter of Dedication to *Basil*, he saw the novel and the play as 'twin-sisters in the family of Fiction . . . [the] one is a drama narrated, as the other is a drama acted; and . . . all the strong and deep emotions which the Play-writer is privileged to excite, the Novel-writer is privileged to excite also'. Like many authors who published fiction in serial form Collins made a great deal of use of dramatic scenes, especially at the end of an episode. He also relied heavily on dialogue, and his novels were often dramatic in structure. *No Name* (1862) and *The Black Robe* (1881) were organized as a series of 'scenes', while in both *The Woman in White* and *The Moonstone* the narrative is dispersed across a range of narrators who are also actors in the story. Moreover, as was quite common in the mid-nineteenth century, many of Collins's novels were adapted for the stage, either by the author himself, or, by a professional playwright, with or without the permission of the author of the original novel. As Collins noted in a letter to John Hollingshead:

My 'Poor Miss Finch' has been dramatised (without asking my permission) by some obscure idiot in the country.

I have been asked to dramatise it, and have refused, because my experience in the matter tells me that the book is eminently *unfit* for stage performances. What I dare not do with my own work, another man (unknown in literature) is perfectly free to do against my will, and (if he can get his rubbish played) to the prejudice of my novel and my reputation. (*Letters*, ii. 362)

Collins also wrote directly for the stage. He made his own acting debut on the professional stage in 1850 in *A Court Duel!*, which he adapted from a melodrama set in the French court of 1726. He also wrote (as well as acted in) two other melodramas in the 1850s, *The Lighthouse* (1855) and *The Frozen Deep* (1857), which later appeared as a short story. Another play, *The Red Vial*, whose plot he subsequently used in his novel *Jezebel's Daughter* (1880), was produced—unsuccessfully—at the Olympic Theatre in 1858. *The New Magdalen* and *The Evil Genius* (1886) were written simultaneously as both novels and plays, although *The Evil Genius* was never produced on stage. One of Collins's most successful plays, *No Thoroughfare* (co-authored with Dickens), appeared first as a mystery story in the Christmas number of *All the Year Round* on 12 December 1867, to be followed a fortnight later by a stage version at the Adelphi Theatre in London. Collins enjoyed another stage success with *Man and Wife*, initially conceived as a play, but in the event published first as a novel. The play version of *Man and Wife* opened at the Prince of Wales Theatre in London on 22 February 1873. By all accounts extremely well acted, and staged in a very up-to-date way, this play enjoyed a very successful London run before going on tour. In May 1873, *The New Magdalen* opened at the Olympic Theatre, a day before the two-volume version of the novel was published by Bentley. Again, the play was a great success with the public, although the critics took issue with its verbosity, and what they perceived to be its immorality.

By the 1870s Collins had become quite a successful dramatist who was usually most successful when adapting a plot which he had already developed for a novel or story. On more than one occasion Collins wrote that in other circumstances he would have become a playwright rather than a novelist:

If I had been a Frenchman—with such a public to write for, such rewards to win, and such actors to interpret me, as the French Stage presents—all the stories I have written from 'Antonina' to 'The Woman in White' would have been told in dramatic form. Whether their success as plays would have been equal to their success as novels, it is not for me to decide; But if I know anything of my own faculty, it is a dramatic one. (*Letters*, i. 208)

Collins sometimes seemed to suggest that he became a novelist rather than a playwright simply because he was writing at a time when the novel was in the ascendant in England and the drama and theatre were in decline. One form of theatre that was clearly not in decline during Collins's writing life was the melodrama. Originally a lower-class form, melodrama also became one of the dominant forms of middle-class theatre, just as it became one of the dominant modes of the novel at mid-century. As Michael Booth notes, melodrama had something for everyone: strong and extreme emotions, pathos or tragedy, comedy, domestic sentiment, extraordinary incidents, plot suspense, romantic or exotic touches, domestic scenes and settings, and 'sharply delineated stock characters . . . love, joy, suffering, morality, the reward of virtue and the punishment of vice'.[34] In an important book on *The Melodramatic Imagination* (1976), Peter Brooks has argued that melodrama is a mode particularly associated with periods of rapid social change and ideological uncertainty, when it can function either as a form of subversion or escapism. In the early Victorian period the stage melodrama became increasingly

LYCEUM THEATRE.

Licensed by the Lord Chamberlain to MRS. BATEMAN,
Actual and Responsible Manager.

THIS AND EVERY EVENING UNTIL FURTHER NOTICE,

Will be presented,

A NEW PLAY,

Adapted, by the Author's express permission, from the Popular
Novel of

WILKIE COLLINS',

ENTITLED, THE

DEAD SECRET,

IN WHICH

MISS BATEMAN

(MRS. CROWE,)

WILL APPEAR.

Produced under the Personal Superintendence of

MR. HENRY IRVING.

The Lyceum Theatre's programme for the 1877 stage production of *The Dead Secret*

Illustration to *The Woman in White* play published in the *Illustrated London News*

urban in its settings and dealt with social and political anxieties in the form of emotional dramas focused on the family. By the 1860s both the content and the staging of melodrama had become more sensational and spectacular, particularly in the larger theatres with technical equipment for the staging of shipwrecks, avalanches, and railway crashes. The 'sensation drama' raised the stakes in providing audience excitement, and the challenge was taken up in the sensation novel. There was considerable overlap between the stage melodrama and the sensation novel in content as well as technique. The sensation novel took up the melodrama's preoccupation with class conflict or tension, cross-class sexual liaisons, social mobility, financial instability (plots revolving around loss of place, bankruptcy, or business failure), and with business crime (such as fraud, forgery, swindles, and embezzlement).

The Novelist as Journalist and Journeyman-of-Letters

As the earlier sections of this chapter indicate, Collins, like many novelists and aspiring novelists in the nineteenth century, made his living by writing in a variety of forms, modes, and genres: the drama and the short story, as well as in various genres of novel (domestic, detective, sensational, and the didactic novel-with-a purpose). In common with many of his contemporaries, Collins was also a journalist—in the sense that he wrote regularly for weekly, fortnightly, or monthly magazines, particularly in the first decade of his career. From 1851 until 1855 he wrote articles and reviews for the radical weekly, the *Leader*, in whose prospectus (written by Thornton Hunt), we can see a considerable degree of overlap with Collins's fictional concerns in the 1850s and 1860s.

THE LEADER will be thoroughly a *news*-paper: the news of the week is the history of the time as it passes before our eyes, informing and illustrating political and social science . . . [Nothing] will be overlooked as alien or inferior to the regard of the true politician: the news should reflect the life of our day, as it is; its materials must be accepted from whatsoever source—from the Parliament or the police-office, from the drawing-room or the workhouse. The utmost care of experienced journalists will be used to collect for the reader every striking incident in the eventful story of Humanity, and to convey it in such manner as to combine fullness of statement with the avoidance of offence.[35]

After *Antonina*, Collins's novels were also a version of the history of the time, full of 'striking incident' and taking their materials 'from whatsoever source', often from the newspapers of the day.

In October 1856 Collins accepted Dickens's offer of a position on the staff of his weekly magazine *Household Words*: 'I have been thinking a good deal about Collins,' Dickens wrote to his sub-editor W. H. Wills on 16 September 1856, 'and it strikes me that the best thing we can do just now for H.W. is to . . . offer him Five Guineas a week. He is very suggestive and exceedingly quick to take to my notions. Being industrious and reliable besides . . . I think it would do him, in the long run, a world of good' (Pilgrim, viii. 188). For the next five years Collins wrote articles and stories for Dickens and in collaboration with him. Journalism remained Collins's main employment and source of income until the popular success of *The Woman in White* enabled him to give up his position on the staff of *All the Year Round*, the successor to *Household Words*. In the course of his employment on Dickens's weeklies, Collins published over fifty short stories and articles. *My Miscellanies* (1863) includes a couple of dozen examples of the pieces which Collins produced weekly for *Household Words* and in the first year of *All the Year Round*. They include humorous essays on (what he described as) 'social grievances' such as 'Give Us Room' (on the problems posed by crinolines in confined spaces); biographical sketches on fellow writers such as Balzac and Douglas Jerrold; narratives of historical events; 'Fragments of Personal Experience' (as he described them in the 1875 edition of *My Miscellanies*) such as 'Laid Up in Lodgings' (accounts of his experiences in lodging houses in London and Paris); and character sketches. Collins also wrote more polemical pieces on the state of modern culture: 'A Petition to the Novel-Writers' (a complaint about the dullness of much modern fiction); 'The Unknown Public' (on the potentially huge audience for the mid-nineteenth-century novelist to be found among the readers of penny fiction); and 'Dramatic Grub Street' (on the parlous state of the contemporary theatre).

In the course of his journeyman work for *Household Words* and *All the Year Round*, Collins also produced numerous short stories (several of which were collected in *After Dark*, published in 1856), which both revealed and developed his talent for describing and creating fear and mystery. They included the Gothic-influenced, locked-room mystery 'A Terribly Strange Bed', a 'Dickensy' curiosity about a man who recognizes the scene of a narrow escape from death in his misspent youth and tells the tale of how he had been tricked into sleeping in a specially adapted bed after breaking the bank at a low-life gambling den in Paris (the bed was designed so as to crush its occupant to death and allow the plotters to escape with his winnings); 'Gabriel's Marriage', set in revolutionary France, whose plot concerns a mysterious priest and the estrangement of a father and son over a crime that was never committed (the plot was later reused in *The Lighthouse*); 'Sister Rose', also set in the French Revolution and a probable influence on the characters and plot of Dickens's *A Tale of Two Cities*; and 'The Yellow Mask' (based on Edgar Allan Poe's, 'The Masque of the Red Death'), which involves a plot to trick a young sculptor into believing that the ghost of his dead wife has returned to haunt him. Quite early in his period on *Household Words*, Collins wrote another story with supernatural overtones, entitled 'The Monktons of Wincot Abbey', whose plot turns on the fear of hereditary insanity. Dickens rejected it as unsuitable for a family magazine, but it was subsequently accepted for publication in *Fraser's Magazine* and it has proved quite popular with readers as 'Mad Monkton'.

One of the most interesting aspects of Collins's work for *Household Words* and *All the Year Round* was his collaboration with Dickens. Collins was a privileged member of the group which has been described as Dickens's young men, and the younger writer worked closely with his editor and mentor at a very formative stage of his development as a professional writer. Together, Collins and Dickens produced 'The Lazy Tour of Two Idle Apprentices', a humorous narrative of their walking holiday in Cumberland. Collins wrote in the person of a natural born idler, while Dickens took on the persona of one who had had to work hard to perfect his idleness. Collins was also one of Dickens's regular co-authors for the linked narratives that he produced as special 'extra' numbers which became a regular feature of the Christmas edition of *Household Words* from 1851. These Christmas stories were, perhaps, the most interesting and important of the Dickens–Collins collaboration and included detective stories, tales of the uncanny and supernatural, and 'The Perils of Certain English Prisoners'—in response to Dickens's request for a story of civilian heroism that might be made relevant to the Indian Mutiny.

The collaboration continued briefly in the Christmas numbers for *All the Year Round*. Their last collaborative work was 'No Thoroughfare' (1867), a mystery story which turns on the secrets surrounding the birth (and legitimacy) of two of its main characters.

The pattern of mentorship and collaboration between Dickens and Collins was by no means uncommon in the nineteenth century. Collins was fortunate to have attracted the attention of one of the most successful writers of his day, but the process of influence was a two-way street. As Sue Lonoff notes, Dickens taught Collins the art of pleasing digression, while the younger writer taught his mentor something about compression, and careful plotting.[36] Most important of all, perhaps, Collins's employment by Dickens throughout the 1850s provided him with both the opportunity for and the discipline of writing and publishing regularly. For Collins, as for so many nineteenth-century novelists, magazines played an extremely important part in the process by which he became a professional writer and then maintained himself in this role. Collins gave up his staff position on *All the Year Round*, following the success of *The Woman in White*, and at the height of his fame in the 1860s his contact with magazines and periodicals (in Britain and in the United States) was mostly as the means for the serialization of the novels which became his main form of literary output during this decade. However, he returned to writing short stories for magazines in the late 1870s, when the short-story form was beginning to have a revival (particularly in the lucrative American market), and when his declining health and increasing addiction to opium combined to make it more difficult for him to maintain the sustained effort of concentration and labour required for novel production. Most of the stories of the late 1870s and early 1880s are tales of cross-class love and marriage, and some of them have suggestions of the supernatural, or contain detective elements (fourteen of them were revised for Collins's 1887 collection *Little Novels*).

Another aspect of the life of the modern man of letters in which Collins followed Dickens's example was that of the reading tour. Dickens popularized public readings from his own fiction in the early 1850s, and Thackeray undertook a very profitable series of literary lectures in America in 1852–3 and again in 1855–6. In 1873 Collins decided to emulate his predecessors and embark on a reading and lecture tour in the United States. A reading of his early *Household*

Words story, 'A Terribly Strange Bed', which Collins gave at the Olympic Theatre in London in preparation for his American tour, revealed that he was no Dickens when it came to the public performance of his own fiction. He chose 'The Dream Woman' for his American reading, which received mixed reviews for both their style and their content (see Chapter 7).

Collins and the Art of the Novel

Like many of his successful contemporaries Collins had a healthy respect for the literary marketplace and for ordinary novel readers. He claimed not to be interested in the opinions of middle-class reviewers, asserting that he did not 'attach much importance to the reviews—except as advertisements which are inserted for nothing', and that he was more concerned with 'the impression I produce on the general public of readers' (*Letters*, ii. 309). He was alert to the potentially large new audience for fiction that existed in the 'unknown public' that devoured the penny magazines. He eagerly exploited the numerous opportunities that arose at a time when the market for fiction was growing apace and sought to gain access to new readerships throughout his career. Edward Marston, a partner in the publishing firm of Sampson Low, noted that 'Mr Collins had a perfect knowledge of his own value',[37] and one imagines that Collins would have agreed with George Warrington, Thackeray's sympathetic portrait of a young novelist in *Pendennis*, who proudly announces that he is a 'prose labourer' and that 'capital . . . the bargainmaster . . . has a right to deal with the literary inventor as with any other' (*Pendennis*, Chapter 32).

However, despite Collins's eager participation in the literary marketplace and in the process of literary commodification that was well underway by the time he began publishing novels in 1850, the prefaces that he wrote for the volume versions of his novels reveal that he also wished to be taken seriously as an artist, and to be considered as a serious novelist rather than (or as well as) merely a popular writer and a good hand at a serial—to borrow the words that Thomas Hardy later used to describe his own early aspirations as a writer. From the very beginning of his career, Collins's prefaces variously elaborate his theories of art and the novel, defend his procedures in the particular novel being prefaced, expound upon the care which he has devoted to his narrative and to the details of chronology, development or setting, and deflect or (especially in the case of later additions) rebut critical objections to his work. The tone is set in the Letter of Dedication to *Basil*, in which he seeks to forestall possible objections to the extravagance of his setting and plot and engages in contemporary debates about realism and idealism in fiction, by claiming that his story is thoroughly grounded in reality and experience. The 'main event' out of which his story sprang, he wrote, was founded on 'a fact within my own knowledge', and the narrative was shaped and guided 'by my own experience, or by the experience related to me by others'. He defends the use of 'extraordinary accidents and events which happen to few men' as being just as 'legitimate . . . [as] materials for fiction to work with— when there [is] a good object in using them—as the ordinary accidents and events which may, and do, happen to us all'. Anticipating the arguments of George Eliot and George Henry Lewes in the mid-1850s, Collins contended that an adherence to the 'Actual' was the means to the 'Ideal' which was the proper concern of art: 'Fancy and Imagination, Grace and Beauty, all those qualities which are to the work of Art what scent and colour are to the flower, can only grow towards heaven by taking root in earth. Is not the noblest poetry of prose fiction the poetry of every-day truth?' Like Dickens before him and like numerous novelists later in the century (notably Hardy and George Moore), Collins, in the prefatory letter to his first novel of modern life, defends his portrayal of scenes and experiences which are beyond the confines of respectable life, as being in the interests of both art and morality, and he attacks the hypocrisy and cant of the respectable reader:

Nobody who admits that the business of fiction is to exhibit human life, can deny that scenes of misery and crime must of necessity, while human nature remains what it is, form part of that exhibition. Nobody can assert that such scenes are unproductive of useful results, when they are turned to a plainly and purely moral purpose. . . .

To those persons who . . . deny that it is the novelist's vocation to do more than merely amuse them; who shrink from all honest and serious reference, in books, to subjects which they think of in private and talk of in public everywhere; who see covert implications where nothing is implied, and improper allusions where nothing improper is alluded to . . . whose morality stops at the tongue, and never gets on to the heart—to those persons, I should consider it loss of time, and worse, to offer any further explanation of my motives, than the sufficient explanation which I have given already. I do not address myself to them in this book, and shall never think of addressing myself to them in any other.

By the time Collins wrote the Preface to the first three-volume edition (1860) of *The Woman in White* he was more confident of his relationship with at least one section of his readers—the serial readers whose response had made the novel the success which in some sense authorizes the presentation of the work to a second, 'new class of readers' (the circulating library readers) who will receive the novel 'in its complete form'. Collins was particularly anxious to make this new class of readers (and also potential reviewers) fully conscious of the care which he had taken in revising the novel for volume publication, 'with a view to smoothing and consolidating the story'. He was also at pains to insist on the boldly experimental nature of his narrative form (which assigns the telling of the story entirely to the characters who 'are all placed in different positions along the chain of events', each taking up the chain in turn and carrying it on to the end), and to warn reviewers against prematurely disclosing the significance of any of the links in the narrative chain. The Preface to the New Edition of 1861 also focuses on narrative, this time engaging with the critical debate which had begun to develop about the tendency of the sensation novel to develop story at the expense of character. Collins took the opportunity to reaffirm his adherence to 'the old-fashioned opinion that the primary object of a work of fiction should be to tell a story', and his firm belief that the novelist who properly performed this first condition of his art, was in no danger of 'neglecting the delineation of character' since the two are inextricably interconnected. Collins returns to the issue of the relationship between character and plot in the Preface to the 1868 edition of *The Moonstone*, noting that whereas in 'some of my former novels, the object proposed has been to trace the influence of circumstances upon character', the project in the current novel was to 'trace the influence of character on circumstances'. In this Preface, as in the prefaces to *Basil* and *The Woman in White*, Collins once more emphasizes the psychological reality of his plot and the pains which he has expended on its accurate development.

When *Basil* was reissued in 1862, following the critical and commercial success of *The Woman in White*, Collins added a section to the Letter of Dedication in which he further exonerated his own procedures and attacked small-minded readers and critics:

On its appearance, it was condemned off-hand, by a certain class of readers, as an outrage on their sense of propriety. Conscious of having designed and written my story with the strictest regard to true delicacy, as distinguished from false—I allowed the prurient misinterpretation of certain perfectly innocent passages . . . to assert itself as offensively as it pleased . . . I knew that 'Basil' had nothing to fear from pure-minded readers . . . Slowly and surely, my story forced its way through all adverse criticism, to a place in the public favour which it has never lost since.

The responses of right-minded readers were clearly very much in Collins's mind in 1862. In the same year he wrote a Preface for the first three-volume edition of *No Name* in which he disingenuously uses 'the authority of many readers' of the periodical version of the novel to underwrite the success and truth to 'Nature' of his treatment of Magdalen as an embodiment of 'the struggle of a human creature under the opposing influences of Good and Evil' (he already knew that many readers and critics were disconcerted and offended by his treatment of Magdalen). Similarly in 1866 Collins prefaced *Armadale* with a brief statement indicating that the continuing 'friendly reception' of 'Readers in general' to his work rendered 'any prefatory pleading' for his story unnecessary. Nevertheless, he went on to warn 'Readers in particular' (or critics) that they may be 'here and there disturbed—perhaps even offended—by finding that "Armadale" oversteps, in more than one direction, the narrow limits within which they are disposed to restrict the development of modern fiction—if they can'. He took up this refrain again in his Preface to *Jezebel's Daughter* (1880) in which he complains that 'there are certain important social topics which are held to be forbidden to the English novelist . . . by a narrow-minded minority of readers, and . . . the critics who flatter their prejudices'. This attack on the restrictions imposed by middle-class readers and reviewers on the range of English fiction was to be echoed by a new generation of writers in the 1880s and 1890s, including George Moore in *Literature at Nurse or Circulating Morals* (1885) and Thomas Hardy in his contribution to the debate on 'Candour in English Fiction' which appeared in the *New Review* in 1890. Collins's own defence against such restrictive views remained the same as that which he had outlined in the brief and terse Preface to *Armadale*, which asserts the power and justice of his 'offensive truth' (to borrow the words that Thomas Hardy later used of his own work): 'I am not afraid of my design being permanently misunderstood, provided the execution has done it any sort of justice. Estimated by the Clap-trap morality of the present day, this may be a very daring book. Judged by the Christian morality which is of all time, it is only a book that is daring enough to speak the truth.'

Collins and the Reviewers

Despite his frequent protestations that he neither read nor heeded reviewers, Collins had collected three scrapbooks of reviews of his fiction by the time of his death, and both his letters and prefaces reveal that he was familiar with the details of the critical praise and blame that his novels received. At the beginning of his career, when he was seeking to establish himself as a professional novelist, he went out of his way to bring his work to the attention of influential reviews and reviewers. He sent copies of *Antonina* with an accompanying note to two or three reviews and got his friend Douglas Jerrold to take a copy to the *Athenaeum* and recommend it to two of its regular fiction reviewers. He exploited his connections with the *Leader* and *Bentley's Miscellany* to get a generally favourable notice for his second novel, *Basil*. Collins later recalled that *Antonina* had received 'such a chorus of praise as has never been sung over me since',[38] and indeed the young author was compared to Shakespeare and his first novel was described as a 'remarkable book' (*Observer*) which showed a 'splendour of imagination' (*Harper's*). Collins was, however, taken to task for his over-reliance on description, for a tendency to 'pictorial display' which was 'frequently detrimental to the dramatic character of the work', and he was advised to 'study thoroughly the art of construction, especially in making his story more compact and rapid in action' (*Eclectic Review*).[39] Collins's subsequent novels and prefaces indicate that he took this lesson to heart, and reviews of his novels show that he spent the rest of his career being alternately praised and blamed for having done so.

The tone of the nineteenth-century critical debate on Collins's work was set by the reviews of *Basil*. The *Leader* praised Collins's storytelling abilities, but was critical of the novel's 'air of unreality'.[40]

The *Examiner* pointed to the riskiness of Collins's brand of storytell-ing when it noted 'the skill with which Mr. Collins has wrought out a plot that in worse hands would be nonsense'.[41] The moral objections to his subject matter and his way of treating it, which were to prove a persistent feature of the critical reception of Collins's fiction, were announced in the *Westminster*'s view that the central episode of *Basil* was 'absolutely disgusting',[42] and that the book lacked moral purpose. The *Athenaeum*, perhaps harking back to the Newgate controversy of the 1830s, warned Collins against adopting the 'aesthetics of the Old Bailey',[43] as it had previously warned him, in its review of *Antonina*, 'against the vices of the French school,—against the need-less accumulation of revolting details,—against catering for a prurient taste by dwelling on such incidental portions of the subject as, being morbid, ought to be treated incidentally'.[44]

If Collins devoted considerable space in his prefaces to defending his art of storytelling that was because the reviewers spent a great deal of time pointing out its defects. Many reviewers took Collins to task for being no more than a storyteller, a mere 'plot machinist' and constructor of puzzles who was incapable of creating characters 'which appeal to our feelings'.[45] These words appeared in the *Satur-day Review*'s notice of *The Queen of Hearts*, (1859) a collection of short stories linked together by a connecting narrative. This review also attempted a broader and fairly representative consideration of Collins's achievements as a novelist up until the autumn of 1859.

There are plenty of novels written in these days to unfold the philosophy or to instil the instruction which finds favour with the writer. There are novels in which the author attempts to elaborate character, and to show how certain vices or virtues are revealed or fostered by the circumstances in which the actors of the fiction are placed. There are, again, novels intended to describe states of society which have passed away, or ways of life unfamiliar to the English public, or scenery, customs, and institutions foreign to our usual habits of thought. Mr. Collins considers that all these attempts are divergences from the proper duty of a novelist. A Story-teller should have a story to tell, and should tell it. It is his business not to improve or to instruct mankind, but to amuse. Common life is full of strange incidents. If these are related disjointedly and unmethodically, the attention of a reader or hearer is only momentarily arrested. But here lies the field for the novelist's skill. He can so arrange the story that the interest shall be prolonged. He can devise a number of minute incidents, all converging in a central point. He can bring constantly home to the conviction of his reader that this central point exists, and yet can conceal what it is. He can manage that, when this central point is revealed, all that before seemed obscure shall seem clear, and every main incident shall appear to have occurred independently and naturally, though conducing to the evolution of the final mystery. A story thus becomes a well-managed puzzle.[46]

The notion that Collins was merely a painstaking constructor of plot also featured prominently in the reviews of *The Woman in White*, despite eulogies from countless readers. Such satisfied readers included fellow novelist Thackeray, who read it 'from morning till sunset', and William Gladstone (soon to become Prime Minister), who failed to attend a play because he found the novel 'so very interesting'. Gladstone thought that *The Woman in White* was 'far better sustained than Adam Bede', and though he was not convinced that 'it rises quite so high' as George Eliot's novel he found the characterization 'excellent'.[47] Most early reviews of Collins's best-seller were far from reaching this level of enthusiasm, but eventually it was favourably reviewed in *Blackwood's* and *The Times*. One early notice, which appeared in the *Saturday Review*, praises Collins's storytelling and plotting, but takes up the refrain from the review of *The Queen of Hearts* (quoted above), arguing that storytelling is *all* that he can do: 'he is a good constructor. Each of his stories is a puzzle, the key to which is not handed to us till the third volume.'[48] On the other hand, 'character, passion, and pathos' are said to be 'mere accessory colouring': his people 'have characteristics, but not character'.[49]

The debate about Collins's privileging of plot over character continued to mark the critical reception of his fiction throughout the 1860s where it became further complicated by becoming entangled with the sensation debate (see also p. 90). *The Woman in White* was reviewed retrospectively as a sensation novel in a *Spectator* review of Frances Browne's *The Castleford Case* which appeared on 28 December 1861:

we are threatened with a new variety of the sensation novel, a host of cleverly complicated stories, the whole interest of which consists in the gradual unravelling of some carefully prepared enigma. Mr. Wilkie Collins set the fashion, and now every novel writer who can construct a plot, thinks if only he makes it a little more mysterious and unnatural, he may obtain a success rivalling that of *The Woman in White*.[50]

Five months later in an unsigned review on 'Sensation Novels'
referred to earlier, Margaret Oliphant was expressing her admiration
for Collins's 'highly-wrought sensation-novel', for which 'the author
has long been engaged in preparatory studies', and congratulating
him on the creation of the pure sensation scene which opened
the novel. *No Name* was drawn into the sensation controversy as
one of the twenty-four examples of sensation fiction attacked by
H. L. Mansel in an unsigned review in the *Quarterly* in 1863. This
review placed Collins in the context of a new 'class of literature'
which aimed merely at the production of excitement, and whose
growth was said to be indicative of the diseased state of the modern
commercial age. Sensation novels, Mansel asserted, were both the
symptoms and cause 'of a widespread corruption . . . and disease',
and they were tainted by a 'commercial atmosphere . . . redolent of
the manufactory or shop'.[51] As far as *No Name* itself was concerned,
the focus of Mansel's attack was less on its plotting than on the
faulty logic and morality of the way in which Collins constructs his
'protest against the law which determines the social position of
illegitimate children'.[52] Alexander Smith, in an unsigned piece in the
North British Review, attacked the unreality of characters such as
Magdalen, Captain Wragge, Noel Vanstone, and Mrs Lecount, noting that 'Such people have no representatives in the living world.
Their proper place is the glare of blue lights on a stage sacred to the
sensation drama'—though he concedes 'yet there are excellent
things in *No Name*'.[53] *Armadale* was similarly reviewed (in the
Athenaeum) as a

'sensation novel' with a vengeance,—one, however, which could hardly
fail to follow *No Name*. Those who make plot their first consideration and
humanity the second,—those, again, who represent the decencies of life as
too often so many hypocrisies,—have placed themselves in a groove which
goes, and must go, in a downward direction, whether as regards fiction or
morals.[54]

Both Magdalen Vanstone and Lydia Gwilt were reviewed as sensation heroines. Lydia—'a bigamist, thief, gaol-bird, forgeress,
murderess, and suicide'—was compared to the 'big black baboon'
that was exhibited when 'Richardson, the showman, went about with
his menagerie'.[55] It was as the work of the leading luminary of the
'sensation school in novels' that *The Times* reviewed *The Moonstone*.

However, for this reviewer the distinguishing characteristic of the sensation school was not its bestial women, nor its faulty morality, but its 'habit of laying eggs and hiding them', a 'propensity for secretiveness' which, it is argued, Collins had in a complex form. While the *Times* reviewer did not find egg-hiding to be incompatible with the creation of interesting and sympathetic characters, other reviewers continued to do so: the words 'puzzle' and 'conundrum' are repeatedly used to describe the narrative and the characters are described as 'puppets'.[56] The American *Lippincott's Magazine*, on the other hand, pronounced *The Moonstone* to be 'a perfect work of art'.[57]

It has often been argued that Collins's reputation as a novelist, and perhaps even his novel-writing abilities, went into terminal decline following *The Moonstone*. Certainly he never repeated the spectacular popular and critical success of *The Woman in White*. However, throughout the 1870s and for most of the 1880s he continued to produce novels which commanded a wide and numerous readership and which attracted critical notice. To be sure, the reviews were not always favourable, and many reviewers deplored what they saw as his increasing use of the novel for propaganda purposes. *Man and Wife*, for example, enjoyed excellent sales when it was serialized in *Cassell's Magazine* in 1870, and several reviewers judged that Collins had lost none of his power as a storyteller. Indeed, the reviewer for the *Saturday Review* claimed to have 'taken the book, so to speak, at one draught' finding it 'too amusing to be laid down unfinished',[58] and *Harper's New Monthly Magazine* pronounced that 'as a romance' it was 'pre-eminently superior to any fiction of the year'. However, *Harper's* also judged it to be a failure 'as an indictment' and the *Saturday Review* noted that:

moral aims generally spoil any novel in which they are prominent, and we think that they have led in this case to some serious artistic faults. If one moral is generally too much, two morals are surely unjustifiable. Mr Collins might be content with assaulting running and boat-racing without breaking a lance at the same moment against all our marriage laws.[59]

Throughout the last twenty years of Collins's career reviewers continued to debate whether he should be taken seriously and on his own professed terms as a moral reformer, or whether he was merely a storyteller. Thus, J. A. Noble in his *Spectator* review of Collins's last completed novel, reflects on the 'intellectual scheme' of *The Legacy of Cain* (1889) only to conclude that he may be 'considering too curiously, and breaking an intellectual butterfly on a critical wheel'. Collins, he asserted, 'may occasionally have a theory to illustrate, but he always has a story to tell, and the story is more important both to him and his readers'.[60] And on the question of Collins's merits as a storyteller, the critical refrain remained substantially the same in the closing decades as it had been in the first decades of his career: he was by turns praised for his skill in storytelling and plotting, and blamed for being a mere or mechanical plotter. The only new note, perhaps inevitably given the length of his career, was that he was now accused of repeating himself, and even of self-parody.

CHAPTER 4

MASTERS, SERVANTS, AND MARRIED WOMEN
CLASS AND SOCIAL MOBILITY IN COLLINS'S NOVELS

> There are certain important social topics which are held to
> be forbidden to the English novelist ... by a narrow-minded
> minority of readers and ... the critics who flatter their prejudices.
>
> (Preface to *Jezebel's Daughter*)

COLLINS's fiction both exemplifies and engages with a range of
contemporary social and cultural concerns and anxieties. Throughout
his career he used both his fiction and his journalism as vehicles for
social critique, and his own equivocal social position is reproduced
in his continuing fascination with marginal and liminal figures.
Sometimes, particularly in the last two decades of his writing career,
Collins devoted whole novels to specific issues: 'certain important
social topics' (as he puts it in the Preface to his late sensation novel,
Jezebel's Daughter, 1880), such as the reform of prostitutes (in *The
New Magdalen* and *The Fallen Leaves*), or anti-vivisectionism (*Heart
and Science*). From the beginning of his writing career Collins was
preoccupied with issues of class and gender. Class inequality and
social mobility, and changing social relations feature prominently in
his fiction, as does an interest in changing conceptions of masculinity and femininity and changing gender roles. Many of his novels
focus on the rights of women and children and explore the role
played by the law and government in constructing and regulating the
family, not least through their investigation of contemporary controversies about the property rights of married women and the 'chaos'
of the laws governing marriage and divorce. More generally, Collins's
novels explore contemporary modes of policing individual and social
behaviour through social, sexual, and religious codes.

Class

In 'A New View of Society', published in *All the Year Round* in 1860, Collins informs his readers that his most enjoyable party during 'the course of a long experience of Society' was one which he had observed in the company of 'worthy fellow-outcasts' out on the street. Collins describes how, having decided against attending the formal ritual of the dinner party to which he had been invited, he had put on comfortable clothes and had gone to lounge with the lower-class people gathered outside the house where the dinner was being held, and had shared in their pastime of looking through the uncurtained window at the spectacle within:

There [the guests] were, all oozing away into silence and insensibility together; smothered in their heavy black coats, and strangled in their stiff, white cravats!

There is a fourth place vacant . . . *My* place . . . I see my own ghost sitting there: the appearance of that perspiring spectre is too dreadful to be described . . . I turn away my face in terror, and look for comfort at my street-companions, my worthy fellow-outcasts.[1]

This passage gives both the middle-class reader and the writer a new perspective on the world of 'Society', whilst it also gives a very familiar picture of the class distinctions and divisions of nineteenth-century society. It is clear that the writer belongs to the world of 'Society', but it is equally clear that he feels uncomfortable with its rituals, and that he surveys it from an ironic distance which renders his own identity and position problematic. The new view of society he obtains when he is at ease with his street companions also gives a new—and troubling—perspective on the self, one which involves a form of self-splitting. Both the insider–outsider perspective on the world of 'Society', and the sympathetic identification with the lower classes which are seen in this passage are characteristic of much of Collins's fiction. So too is the shifting sense of class identity that is inherent in the suggestion that it can be put on and off like (or, indeed, by) a change of clothing. This point is reinforced by Magdalen Vanstone's adoption of a series of different class identities in *No Name*, and by her assertion that 'A lady is a woman who wears a silk gown, and has a sense of her own importance' (*No Name*, The Sixth Scene, Chapter II).

The plot of *Basil* (1852), the first of Collins's novels of modern life, turns on issues of social mobility and straying across class boundaries, as well as on cross-class tensions and resentment, all seen mainly from the perspective of a confessional narrator who is also the novel's chief protagonist. One strand of the narrative, the secret cross-class marriage between Basil, the younger son of a man who takes pride in his noble and ancient lineage, and Margaret Sherwin, a linen-draper's daughter, originates in a chance meeting on an omnibus. In 1852 this was a distinctively modern form of transport; as Basil puts it, 'a perambulatory exhibition-room of the eccentricities of human nature'(*Basil*, Part I, VII), which brought together 'persons of all classes' in an unfamiliar proximity. The other main driver of this early sensation narrative is the cross-class rivalry for Margaret's affections of Basil and Robert Mannion, clerk to Mr Sherwin, and (it turns out) son of a disgraced former associate of Basil's father.

The early part of the narrative focuses minutely on Basil's experiences of various signifiers of class. His own boyhood and education are dismissed as of little interest, being merely those of 'hundreds of others in my rank of life' (Part I, II). His relations with his father are arguably also like those of hundreds of others in the narrator's rank of life—although Basil sees them as peculiarly formative of his own identity; 'We . . . had to share his heart with his ancestors—we were his household property as well as his children . . . [and] were taught . . . that to disgrace our family, either by word or action, was the one fatal crime that could never be . . . pardoned' (Part I, III). Uncomfortable and insecure in his own class role, Basil nevertheless reveals himself as formed by it. As he narrates what he retrospectively presents as the story of the entrapment of a naive and vulnerable young man by the socially ambitious Sherwins, Basil presents himself as a visitor to an alien world of the newly built North London suburbs, a gimcrack world of glaring novelty and display which assaulted his more refined sensibilities:

Everything was oppressively new. The brilliantly-varnished door cracked with a report like a pistol when it was opened; the paper on the walls, with its gaudy pattern . . . looked hardly dry yet; the showy window-curtains . . . and the still showier carpet . . . seemed as if they had come out of the shop yesterday . . . the morocco-bound picture books . . . looked as if they had never been moved or opened since they had been bought; not one leaf even of the music on the piano was dogs-eared or worn. Never was a richly-furnished room more thoroughly comfortless than this—the eye ached at looking at it. There was no repose anywhere. (Part I, X)

Basil is an early example of the way in which Collins's modernization of Gothic reverses some of its key terms, including those of class. Whereas traditional Gothic habitually puts its middle- or upper-class heroine at the mercy of a sinister ecclesiastical or aristocratic power, Collins's modern Gothic entraps its upper-class male protagonist in a secular lower-middle-class world, whose power to trap and terrify stems in part from the hero's inability to read it correctly. Basil ultimately survives his adventures in the suburbs and is reconciled with his father, but he does not fully rejoin his father's world, and his narrative ends with his father's death, his brother's inheritance of the family home, and his own retreat into rural retirement with his sister.

Basil charts the social and self-estrangement of an aristocratic hero through his sexual attraction to and subsequent obsession with a lower-middle-class woman and his obsessive jealousy and hatred for her scheming lover, the confidential clerk Mannion. The clerk, in his turn, is obsessively jealous and resentful of his social superior 'who, in his insolence of youth, and birth, and fortune, had snatched from me the one long-delayed reward for twenty years of misery, just as my hands were stretched forth to grasp it', and who, to add insult to injury, 'was the son of that honourable and high-born gentleman who had given my father to the gallows' (Part III, V). *The Woman in White*, on the other hand, charts the social advancement of a middle-class drawing master through his involvement with an upper-class woman and his dogged pursuit of her scheming aristocratic husband. Walter Hartright's story of 'what a Woman's patience can endure, and what a Man's resolution can achieve' (*The Woman in White*, The Story begun by Walter Hartright, I) is one which, as Ann Cvetkovich has argued, 'serves as a vehicle for his accession to patriarchal power and property, making it possible for him to marry [Laura Fairlie] despite their class difference'.[2] Walter, the narrator of part of his own story and the editor of the stories of the other protagonists in, and 'witnesses' to, the events, presents that story as one in which he seeks to achieve the justice which is denied to Laura by the patriarchal power of the aristocracy and the 'long purse' of the law. The story of

Walter's unmasking of the crimes and misdemeanours of aristocratic men, such as Sir Percival Glyde and Laura's own father, is also a story which (as Cvetkovich points out) provides a cover for the story of his own acquisition of their power through marrying Laura—after restoring her identity.

The different social positions of Walter, Laura, and Marian and the changes which they undergo during the course of the novel are very interesting. Like many of Collins's (and Dickens's) heroes, Walter is, at the beginning of the novel, a young man who has no clear social position, no secure income, and no clear vocation. He is middle class, but his family lives in reduced circumstances and must make what they can of such social connections that they have. He has made a half-hearted attempt at one profession—the law—and is trying to make his way as an artist and drawing master, when he first gains employment at Limmeridge. Laura, his pupil, and the heiress of Limmeridge, is the daughter of an aristocratic father and a mother whose social origins, habits, and tastes are middle class. Laura's modest bearing and dress align her with her mother's middle-class gentility, rather than with her father's aristocratic heritage. In contrast, the lower-born Marian, whose social position depends, to a large extent on the good grace of her half-sister, is described (by Walter) as having the 'unaffected self-reliance of a highly-bred woman' (*The Woman in White*, The Story begun by Walter Hartright, VI). As John Kucich notes, these three characters 'undergo an unmistakable realignment with middle-class social identities'[3] in the later part of the narrative, when the more showy and independent Marian adopts housewifely duties, and Walter becomes an illustrator for journals, a profession in which it is possible to earn a reliable income by one's own efforts and the exploitation of professional networks, rather than being dependent on the patronage of the upper classes. Even Laura play-acts (unbeknown to her) a genteel occupation, by 'earning' pennies (from Walter's pocket) for her own illustrations. Thus when the three return to Limmeridge House at the end of the novel, they can be seen as both replacing an outmoded aristocratic world, and, in the case of Walter and Laura, as taking their own middle-class values up a social notch.

The fascination with cross-class sexual liaisons evident in *Basil* and *The Woman in White* was one which Collins retained throughout his career, and he repeatedly represented sexual attraction as 'a state of mind' (as he puts it in *The Guilty River*, 1886) which rendered his characters 'insensible to the distinctions that separate the classes in England' (Chapter VII). Cross-class marriages also feature prominently in his fiction, from Basil's downwardly mobile marriage to the linen-draper's daughter, through Walter's upwardly mobile marriage to his aristocratic pupil, to the marriage of a former prostitute (Mercy Merrick) to a clergyman (Julian Gray) in *The New Magdalen*, the matching of an elderly aristocrat to a woman of uncertain social position who has been seduced and betrayed by the father of her illegitimate stillborn child (Sir Patrick Lundie and Anne Sylvester in *Man and Wife*), and the marriage of a well-born man to a miller's daughter in *The Guilty River*. Among other things cross-class marriages are symptomatic of the social mobility which characterized mid-Victorian society, and Collins's novels repeatedly focus on anxieties about the signifiers of social status. One of the reasons that Basil agrees to the proposal that his secret marriage to Margaret Sherwin should not be consummated for a year, is his belief that during this period—which will permit 'the finishing off of her education and the formation of her constitution' (*Basil*, Part I, XI)—she will lose some of the marks of the social difference between them. Similarly, the plot complications of *The Guilty River* are used to keep apart the hero and his lower-class beloved while her education and accomplishments are improved by her aristocratic patroness.

While many of Collins's plots turn on the desire for upward social mobility, or track its progress through the narrative, some of them focus on downward mobility and the precariousness of social rank. In *The Dead Secret* (1857), for example, Rosamond Frankland, the heroine and inheritor of the fortune of Captain Treverton (whom she and the world at large has always believed to be her father), loses her fortune and is in danger of losing social caste when she discovers that she is the daughter, not of Captain Treverton and his wife, but of Mrs Treverton's lady's maid, Sarah Leeson and a tin miner. Similarly, in *No Name* the Vanstone sisters lose their name and rank as well as any entitlement to their father's estate when it is discovered, after the death of their parents, that Mr and Mrs Vanstone were not in fact legally married at the time of their daughters' birth (indeed Mr Vanstone was legally married to someone else at that time).

The detective investigation upon which Rosamond embarks in *The Dead Secret*, and the detective-cum-fraud plot in which Magdalen Vanstone becomes embroiled in *No Name*, are used by Collins both to explore the grounds on which class and social identities were constructed in Victorian England, and to expose their shifting nature. Both these novels employ plot situations which involve a 'lady' exchanging identities with a lower-class character. For example, in the deception at the centre of *The Dead Secret*, Mrs Treverton briefly exchanges both clothes and roles with her unmarried and pregnant maid, Sarah Leeson, in order to protect the maid's reputation and to provide Captain Treverton with a much-wanted child. In order to further her schemes to avenge herself against the man who has displaced the Vanstone sisters as their father's heir and to restore her family name, Magdalen, the heroine of *No Name*, impersonates her former governess, Miss Garth. Later, having been tutored by her own maid Louisa, she enters the household of Admiral Bartram in the role of a parlourmaid.

As some of these examples might suggest, as well as exposing and exploring—often with satirical intent—the somewhat minute concern of his contemporaries with social codes, social gradations within the growing middle classes, and relations between the middle classes and aristocracy, Collins also focuses sympathetically on some aspects of lower-class life, particularly through his portrayal of servants. Something of Collins's views of the artistic representation of servants and the working classes was evident in his first published work, *Memoirs of the Life of William Collins, Esq., RA*, in which he had implied that his father, like many artists of his generation, had sentimentalized the poor and failed to render adequately the 'fierce miseries or coarse contentions which form the darker tragedy of humble life' (*Memoirs*, ii. 311). In his 1856 *Household Words* essay, 'Laid up in Two Lodgings', Collins offers a comic but sympathetic study of 'those forlorn members of the population called maids-of-all-work' who pass through the clutches of his unsavoury London landlady Mrs Glutch. For these 'apprentices to the hard business of service' and 'drudgery':

Life means dirty work, small wages, hard words, no holidays, no social station, no future . . . No human being ever was created for this. No state of society which composedly accepts this, in the cases of thousands, as one of the necessary conditions of its selfish comforts, can pass itself off as civilized except under the most audacious of false pretences. These thoughts rise in me often, when I ring the bell, and the maid-of-all-work answers it wearily. I cannot communicate them to her: I can only do my best to encourage her to peep over the cruel social barrier which separates her unmerited comfortlessness from my undeserved luxury, and encourage her to talk to me now and then on something like equal terms.[4]

In some of his novels Collins both focuses on the 'cruel social barrier which separates [the servant's] unmerited comfortlessness from [the] undeserved luxury' of their masters and social superiors, and makes his fictional servants 'talk to' his readers on something like 'equal terms', by claiming common humanity with them. For example, Rosanna Spearman in *The Moonstone* is not only an important plot device, she is also a sympathetic and admonitory portrait of the sufferings of a lower-class woman who transgresses class boundaries by becoming infatuated with her social superior Franklin Blake. Rosanna's friend Lucy Yolland ('Limping Lucy') speaks up for the dead servant and articulates the class resentment of that procession of maids-of-all-work noted by Collins in 'Laid up in Two Lodgings' when she rebuts Betteredge's view of the respect due to 'Mr Franklin Blake', with the revolutionary sentiment that 'the day is not far off when the poor will rise against the rich' (*The Moonstone*, First Period, Chapter XXIII). Significantly, in the novel's calendar of events Lucy issues her warnings about the imminent toppling of the rich by the poor in 1848, the year of the climax of the Chartist movement and the year of revolutions in Continental Europe. Lucy's own call for social revolution follows what she perceives to be Blake's thwarting of her own plan to rescue Rosanna from a life of servitude by establishing her in a sisterhood of dignified labour in which they would live 'by our needles' (*The Moonstone*, First Period, Chapter XXIII). Similarly, both Sarah Leeson and Hester Dethridge, the servants-with-a-secret in *The Dead Secret* and *Man and Wife*, are more than merely plot devices and stereotypes, and their sufferings are presented sympathetically, if melodramatically.

Anthea Trodd has linked Collins's (and other nineteenth-century novelists') portrayal of servants to the 'widespread perception of a crisis in employer–servant relations' in the mid-Victorian period, a state of affairs which was much discussed in the contemporary press. She has argued persuasively that this crisis found literary expression in the unusually 'high visibility' of servants in mid-century crime and detective fiction.[5] As many social historians have pointed out, the number and nature of the complement of servants in a nineteenth-century household served to signify the status and gentility of that household. However, there was also a persistent anxiety, especially amongst the new middle classes, that the presence of lower-class people in the upper- or middle-class household threatened the domestic privacy upon which middle-class gentility was increasingly constructed. Hence servants were frequently represented by Collins and his contemporaries as invaders or interlopers, plotters and spies.

On a number of occasions Collins placed a servant (or servants) at the very heart of his plot. Sarah Leeson, in *The Dead Secret*, is a servant who bears the guilty burden of her own and her mistress's secret, and her disturbed and disturbing appearance signals the presence of a mystery that the characters and readers want to solve. Indeed there would not be a mystery in this novel if it were not for Sarah's action in concealing the deathbed confession which Mrs Treverton writes for her husband. Servants are often close either to the centre of the mystery or to the prolongation of the mystery in Collins's novels. The high visibility of servants in plot terms derives from Collins's exploitation of their invisibility in class terms. Thus the retired ladies' maid, Mrs Catherick, in *The Woman in White* and Rosanna Spearman, the crippled 'second housemaid' with a criminal record in *The Moonstone*, both write letters which contain vital clues which the heroes of those novels fail to read correctly in their too hasty dismissal of the servants' missives. Moreover, Rosanna also prolongs the mystery of the theft of the Moonstone partly as a consequence of misinterpreting the 'evidence' of Franklin's nightshirt and by seeking to exploit her 'knowledge' in order to gain emotional access to him. The mystery is also prolonged by the difficulty which Rosanna has in gaining any kind of access to Franklin by virtue of their class difference and their relative positions as 'family' and servant in Lady Verinder's household. To Franklin Blake the besotted Rosanna is to all intents and purposes invisible as she pursues her duties in the house in which he is a guest and she is merely part of the system that keeps the household functioning for his (and the others') comfort. She may inhabit the same house, but she traverses it by different pathways and staircases. A kind of class blindness also causes Geoffrey Delamayn to misread the desperation of the crazed, speechless, persecuted cook Hester Dethridge whose secret he seeks to exploit in *Man and Wife*. Hester is an interesting case. Viewed from one perspective she is the ideal servant, and perhaps the misogynist's ideal woman: 'A woman who *can't* talk, and a woman who *can* cook—is simply a woman who has arrived at absolute perfection. Such a treasure shall not go out of the family, if I can help it' (*Man and Wife*, Chapter XXVI). However, her odd behaviour (and the story behind it), reveal some of the fears and fantasies of the middle classes about the domestic 'treasures' upon whom their own treasured domesticity depended.

Servants are not simply associated with the crimes or mysteries that lie at the heart of some of Collins's fictions, they are also, in some cases, themselves criminals. Hester's secret—and the cause of her dumbness and her odd behaviour—is that she has countered prolonged domestic violence with violence and has planned, executed, and concealed a murder. Rosanna is a reformed thief, whom the philanthropic Lady Verinder has taken into her household as part of her rehabilitation, and who conceals what she takes to be the evidence of Franklin's guilt of a crime in order to protect the man she loves. In other novels, Collins exploits the contemporary association of professional servants and crime even more sensationally. For example, Lydia Gwilt, the *femme fatale* of *Armadale*, who adopts the guise of governess to further her scheming, began her life of crime as a 12-year-old lady's maid. In a life history that has enough material for several sensation plots, Lydia has, among other things: exploited her privileged position as a lady's maid to capitalize on the family secrets in which she becomes involved, and used her position and ill-gotten gains in order to acquire an education and accomplishments (first, during periods as a pupil at a French school, and then, following a scandal, a Belgian school for young ladies); become the lure working with a group of professional swindlers and card-sharpers; snared a wealthy young man into marriage; been imprisoned for poisoning him; gained a pardon and a retrial. Like Mary Elizabeth Braddon's Lady Audley, the chameleon-like Lydia Gwilt both plays out a fantasy of upward social mobility and represents a pervasive middle-class insecurity about the unreliability of class signifiers in a period of rapid social change.

Collins shows more sympathy for lower-class characters who are drawn into crime than he does for his aristocratic and upper-middle-class criminals such as Sir Percival Glyde and Godfrey Ablewhite who seek to manipulate the law to their own ends and to prey on the social, economic, and emotional vulnerability of women. Thus, one of his early stories, published in *Harper's New Monthly Magazine* in 1857, depicts the heroic efforts of Bessie, a stone-mason's daughter, to resist the violent attempts of burglars to steal a pocketbook whose safekeeping has been entrusted to her. Perhaps echoing the views of her creator, Bessie notes: 'It is one thing to write fine sentiments in books about uncorruptible honesty, and another thing to put those sentiments into practice, when one day's work is all that a man has to set up in the way of an obstacle between poverty and his own fireside' ('Brother Owen's Story of the Black Cottage' in *The Queen of Hearts*). The plight of the poor and the socially disadvantaged is given greater prominence in some of the later novels, such as *The New Magdalen* and *The Fallen Leaves*, in which Victorian capitalism is observed from the perspectives of their respective heroes, the radical clergyman Julian Gray and the Christian Socialist Amelius Goldenheart. 'I had no idea . . . of what the life of a farm labourer really was, in some parts of England,' proclaims the 'Radical, Communist, Incendiary Clergyman' (Julian) in *The New Magdalen*:

never before had I seen such dire wretchedness as I saw in the cottages . . . the martyrs of old could endure, and die. I asked myself if they could endure and *live* . . . year after year on the brink of starvation, and see their pining children growing up around them; live with the poor man's parish-prison to look forward to as the end, when hunger and labour have done their worst! (*The New Magdalen*, Chapter 8)

Collins's novels are fairly consistent in their sympathetic portrayal of the predicament of the poor and outcast. They are also consistent in their treatment at the other end of the social spectrum: the upper classes are almost always portrayed as outmoded, and either barbaric or effete. Collins also fairly consistently satirized and criti-cized the pretensions of a middle-class gentility that aped the aris-tocracy. However, as John Kucich argues, he also wrote about, and to some extent for, a middle-class elite of 'cultural intellectuals'. As Kucich points out, Collins's central characters 'tend to be drawing masters, writers, actresses, amateur painters and philosophers—especially in his major novels of the 1860s, when he was consolidating his literary success'.[6] These protagonists are usually presented as being in conflict and competition with both superannuated aristocrats, and also—perhaps even more so—with other more secure middle-class and upper-middle-class professionals who had recently established a position of power in the social hierarchy: lawyers, doctors (whose social pretensions are mocked in *A Rogue's Life*), and scientists (in *Heart and Science*). Perhaps unsurprisingly, given Collins's persistent attacks on the law and the legal system, lawyers seem to be the most despised amongst the new professionals. Lawyers are often presented as being merely self-serving, but they are always presented as being the servants of double-thinking. Thus, Mr Gilmore in *The Woman in White* is a decent enough fellow, but morally blinded by that 'great beauty of the Law' which enables it to 'dispute any human statement, made under any circumstances'. When called upon to respond to the evidence that Marian and Walter have provided about Sir Percival Glyde's dealings with Anne Catherick, he concludes:

If I had felt professionally called upon to set up a case against Sir Percival Glyde, on the strength of his own explanation, I could have done so beyond all doubt. But my duty did not lie in this direction: my function was of the purely judicial kind. I was to weigh the explanation we had just heard; to allow all due force to the high reputation of the gentleman who offered it; and to decide honestly whether the probabilities . . . were plainly with [Sir Percival], or plainly against him. My own conviction was that they were plainly with him. (*The Woman in White*, The Story continued by Vincent Gilmore, I)

Of course, Gilmore is also blinded by class and by gender: he is more inclined to accept the word of a male member of the aristocracy than of an enfeebled girl. As far as Collins is concerned, their tendency to identify with the social status quo is one of the main problems with lawyers. They tend to be insufficiently questioning of those with social power, and universally suspicious of those without it.

Collins reserves the full force of his animus for 'imitation' professionals or quacks who consciously exploit the modern rise of specialist professional expertise, turning its language and methods to their own ends, rather than merely following them slavishly or unthinkingly colluding in their obfuscations. Collins's quacks include the 'moral agriculturalist', Captain Wragge (in *No Name*), an early example of a public relations professional who also bamboozles Mrs Lecount with his fake scientific talk; 'Doctor' Downward (in *Armadale*), an abortionist turned quack psychologist and Principal of a sanatorium which is used to exploit the ignorant as well as acting as a cover for more nefarious activities; even Count Fosco is a kind of quack, an amateur of medicine who 'treats' both Marian and Laura with drugs at various times. As these last two examples indicate, Collins's quacks or imitation professionals are often also criminals, and as such are directly involved in the central crimes and mysteries in the novels in which they appear. The real 'expert' professionals are usually simply involved in the prolongation of the mystery through the failure and failings of their expertise. As John Kucich notes, Collins's championing of his own preferred elite of cultural intellectuals can be seen in their plot role as solvers of the mystery.[7] Thus Walter Hartright, the socially liminal artist, joins forces with a woman to outwit the quacks and to achieve what the professionals are unable to do. Similarly Franklin Blake, the German-educated philosopher, is assisted by the social outcast Ezra Jennings (an 'under-professional' with a self-taught knowledge of both opium and the operations of the human mind) in providing explanations which elude Cuff the famous policeman, Bruff the lawyer, and Candy the medical man.

Gender

From his first novel *Iolani* (unpublished in his life time) to *Blind Love*, the novel he left for Walter Besant to finish after his death, gender roles and gender relations were a recurring preoccupation in Collins's work. In particular his novels repeatedly focused on the victimization of women by men who plot against, mistreat, and imprison them, very often with the support of the law or social custom. However, instances of female victimization were, from the outset, always accompanied by counter-examples of female resistance. From 'primitive' Tahiti (in *Iolani*), through ancient Rome (in *Antonina*), to nineteenth-century England (in most of his novels), 'culture' made victims of women who were by 'nature' made of sterner stuff. In his best-known fiction Collins repeatedly explored the social construction of both femininity and masculinity, and also dramatized pervasive cultural anxieties about changing gender roles. Nevertheless, his fiction often worked with and within the very assumptions about gender difference—and particularly about femininity—which they purported to explore and question. This reflection by the male narrator of *Iolani* is not untypical:

In women, more universally than in men, the necessity for action generates the power. Their energies, though less various, are more concentrated and—by their position in existence—less over-tasked than ours; hence in most cases of extremity, where *we* deliberate, *they* act; and if, in consequence, their failures are more deplorable, their successes are, for the same reason, more triumphant and entire.[8]

Although they repeatedly focus on what it means to be a man or a woman in a particular kind of society at a particular historic moment, Collins's novels also repeatedly return to the universal and essentialist 'truth' about the real natures of men and women offered in the above statement. Thus a significant part of the action of *Antonina* is motivated by the powerful intuitive resolve of a mother (the Goth, Goisvintha) seeking to avenge the slaughter of her children by the Romans. The fall of Rome in Collins's account was, at least in part, attributable to the actions of a primitive mother who was also an emasculating woman. In his novels of contemporary British life, the social fabric of a modern imperial nation is by turns, and sometimes simultaneously, threatened by an 'emasculating' primitive womanly nature, by women who do not know—or who refuse to accept—their assigned place in society; by feminized men, or by coarse brutal masculinity.

Basil, as Jenny Bourne Taylor has noted, offers an exploration of the 'formation and breakdown of the codes that shape masculine upper-middle-class identity'.[9] It does this, among other things, by focusing on the way in which such an identity is constructed in relation to available versions of femininity, as well as being actively shaped by particular women. Thus Basil's precarious masculine identity is shaped, on the one hand, by his feelings of alienation from his father and his father's conceptions of upper-middle-class masculinity, and, on the other, by a complex set of responses to a variety of femininities. These include his idealization of his younger sister, Clara, who is an embodiment of the nineteenth-century womanly ideal and a substitute for the mother who had died shortly after giving birth to her, and his nervousness about a new kind of femininity which threatens both his father's conception of masculinity and Clara's version of 'womanliness'. It is worth quoting at length from the fifth chapter of Basil's narrative, because the opposing versions of femininity which he articulates here recur throughout Collins's fiction. For Basil, it is women such as Clara who preserve 'that claim upon the sincere respect and admiration of men on which the power of the whole sex is based':

There was a beauty about [Clara's] unassuming simplicity, her natural— exquisitely natural—kindness of heart, and word, and manner, which preserved its own unobtrusive influence over you, in spite of all other rival influences . . . You remembered a few kind, pleasant words of hers when you forgot the wit of the wittiest ladies, the learning of the most learned. The influence thus possessed, and unconsciously possessed, by my sister over every one with whom she came in contact—over men especially—may, I think, be very simply accounted for, in very few sentences.

We live in an age when too many women appear to be ambitious of morally unsexing themselves before society, by aping the language and manners of men—especially in reference to that miserable modern dandy-ism of demeanour, which aims at repressing all betrayal of warmth of feeling . . . Women of this exclusively modern order, like to use slang expressions in their conversation; assume a bastard-masculine abruptness in their manners, a bastard-masculine licence in their opinions . . . Nothing impresses, agitates, amuses, or delights them in a hearty, natural, womanly way. (*Basil*, Part I, V)

Margaret Sherwin is one such modern woman who not only 'unsexes' herself by flaunting her sexual attractiveness and conspiring to entrap Basil into marriage, but also unsexes or unmans him by the 'humiliating terms of dependence and prohibition' (*Basil*, Part II, V) which she and her father impose upon that marriage. Like her lover, the upstart clerk Mannion, Margaret is expelled from the narrative, which comes to rest in a world which is isolated and insulated from both modernity and insurgent modern women, as Basil relates his retreat into a feminized world of rural domesticity—'this last retreat, this dearest home' (*Basil*, Letters in Conclusion, Letter III)—with his sister on a small estate which she has inherited from her mother.

At the end of his narrative Basil presents himself as having freely chosen a version of feminine domesticity which for many of Collins's later female characters is a humiliating, dependent, and prohibitive condition, imposed upon them by social custom. Indeed, Collins's novels of modern life are full of women who variously chafe against the bonds of what Marian Halcombe describes as their petticoat existence. Basil may be quite content with his retreat from the world, and, in the end, the narrative of *The Woman in White* reconciles Marian to a domestic existence as the helpmeet of Walter and Laura and a kind of co-parent to their child. However, at the beginning of the novel Collins's early example of one of those strong heroines who were alternatively admired and decried by fiction reviewers of the 1860s is outspoken in her hostility to the limitations of feminine domesticity. It is unreasonable, she objects, to expect four women to dine together alone every day, and not quarrel: 'We are such fools, we can't entertain each other at table. You see I don't think much of my own sex . . . no woman does . . . although few of them confess it as freely as I do' (The Story begun by Walter Hartright, VI). In fact, Marian does not think much of either sex, as presently constituted, and rages over Sir Percival's arrangements for his wedding to her half-sister, Laura: 'Men! They are the enemies of our innocence and our peace—they drag us away from our parents' love and our sisters' friendship—they take us body and soul to themselves, and fasten our helpless lives to theirs as they chain up a dog to his kennel' (The Story continued by Marian Halcombe, II). Collins uses Marian's proto-feminist pronouncements and her active involvement in rescuing Laura and helping Walter to restore her half-sister's identity as a way of questioning and challenging current gender roles. She is also one of a number of characters who are used to destabilize gender boundaries. As first seen through the eyes of Walter Hartright (a man whose own class and gender identity is presented from the outset as being extremely unstable), Marian is both masculine and feminine: 'the rare beauty' of her uncorseted feminine figure being belied by her 'large, firm, masculine mouth and jaw', and an expression, 'bright, frank, and intelligent' which was 'altogether wanting in those feminine attractions of gentleness and pliability' (The Story begun by Walter Hartright, VI), Marian, in turn, sees Walter as feminine, and repeatedly exhorts him to act like a man: 'Don't shrink under it like a woman . . . trample it under foot like a man' (ibid., X). In fact Walter's story is, in part, the story of how he learns to be a man: it is a story which involves going off and dicing with death in the Brazilian jungle, and vying with a man with more social power than himself for the possession of a dependent woman.

In *The Woman in White* sex–gender hybridity is not restricted to Marian and Walter: it is everywhere. Frederick Fairlie, Laura's uncle, is unpleasantly feminized, both in his appearance, which is described as 'frail, languidly-fretful, over-refined' (The Story begun by Walter Hartright, VII), and in his constitution, which is defined in terms of his invalidism and a susceptibility to 'nerves'. Sir Percival Glyde, seen by Marian as a typical male predator, is also presented as an effete aristocrat with a nervous disposition, and his accomplice, Fosco is 'nervously sensitive', and, in Marian's words, is 'a fat St Cecilia masquerading in male attire' (Second Epoch, The Story continued by Marian Halcombe, III). Fosco is, of course, also Italian, and thus outside a conception of masculinity that is constructed in terms of (upper-) middle-class Englishness. Collins's representation of the feminized nervous sensitives Ozias Midwinter in *Armadale* and Ezra Jennings in *The Moonstone* also foregrounds the ways in which class, gender, and nationality intersect in the construction of identity. Midwinter is said to have a 'sensitive feminine organization' (*Armadale*, Book the Second, Chapter VI) and Jennings has a self-proclaimed female constitution: 'Physiology says, and says truly, that some men are born with female constitutions— and I am one of them!' (*The Moonstone*, Second Period, Third Narrative, Chapter IX). In both cases their feminine organization is associated with their liminal position in English society and with their foreignness and racial otherness. Both men are described as dark skinned, and both are of mixed parentage: Midwinter is the son of a white British father and a mother whose 'hot African blood burnt red in her dusky cheeks' (*Armadale*, Prologue, Chapter III), and Jennings is a sort of racial melting pot, whose 'complexion was of a gypsy darkness', and whose 'nose presented the fine shape and modelling so often found among the ancient people of the East, so seldom visible among the newer races of the West' (*The Moonstone*, Second Period, Third Narrative, Chapter IV).

Collins's representation of the blurring of gender boundaries is sometimes (as in the case of Frederick Fairlie) associated with grotesqueness, and this is certainly the case in his portrayal of

Miserrimus Dexter in *The Law and the Lady* (1875). Dexter, who has 'the eyes and hands of a beautiful woman' and a legless body of otherwise 'manly proportions' is (as he is described in the report of Eustace Macallan's trial) quite 'literally the half of a man' (*The Law and the Lady*, Chapter XX). Feminized by his nerves and his propensity to hysteria, yet at the same time aggressive and sexually predatory, Dexter is a grotesque hybrid. He is not only the physical embodiment of the question of what it means to be a man, but he also calls attention to the mutability of gender norms, as for example, when he explains his own elegant garb by giving a potted history of fashion, concluding that: 'Except in this ignoble and material nine-teenth century, men have always worn precious stuffs and beautiful colours as well as women. A hundred years ago, a gentleman in pink silk was a gentleman properly dressed' (Chapter XXVII). This novel's blurring and relativizing of gender boundaries through its presentation of Dexter is complicated (or off-set) by its representa-tion of the heroine, Valeria Macallan, who seeks to defend her marriage by becoming one of the 'lawyes in petticoats' (Chapter XIV). Although, like Marian Halcombe, she turns detective partly in order to escape the constraints of a conventionally defined feminine role, in the end she could be said to collude in the oppression of women by perpetuating the womanly protection of men from the consequences of their actions when she advises her husband against reading the suicide letter left by his first wife.

While most of Collins's novels explored the ways in which gender roles were constructed, and, at the same time, explored various pres-sures for and anxieties about changes in gender roles in the mid-nineteenth century, one novel in particular was a very self-conscious indictment of a specific version of masculinity. *Man and Wife*, published a year after Matthew Arnold's *Culture and Anarchy* (1869), echoes Arnold's attack on an increasingly rough and unruly populace, and, more particularly, on a 'barbarian' aristocracy in its study of the savage brutality of Hester Dethridge's drunken husband and the barbarity and savagery of the cult of athleticism and the ideals of upper-middle-class masculinity, as exemplified by Geoffrey Delamayn. As Collins notes in his 1870 Preface:

We have become so shamelessly familiar with violence and outrage, that we recognise them as a necessary ingredient in our social system, and class our savages as a representative part of our population, under the newly invented name of 'Roughs'. Public attention has been directed by hundreds of other writers to the dirty Rough in fustian . . : [but just as important is] the Rough with the clean skin and the good coat on his back [who] is easily traced through the various grades of English society, in the middle and upper classes.

Or, as Sir Patrick Lundie, one of the novel's more sympathetic characters puts it:

There is far too much glorification in England, just now, of the mere physical qualities which an Englishman shares with the savage and the brute . . . We are readier than we ever were to practise all that is rough in our national customs, and to excuse all that is violent and brutish in our national acts. Read the popular books; attend the popular amusements—and you will find at the bottom of them all, a lessening regard for the gentler graces of civilized life, and a growing admiration for the virtues of the aboriginal Britons. (*Man and Wife*, Chapter III)

As well as being an attack on brute masculinity, *Man and Wife*—in common with many of Collins's novels—is also an attack on the 'rough' national customs and laws relating to marriage in mid-nineteenth-century Britain.

Marriage, Family, and the Law

The general idea of the scope and purpose of the institution of marriage is a miserably narrow one. The same senseless prejudice which leads some people, when driven to extremes, to the practical confession . . . that they would rather see murder committed under their own eyes, than approve of any project for obtaining a law of divorce which shall be equal in its operation on husbands and wives of all ranks who cannot live together, is answerable also for the mischievous error in principle of narrowing the practice of the social virtues, in married people, to themselves and their children . . . The social advantages which [marriage] is fitted to produce ought to extend beyond one man and woman, to the circle of society amid which they move'. ('Bold Words by a Bachelor')[10]

You marry the poor man whom you love . . . and one half your friends pity, and the other half blame you . . . you sell yourself for gold to a man you don't care for; and all your friends rejoice over you; and a minister of public worship sanctions the base horror of the vilest of all human bargains (Count Fosco in *The Woman in White*, Second Epoch, The Story continued by Marian Halcombe, III).

Nearly all of Collins's novels are very obviously concerned with the role of the law in constructing and controlling family life—especially the lives of the property-owning classes. Many of his plots are organized around legal issues, such as wills, inheritance laws, property rights, and marriage laws, and, as several critics have pointed out, 'in most cases it is women who are depicted as the victims of inequities in the law'.[11] One of the exceptions to this general rule is Collins's first novel of modern life, *Basil*, which is concerned, among other things, with the law of primogeniture, and focuses on the predicament of the younger son who cannot in the normal course of events inherit a fair share of his father's property. As Basil complains:

When a family is possessed of large landed property, the individual of that family who shows least interest in its welfare; who is least fond of home, least connected by his own sympathies with his relatives, least ready to learn his duties or admit his responsibilities, is often that very individual who is to succeed to the family inheritance—the eldest brother.

My brother Ralph was no exception to this remark. (*Basil*, Part I, IV)

It is, in large part, Basil's dependent position which renders him vulnerable to the Sherwins' marriage plot, and which also aligns him with female characters and his social inferiors. Unusually, in this novel Collins uses the 'reformed rake' plot to make Basil's older brother, Ralph, worthy of his inheritance: Ralph is redeemed by 'a reformatory attachment to a woman older than himself, who was living separated from her husband', whilst the younger son remains in a dependent role, living in retirement with his sister.

However, from the beginning of the 1860s with the publication of *The Woman in White*, the first of his novels to be reviewed as a sensation novel, Collins turned his attention to the law as it affects women. He took the plot for *The Woman in White* from Maurice Méjan's *Recueil des causes célèbres*, which tells of the successful conspiracy in 1788 by the brother of Madame de Douhault to obtain the money that she had inherited from their father by incarcerating her in a lunatic asylum under a false name. Madame de Douhault was presumed dead and as a consequence her brother and a male cousin inherited her fortune. Although she subsequently regained her freedom she was unable to prove her identity, or regain her estate. In Collins's novel, Sir Percival Glyde and his co-conspirator Count Fosco obtain Laura Fairlie's fortune by falsifying her death and incarcerating her in a lunatic asylum; they substitute her for a long-term inmate, her half-sister Anne Catherick, who dies of heart disease after having been given Laura's identity. Sir Percival's schemes take advantage of the scandalous ease with which men could confine their female relatives to lunatic asylums in mid-nineteenth-century England (as well as in pre-revolutionary France). This scandal was one of the issues addressed by the Parliamentary Select Committee *Inquiry into the Care and Treatment of Lunatics and their Property* in 1858–9, whose findings were the subject of much discussion during the writing and publication of *The Woman in White*. The Select Committee and its report marked an important stage in a continuing debate about the definition and treatment of madness. Collins would have been very familiar with these debates as there had been several articles in Dickens's *Household Words* on the topic of madness, the boundaries between sanity and insanity, and the incarceration of the mad (or those deemed to be so). Stories and articles on madness and the treatment of the mad continued when *Household Words* was replaced by *All the Year Round* and included *The Woman in White* as one of its first serialized novels. For example, one episode of Collins's novel appeared alongside two pieces which gave opposite views of lunatic asylums. In 'Without a Name', a woman who had spent a period in Bedlam tells of her positive experience of treatment for a condition which left her 'silent and moody'.[12] On the other hand *The Black Tarn*, a novella in three parts which appeared at the same time as some of the episodes of *The Woman in White*, tells of a husband who kills his wife after having failed in his attempts to have her locked up on grounds of insanity; his second wife becomes mad and dies when she discovers her predecessor's fate.

Sir Percival resorts to his substitution and confinement plot because his initial attempt to obtain Laura's fortune by the simple tactic of marrying her is thwarted by the terms of the marriage settlement drawn up by her lawyer. This marriage plot thus focuses attention on the problems and complexities of the laws affecting the property of married women of the middle and upper classes, and the vulnerability of these women to the tyranny of their husbands.

Gilmore, the Fairlies' lawyer, seeks to protect Laura from the legal disadvantages of the common law (by which all her property would become her husband's upon marriage), through a marriage settlement (under the law of equity) which seeks to allow Laura to retain control of her property, under the management of a trustee, and to allow her the sole use of the income deriving from it during her lifetime. He proposes that Sir Percival's interest in her property should be restricted to the inheritance of the income in the event of her death, and that the principal or capital should be inherited by her children or, in the absence of children, by her named heirs. However, Sir Percival is able to take advantage of the fact that, as a woman, Laura lacks legal agency, and, in the absence of support from her only male relative (Frederick Fairlie), Gilmore is forced to concede a vital clause to Sir Percival which will allow him to inherit all of Laura's fortune in the event of her death. After a short period of marital bullying during which he fails to persuade Laura to sign away those rights that Gilmore's settlement has secured for her, Sir Percival resorts to the substitution plot which will remove Laura's legal and social identity, and give him control of all of her property as her heir.

The plot of *The Woman in White* depends on a wilful manipulation of the laws affecting married women's property; that of *No Name* depends on the laws concerning inheritance and the legitimacy of children. Having made a foolish marriage during a period of military service in Canada, and being unable to divorce his wife, Andrew Vanstone has entered what Collins was wont to describe in his own case as a morganatic marriage, with a woman with whom he subsequently has two daughters. Although Norah and Magdalen Vanstone are illegitimate, and thus have no legal right to his property, their father has provided for them in his will. The complications of *No Name* result from Andrew's unwitting disinheritance of his daughters when news of the death of his Canadian wife enables him to legalize his union with their mother. When both Vanstone and his wife die shortly after their marriage, their daughters are left penniless as well as nameless, since their parents' marriage does not confer retrospective legitimacy upon the children they bore out of wedlock, and, as their lawyer Pendril points out, a man's marriage 'destroys the validity of any will which he may have made as a single man' (*No Name*, The First Scene, Chapter XIII). As a result,

Vanstone's property passes first to his brother, Michael Vanstone, and, when he dies, to Michael's son Noel: neither man acknowledges any moral claim that the daughters might have to a portion of their father's property. Subsequently the Vanstone inheritance passes to Noel's cousin, Admiral Bartram, and finally to the Admiral's nephew, George Bartram, who (in Collins's squaring of the circle of injustice) has recently married Norah Vanstone.

Although the most impassioned outbursts in the novel are directed at what Pendril and Miss Garth describe as the 'cruel law', the 'disgrace to the nation' (The First Scene, Chapter XIII) which visits the sins of the parents on their illegitimate children, this novel like its predecessor shifts its focus from the rights of children to the legal and property rights of married women, and to contemporary marriage customs. The adventures of Magdalen, the scandalous heroine who adopts a range of disguises in order to entrap Noel Vanstone into marriage, are used to foreground the hypocrisies and machinations in which numerous nineteenth-century men and women engaged in order to make an advantageous marriage. By making 'the general Sense of Propriety [her] accomplice' (*No Name*, Between the [Third and Fourth] Scenes, X), Magdalen acquires the legal right to her family name and, after a period of social marginalization as a professional actress, she also acquires a legitimate social identity via marriage. As Magdalen writes to her former governess:

I am a respectable married woman . . . I have got a place in the world, and a name in the world, at last. Even the law, which is the friend of all you respectable people, has recognized my existence, and has become *my* friend too . . . my wickedness . . . has made Nobody's Child, Somebody's Wife. (Between the [Fifth and Sixth] Scenes, III)

However, when her husband dies having excluded her from his will, Magdalen soon learns that the common law offers as little protection to a wife as it does to an illegitimate child. As in the case of Laura Fairlie, the only protection open to Magdalen is the love of a good man. Although, in *The Woman in White*, Hartright presents his narrative as the story of the process by which Laura's identity is restored to her, it is in fact the story of how she takes on a different identity—that of Mrs Walter Hartright, the wife and dependent of a prosperous artist, and the mother of the male heir of Limmeridge House. Similarly, the resourceful and independent Magdalen fails in her attempts to regain her father's property, and exchanges her legally acquired name of Vanstone for that of her father's closest friend, whose son rescues her from illness and penury and marries her.

If *The Woman in White* and *No Name* were responses to the debates around the Divorce and Matrimonial Causes Act of 1857 and the defeated Married Women's Property Bill of 1856, then *Man and Wife* (1870) was Collins's response to the 1865 Royal Commission which inquired into the state of the marriage laws, and to the debates surrounding the Married Women's Property Bill which came before Parliament in 1868. The Preface which Collins wrote in 1870 emphatically announces *Man and Wife* as a novel-with-a-purpose.

This . . . fiction is founded on facts, and aspires to afford what help it may towards hastening the reform of certain abuses which have been too long suffered to exist among us unchecked.

As to the present scandalous condition of the Marriage Laws of the United Kingdom, there can be no dispute. The Report of the Royal Commission, appointed to examine the working of those laws, has supplied the solid foundation on which I have built my book. Such references to this high authority as may be necessary to convince the reader that I am not leading him astray, will be found collected in the Appendix. I have only to add that, while I write these lines, Parliament is bestirring itself to remedy the cruel abuses which are here exposed in the story of 'Hester Dethridge'. There is a prospect, at last, of lawfully establishing the right of a married woman, in England, to possess her own property, and to keep her own earnings. Beyond this, no attempt has been made by the Legislature, that I know of, to purify the corruptions which exist in the Marriage Laws of Great Britain and Ireland.

As the Preface indicates, *Man and Wife* takes as its starting point the inconsistencies within and between the Irish, Scottish, and English marriage laws. It is these inconsistencies—and specifically 'the Irish Statute of George the Second' (Prologue, Part the First, III)—which, in the prologue to the main story, allow the lawyer Delamayn to secure the annulment of Anne Sylvester's marriage to John Vanborough when the latter seeks to make a better match with an aristocratic widow. In the main narrative, the daughter of Anne Sylvester falls foul of the Scots custom of 'irregular marriage' which permits a couple to marry merely by making a public declaration that they are man and wife. As a result of this practice Anne finds herself legally bound to her seducer, Geoffrey Delamayn, the son of the lawyer who had undone her parents' marriage, though not before she has escaped from being deemed to have married her best friend's fiancé, Arnold Brinkworth. The confusion arises because, when acting as an intermediary for Delamayn, Brinkworth had been persuaded to pretend to be Anne's betrothed in order to gain access to the inn where she was staying. He had subsequently been forced to spend the night in her room because of a storm, and under Scots law these two circumstances were regarded as constituting a public declaration of marriage. However, what begins as an attack on the confused state of the marriage laws subsequently develops into a continuation of Collins's attack on the position of women within marriage, and, at points, into an attack on marriage as an institution. As in *The Woman in White*, an important part of the plot of *Man and Wife* turns on the right of a man to regard his wife as his property and to imprison her in his home. In the later novel, however, Collins brings the full force of his rhetorical power as well as his plotting skills to bear on this situation. Thus when Geoffrey Delamayn (for his own purposes) finally claims the wife whom he has unwillingly and inadvertently married with the words, 'the law tells her to go with her husband . . . The law forbids you to part Man and Wife', the narrator responds:

True. Absolutely, undeniably true. The law sanctioned the sacrifice of her, as unanswerably as it had sanctioned the sacrifice of her mother before her. In the name of Morality, let him take her! In the interests of Virtue, let her get out of it if she can!

. . . Done, in the name of Morality. Done, in the interests of Virtue. Done, in an age of progress, and under the most perfect government on the face of the earth. (Chapter LI)

The horrors of marriage under the unreformed marriage laws are graphically portrayed in the Gothic drama of the final two 'scenes' of the novel in which Anne is, in effect, imprisoned by her husband in a lonely cottage in Fulham which is surrounded by a large garden and a high wall. Wishing to be rid of her, and having no legal grounds for divorce, Geoffrey plans to murder her. Although her relatives fear for her welfare and safety, the law sanctions Delamayn's tyranny:

There were outrages which her husband was privileged to commit, under the sanction of marriage, at the bare thought of which her blood ran cold . . . Law and Society armed her husband with his conjugal rights.

Law and Society had but one answer to give, if she appealed to them:—
You are his wife. (Chapter LV)

The legally sanctioned marital sufferings of the middle-class heroine, which lead up to the novel's denouement, are counter-pointed by the story of the marital trials of a working-class woman which is retrospectively narrated in Hester Dethridge's 'Confession' of how she came to murder her brutal husband. It is the discovery of the manuscript containing this 'Confession' that gives Geoffrey the idea for how he might dispose of Anne. Hester's narrative is a vivid illustration of the legal disabilities of the married woman, and of the fact that there 'is no limit, in England, to what a bad husband may do—as long as he sticks to his wife' (Chapter LIV). Tied to a violent husband who drinks away her small inheritance, and periodically returns to rob her of (i.e. claim his legal right to) any money and possessions which she manages to acquire as a result of her labours, Hester has no recourse in law. As the officer in the Police Court to which she appeals after one incident informs her:

Yours is a common case . . . [i]n the present state of the law, I can do nothing for you. . . . you are a married woman. The law doesn't allow a married woman to call anything her own—unless she has previously (with a lawyer's help) made a bargain to that effect with her husband, before marrying him. You have made no bargain. Your husband has a right to sell your furniture if he likes. I am sorry for you; I can't hinder him. (Chapter LIX)

Hester's account of her own bemused response and of the conversation between the officers on the bench dramatize the fact that the working-class woman is even more disadvantaged by 'the present state of the law' than her middle-class counterpart, since, as the court officer observes: 'Poor people in this condition of life don't even know what a marriage settlement means. And, if they did, how many of them could afford to pay the lawyer's charges?' (Chapter LIX).

Collins wrote the first Preface to *Man and Wife* just as the 1870 Married Women's Property Bill was about to be enacted. However, as he noted in an addition to the Preface in 1871, the passing of this Act (which still did not give married women the same property rights as men) did not mean that his novel was immediately outmoded: 'Being an Act mainly intended for the benefit of the poor, it was, of course, opposed by the House of Commons at the first reading, and largely altered by the House of Lords . . . it is, so far, better than no law at all'[13] *Man and Wife* is Collins's most overt attack on nineteenth-century marriage laws and marriage customs, but from *Basil* onwards virtually all of Collins's novels seek to demonstrate and explore changing expectations about marriage in an age in which the roles and aspirations of both men and woman were subject to change and questioning.

CHAPTER 5

SEX, CRIME, MADNESS, AND EMPIRE

As well as examining marriage as a legal, social, and economic entity (as shown in the last chapter), Collins's novels also focus on marriage as a means of regulating sexuality and explore sexual mores on the fringes of and outside marriage. Contemporary sexual mores and morality come under scrutiny as Collins investigates the hypocrisies of 'respectable' Victorian society and the relationship between respectable society and the *demi-monde*, and, like many of his contemporaries, joins in the debate on the social evil of prostitution. His fascination with social outsiders is matched by a well-developed interest in crime and criminality. Another contemporary social issue which figures prominently in Collins's fiction and journalism is the categorization and treatment of mental disorders, and particularly the ease with which women could be incarcerated in asylums by their male relatives. Collins's interest in 'others' is also evident in the way his fiction engages with issues of race and empire, and in his depiction of exiles, including that diverse London community of exiles and fugitives from the social upheavals of nineteenth-century Europe.

Sexual Mores and Social Evils

The narrator and chief protagonist of *Basil* tells the story of how he falls in love at first sight with a veiled woman, whom he marries, subject to her father's condition that the consummation of the marriage will be delayed for one year. This tale of Basil's sexless marriage and (what turns out to be) his permanently deferred sexual gratification, is framed by the tale of his older brother's sexual adventures outside marriage. Basil presents his brother Ralph as a typically dissolute eldest son bent on avoiding 'the domestic conspiracy of which he was destined to become the victim', and putting off for as long as possible the evil day when he must marry a girl of his own class and take up his place in English society.

Ralph had never shown much fondness at home, for the refinements of good female society. Abroad, he had lived as exclusively as he possibly could, among women whose characters ranged downwards by infinitesimal degrees, from the mysteriously doubtful to the notoriously bad. The highly-bred, highly-refined, highly-accomplished young English beauties had no charm for him. (*Basil*, Part I, IV)

Ralph's conduct puts him temporarily beyond the pale of polite society. Protective society mothers remove their daughters from the immediate danger of his predatory presence, and his father sends him abroad. However, it does not permanently affect his social position: according to the double standard of sexual morality, male rakes can be welcomed back into the fold if they repent their youthful excesses (especially if they also inherit a large estate at the same time). In fact, Ralph is an interesting variation on the theme of the reformed rake, since he reforms according to 'the continental code of morals', and enters into a 'morganatic' marriage with an older woman to whom he refers as 'Mrs Ralph'. The worldly Ralph, who ultimately proves his worth by his actions on Basil's behalf, will have no truck with his more conventional brother's 'second-rate virtue' when the latter complains about his mentioning 'that woman' in the same breath as their virtuous and virginal sister Clara (*Basil*, Part III, VI).

Ralph attributes his own moral progress to the influence of this 'really superior woman', who, as he jokes to his prim brother, has been responsible for his 'dropping down to playing the fiddle, and paying rent and taxes in a suburban villa! How are the fast men fallen!' (*Basil*, Part III, VI). It is not clear what happens to the 'morganatic Mrs Ralph' when Ralph assumes his place as 'the head of our family', and is 'aroused by his new duties to a sense of his new position' (*Basil*, Letters in Conclusion, Letter III). Perhaps she becomes the legal Mrs Ralph, or perhaps she has to remain in her suburban villa having trained Ralph to be the husband of a highly bred young English beauty. In the 1850s and 1860s there was quite a lot of debate in the press about the growing tendency for quite ordinary (as well as rather 'fast') middle- and upper-middle-class men to set up accomplished and experienced women in suburban villas, as an alternative to marriage, or (more usually) as a stop-gap measure until they were ready to take on the role of husband to a wife who was much less experienced in the ways of the world than the mistress whom she replaced. As W. R. Greg observed in his 1862 essay, 'Why Are Women Redundant?':

Society—that is, the society of great cities and of cultivated life—high life—has for some years been growing at once more expensive and less remunerative . . . All this time, while the *monde* has been deteriorating, the *demi-monde* has been improving . . . The ladies *there* are now often clever and amusing, usually more beautiful, and not infrequently (in external demeanour at least) as modest, as their rivals in more recognised society.[1]

Ralph is quite open about his domestic arrangements, not least because as the heir to a large estate and a family name of distinction he can afford to be. The young men in Greg's article tended to be more discreet, or, like Collins's Godfrey Ablewhite, more secretive. In a late section of *The Moonstone*, we not only learn what Ablewhite has done with the Diamond, but we are also given an explanation of his motive for taking it. Sergeant Cuff's revelations about Godfrey's double life both exploit and feed Victorian anxieties about the secrets upon which respectable life was built. It is worth quoting at length.

I may state, at the outset, that Mr Godfrey Ablewhite's life had two sides to it.

The side turned up to the public view, presented the spectacle of a gentleman, possessed of considerable reputation as a speaker at charitable meetings, and endowed with administrative abilities, which he placed at the disposal of various Benevolent Societies, mostly of the female sort. The side kept hidden from the general notice, exhibited this same gentleman in the totally different character of a man of pleasure, with a villa in the suburbs which was not taken in his own name, and with a lady in the villa, who was not taken in his own name, either.

My investigations in the villa have shown me several fine pictures and statues; furniture tastefully selected . . . and a conservatory full of the rarest flowers . . . My investigation of the lady has resulted in the discovery of jewels which are worthy to take rank with the flowers, and of carriages and horses which have (deservedly) produced a sensation in the Park . . .

All this is, so far, common enough. The villa and the lady are such familiar objects in London life, that I ought to apologise for introducing them to notice. But what is not common and not familiar (in my experience), is that all these fine things were not only ordered, but paid for . . . the villa . . . had been bought, out and out, and settled on the lady. (*The Moonstone*, Second Period, Sixth Narrative, Chapter III)

One of the causes of the disruption of the domestic peace of what Betteredge describes as 'our quiet English house', is its opposite (or inversion), the luxurious sexualized space of the villa in the suburbs (not to be confused with Sherwin's gimcrack new edifice in *Basil*). Like Greg's article, Ablewhite's life story suggests that Victorian respectability is built upon 'fallen' women and the social evil of prostitution, as well as upon an idealized conception of the family headed by a chaste husband and wife.

The parallels between the lives of respectable women and those of their fallen sisters were a frequent topic in Collins's novels. Several of his most resolute and independent female characters—Magdalen Vanstone and Lydia Gwilt are good examples—trade on their sexuality in the same way that prostitutes do. The marriage plot of the scheming actress Magdalen Vanstone in *No Name* is used to suggest that marriage itself can be seen as a form of legalized prostitution. Like Braddon's Lady Audley, Magdalen cites contemporary marriage customs as a justification for her own mercenary marriage to her cousin Noel Vanstone: 'Thousands of women marry for money . . . Why shouldn't I?' (*No Name*, The Fourth Scene, Chapter XIII). Magdalen has better cause than many to make such an alliance, since she marries not to gain a name and fortune but to reclaim her father's name and fortune of which the law on illegitimate children has robbed her. The natural justice of her cause and Collins's sympathetic, if sensational, presentation of the self-loathing which her schemes induce both tend to press the reader towards a sympathetic response to the woman, if not to her apparently cynical, criminal and 'unwomanly' conduct. Nevertheless, the reader is repeatedly reminded of the connections between Magdalen's name (prostitutes or fallen women were often referred to as 'Magdalens') and her actions. Much is made of her sense that she has prostituted herself in marrying Noel. Moreover, following his death she actively compares herself to a fallen woman first in her response to her maid Louisa's revelation that she is an unmarried mother who has forged her own character reference prior to taking up her current post, and second by taking on Louisa's identity in order to pursue the next phase of her plotting. Magdalen's response to Louisa's falling to her knees to pronounce herself a 'miserable, degraded creature' who is not fit to be in the same room as her mistress, is to proclaim: 'For God's sake, don't kneel to *me!* . . . If there is a degraded woman in this room, I am the woman—not you!' (The Sixth Scene, Chapter I). Magdalen's recognition of her degradation—rather than her mere acceptance of society's labels—is one step on her route to reclamation, although many readers and reviewers found it difficult to accept that such a brazen hussy was a suitable candidate for redemption. Margaret Oliphant was not alone in disapproving of Magdalen's 'career of vulgar and aimless trickery' nor in expressing her surprise that Collins should expect his readers to believe that his heroine could emerge from the 'pollutions' of such a career 'at the cheap cost of a fever, as pure, as high-minded, and as spotless as the most dazzling white of heroines'.[2]

If Magdalen exploits her sexuality to regain what she sees as her rightful place in the social and economic hierarchy, Lydia Gwilt, the heroine of the novel that followed *No Name*, exploits her sexual attractiveness in a much longer career of trickery in order to gain wealth and social position. Lydia enters the dramatic present of the plot of *Armadale* as a scheming governess, like Thackeray's Becky Sharp and Braddon's Lucy Graham/Audley. However, like so many sensation heroines or villainesses, she is a woman with a past—in this case a very mysterious past whose details are revealed sporadically and partially throughout the narrative. The history which Collins constructs for Lydia makes her the repository of a range of Victorian fascinations with and anxieties about the social outsider, the *femme fatale*, the fallen woman, and the female social schemer. Lydia Gwilt is a woman of dubious origin. She may be the child of a nobleman or a streetwalker (or both), but she is the foster child of Mrs Oldershaw and her husband, who use her to lure customers to their travelling shop to buy cosmetics. When she is 12 she is taken on as a lady's maid by a spoiled young heiress, Jane Blanchard, who is attracted by her flaming red hair (a badge of villainy to many Victorians). She is spoiled by her mistress, persuaded into the crime of forgery by her mistress's husband Allan (Ingleby) Armadale, and possibly seduced by him. The price of her silence is an education in France and an income which depends on her permanent removal from England. Whilst still in her teens she is the cause of the attempted suicide of a married music teacher, and she is subsequently taken up by a card-sharp who uses Lydia's beauty to attract victims to the card tables. One of these victims exposes the card swindling and seeks to blackmail her into becoming his mistress, but she secures a marriage instead. Once back in England both parties discover the hazards of respectable marriage, when she is mistreated by her jealous husband and he is betrayed and then poisoned by his adulterous wife. Following a sensational trial she is found guilty of murder, but sensational and sentimental newspaper reporting secures a pardon and a reduced sentence for theft. Upon her release she makes a bigamous marriage to the man with whom she had committed adultery (a Cuban who is already married), who subsequently robs her of the money she obtains by blackmailing her former employer, and leaves her. It is her suicide attempt at this stage in her career that starts off the chain of events that lead to the blond blue-eyed Allan Armadale inheriting Thorpe-Ambrose.

Despite (or perhaps because of) her early career, Lydia is presented as an intelligent, articulate, and cultivated woman who—rather like those denizens of the *demi-monde* referred to by W. R. Greg in the article quoted above—is a more interesting companion than Neelie Milroy, the insipid girl who is to marry the heir of Thorpe-Ambrose. What was most surprising in Collins's frank depiction of the exploits of Lydia Gwilt—and what shocked and disgusted some of his reviewers—was the fact that he constructed his novel in such a way as to elicit sympathy for 'one of the most hardened of female villains whose devices and desires have ever blackened fiction'.[3] He does this by portraying her as one who is as much a victim as a villain—a social outsider in an economically and sexually vulnerable position who, to some extent, learns exploitation from the adults who exploit her. The novel also directs the reader's sympathies towards Lydia by progressively presenting the action from Lydia's point of view, most notably in the extracts from her diary in which she scrutinizes her own life and her feelings for Midwinter and provides a very accurate assessment of some of the other characters. Lydia may be a sexual predator who has made a career of exploiting her own sexual power and the sexual weakness of others, but she is also capable of moral introspection and self-criticism. One of the effects of presenting Lydia's self-critical reflections on her own predicament is to make readers compare their own situations with hers. This is done explicitly in an extract from Lydia's diary in which she compares her lot to that of a woman she observes driving by in her carriage: '[s]he had her husband by her side, and her children on the seat opposite. . . . a sparkling, light-hearted, happy woman. Ah, my lady, when you were a few years younger, if you had been left to yourself, and thrown on the world like me—' (Book the Fourth, Chapter I). This is not merely self-justification of the kind that Thackeray's Becky Sharp engages in when she asserts that she could be a good woman if she had five hundred a year.

Further links between the respectably married lady in her carriage and the fallen woman or the prostitute are suggested through the novel's depiction of Mrs Oldershaw (or 'Mother Jezebel' as she is sometimes referred to). Lydia's foster mother (who, as Richard Altick has shown, is partly modelled on Madame Rachel Leverson[4]), offers services to women of all stations and vocations. She is certainly a practitioner in the dark arts of making women maximize their physical attractiveness, with more than 'twenty years' experience . . . in making up battered old faces and worn-out old figures to look like new' (Book the Second, Chapter I). She may also be a procuress and controller of prostitutes, and, through her association with Doctor Downward, an abortionist. Her shop, The 'Ladies' Toilette Repository' in Pimlico, is described (as seen through the eyes of Pedgift Junior) as being 'essentially furtive in its expression', its very bricks and mortar signalling secrecy. 'It affected to be a shop on the ground floor; but it exhibited absolutely nothing in the space that intervened between the window and an inner row of red curtains, which hid the interior entirely from view'. The door, next to the shop door, has a bell marked 'Professional' and 'a brass plate, indicating a medical occupant'. Doctor Downward, who is named on this brass plate, is said to be

one of those carefully-constructed physicians, in whom the public— especially the female public—implicitly trust. . . . His voice was soothing, his ways were deliberate, his smile was confidential. What particular branch of his profession Doctor Downward followed, was not indicated on his door-plate; but [Pedgift Junior] had utterly mistaken his vocation if he was not a ladies' medical man. (*Armadale*, Book the Third, Chapter III)

A further hint about the nature of Downward's work as a ladies' medical man is given in the reference in Lydia's diary to the risks the doctor runs in his particular form of practice.

In some of his later novels Collins focuses more directly and polemically on the social evil of prostitution and on the case of the reformed prostitute, taking up a cause that had been the focus of prolonged press campaigns from the mid-1850s onwards. These campaigns had been orchestrated by feminists and by others campaigning for the moral purity of society who had dedicated themselves, practically and through propagandizing, to the eradication of prostitution and the reform of fallen women. In both *The New Magdalen* and *The Fallen Leaves* it is the prostitute's predicament rather than her trade that is presented as the social evil. Both Mercy Merrick, the heroine of *The New Magdalen*, and Simple Sally, one of the 'fallen leaves' in the later novel, are illegitimate children. Left a 'starving outcast' on the death of her mother, Mercy becomes one of the women 'whom Want has driven into Sin' (*The New Magdalen*, Chapter 2), and Sally ends up on the streets never having known her family (she has been kidnapped by her father and given into the care of a baby farmer).

Mercy's life story is narrated in the form of a confession which she makes to Grace Roseberry, during a pause in a battle on French territory in the Franco-Prussian War (which had just finished when the novel began its serialization in *Temple Bar*). Mercy, who had earlier been rescued from her life of sin by the preaching of the radical clergyman Julian Gray at the refuge for fallen women in which she had been living, is working as a Red Cross nurse in the war. At the time of her first meeting with Mercy, Grace (who has also been left without relatives or money on the death of her father) is en route for England and a job as a paid companion. As Jenny Bourne Taylor has pointed out, Mercy's account of her life is 'not so much a reformed sinner's confession as a philanthropist's case history' told by someone who has thoroughly assimilated the terms of her own ostracism.[5]

I am accustomed to stand in the pillory of my past life. I sometimes ask myself if it was all my own fault. I sometimes wonder if society had no duties towards me when I was a child selling matches in the street—when I was a hard-working girl fainting at my needle for want of food . . . What I *am* can never alter what I *was* . . . Everybody is sorry for me . . . Everybody is kind to me. The lost place is not to be regained. I can't get back! (*The New Magdalen*, Chapter 2)

When Grace is hit by a German shell and left for dead, Mercy seizes upon what she sees as the only way of escaping the taint of her past—she adopts Grace's identity and travels back to England to take Grace's place as companion to Lady Janet Roy. The success of Mercy's impersonation of Grace, and her acceptance as a respectable woman, tends to reinforce Magdalen Vanstone's contention that respectable femininity is a role that involves successful acting on one side and the acceptance of the illusion on the other. However, like *No Name*, *The New Magdalen* also suggests that respectable or genteel femininity is a quality that some women either possess innately, or acquire through painful struggle. Collins's narrative demonstrates that Mercy really has escaped the moral taint of her past, by making her confess the truth of her situation when Grace, who has miraculously recovered, returns to reclaim her identity—even though everyone else believes (or pretends to believe) that Grace is the imposter. However, Mercy is ultimately unable to escape the judgement of society. Collins's reformed prostitute avoids the tragic death which is the usual fate of her fictional sisters, and is granted the alternative ending of marriage (to Julian Gray), but she cannot be assimilated into conservative English society and, like Elizabeth Gaskell's Mary Barton she is dispatched to the New World and a new life in Canada. Like Gaskell before him, Collins represents Canada as a kind of promised land in whose wide open spaces the hero and heroine can build a better English society than the one they leave behind.

Criminality and Roguery in Respectable Society

English society . . . is as often the accomplice as it is the enemy of crime. . . . I say what other people only think; and when all the rest of the world is in a conspiracy to accept the mask for the true face, mine is the rash hand that tears off the plump pasteboard, and shows the bare bones beneath. (*The Woman in White*, Second Epoch, The Story continued by Marian Halcombe, III)

The genteel Marian Halcombe dismisses these words of Fosco's as 'glib cynicism' but we can surmise that Collins, who was just as much a 'a citizen of the world' as was his Italian with white mice, would have had more sympathy with them. Of course, it is one of the triumphs of Collins's narrative method in *The Woman in White* that there is no single authoritative narrative voice, and here, to complicate matters further, Fosco's words are reported by a shocked

Marian. However, Fosco's discourse on the 'clap-trap' with which Society consoles and deceives itself for its own shortcomings states overtly what virtually all of Collins's narratives imply: that conceptions of virtue are culturally defined, and that 'John Englishman' and 'John Chinaman' each define virtue in their own terms; that crime very often does pay, especially if the criminal goes undetected by the police—and the 'resolute, educated, highly-intelligent man . . . in nine cases out of ten' does; that an individual's crime is often simply the response to social injustice—it is only as a result of her crime that the plight of the starving dressmaker who 'falls under temptation and steals' is brought to the attention of 'good-humoured, charitable England' whereas her honest sister is left to starve.

Collins's novels are littered with 'resolute, educated, highly-intelligent' men, and the occasional woman, whose crimes go undetected by the police and who are not dealt with by the legal and penal system. Several of them receive summary justice: Mannion falls to his death after a cliff-top struggle with Basil, Glyde is burnt to death in a fire, Fosco is killed by a fellow countryman (one of his former co-conspirators), Ablewhite is killed by the Indian guardians of the Moonstone, and Geoffrey Delamayn dies from overstraining his weak heart. Lydia Gwilt is, at least in part, an exception to this general rule. Some of her crimes are dealt with by the legal system, albeit rather ineffectually. Ultimately, however, Lydia judges and disciplines herself by committing suicide when Midwinter foils her plot to kill Allan Armadale. Another character who metes out justice to himself is Dr Benjulia, in *Heart and Science* (1883); he sets fire to his laboratory and commits suicide, having first released the animals on which he had been experimenting. On the other hand, Doctor Downward (under his new alias of Le Doux), Lydia's accomplice in her final attempt on Armadale's life, not only evades the law (as a result of Midwinter's desire to protect his wife's reputation) but even prospers from the results of his failed crime. As Pedgift Senior writes to his son:

The doctor's friends and admirers are . . . about to present him with a Testimonial, 'expressive of their sympathy under the sad occurrence which has thrown a cloud over the opening of his Sanatorium, and of their undiminished confidence in his integrity and ability as a medical man.' We live . . . in an age eminently favourable to the growth of all roguery which is careful enough to keep up appearances. In this enlightened nineteenth century, I look upon the doctor as one of our rising men. (*Armadale*, Epilogue, Chapter I)

'Roguery' was also the subject of one of Collins's early novellas, and the only one of his works to have a convicted criminal as its sole narrator. *A Rogue's Life: Written by Himself*, which appeared in five instalments in *Household Words* from 1 to 29 March 1856 (and was reissued in 1879 as *A Rogue's Life: From his Birth to his Marriage*) is a kind of satirical Newgate novel in which Frank Softly recounts the story of his 'strange' life 'for the edification of [his] countrymen':

My life . . . may not seem particularly useful or respectable; but it has been, in some respects, adventurous; and that may give it claims to be read, even in the most prejudiced circles. I am an example of some of the workings of the social system of this illustrious country on the individual native, during the early part of the present century. (*A Rogue's Life*, Chapter 1)

Using the same insouciant tone for his own adventures and his comments on the hypocrisies of his family and contemporary society, Frank tells how he failed to make useful connections, although sent away to boarding school by his snobbish father expressly for the purpose of doing so; how he tried various professions (medicine, portrait painting, administering a scientific institution), and failed at all of them; and how he became an unsuccessful forger of Old Masters, before becoming involved with a gang of forgers of money after falling in love with the daughter of their leader, Dr Dulcifer. Frank's narrative then recounts how he was caught, tried, convicted, and transported to Australia, where, as a model 'ticket of leave man',[6] he was allowed to become a servant to his own wife (who had followed him to Australia disguised as a widow). Like Dickens's Magwitch, the rogue prospers in Australia and by the end of his story he was a 'convict aristocrat—a prosperous, wealthy, highly respectable mercantile man, with two years of my sentence of transportation still to expire'. At this point he brings his story to an abrupt end, asking how as a 'rich and reputable man' he could be expected 'to communicate any further autobiographical particulars . . . to a discerning public of readers', and declaring that he is 'no longer interesting . . . only respectable like yourselves'. Here Collins is not only mocking his respectable readers for finding criminality more interesting than respectability, but he is also reminding them that their vaunted respectability may be built on foundations just as dubious as Frank's, but at least the self-confessed rogue is frank about his roguery.

Frank's career of criminal roguery as a forger and fraudster is typical of the kind of criminality that Collins's novels focus on. There are some violent crimes, and Lydia Gwilt's criminal history is clearly linked to some famous trials and the broader cultural fascination with murderous women in the 1860s. However, much of the crime in Collins's fiction—and particularly in the fiction of the 1850s and 1860s—is the white-collar crime that fascinated many of his contemporaries: crimes such as fraud, swindling, forgery, embezzlement, and blackmail. All these might be described as crimes of advanced capitalism; they are crimes which arise from the traffic in paper currency, from the manipulation of the documents of a bureaucratic culture, and the control, misrepresentation, or misuse of information.

Madness and its Treatment

Another white-collar crime which plays an important part in the plots of *The Woman in White* and *Armadale* and also features in *Jezebel's Daughter* is that of wrongful confinement in lunatic asylums. In *The Woman in White*, Collins's use of the wrongful confinement of both Anne Catherick and Laura Fairlie is one of the ways in which he modernizes and makes more realistic the conventions of Gothic imprisonment: instead of being incarcerated in a monastery or a remote castle, or even a disreputable madhouse run by corrupt owners, Anne and then Laura are confined within a modern lunatic asylum run according to the new humane, non-restraint methods of moral management. In this novel, the incarceration of two of the central female characters in a lunatic asylum is not merely a convenient plot device, but rather, as both Jenny Bourne Taylor and Deborah Wynne have demonstrated,[7] it is a means of exploring contemporary definitions of insanity and intervening in current debates about the diagnosis and treatment of the insane.

At the end of the opening sensation scene of *The Woman in White*, Walter Hartright's reaction to the news that Anne Catherick has escaped from a lunatic asylum plunges the reader directly into a range of issues concerning the definition and treatment of madness in the mid-nineteenth century.

'She has escaped from my Asylum!'

I cannot say with truth that the terrible inference which those words suggested flashed upon me like a new revelation. Some of the strange questions put to me by the woman in white . . . had suggested the conclusion either that she was naturally flighty and unsettled, or that some recent shock of terror had disturbed the balance of her faculties. But the idea of absolute insanity which we all associate with the very name of an Asylum, had, I can honestly declare, never occurred to me, in connexion with her. I had seen nothing, in her language or her actions, to justify it at the time; and, even with the new light thrown on her by the words which the stranger had addressed to the policeman, I could see nothing to justify it now (The Story begun by Walter Hartright, V).

Walter's reaction to the question of Anne's possible madness suggests a spectrum of mental oddity or disturbance ranging from inherent or 'natural' flightiness, through temporary loss of the balance of the mind as a result of shock, to 'absolute insanity'. The latter, it is implied, can be detected through language or behaviour, and the authority for labelling it lies with the Asylum and the medical profession. In this case the authority of the Asylum is thrown into question by Walter's appeal to his own ambivalent experience of the woman in white, and by his subsequent reference to the practice of confinement on the basis of a misreading (deliberate or otherwise) of the signs of madness as 'the most horrible of all false imprisonments': 'What had I done? Assisted the victim of the most horrible of all false imprisonments to escape; or cast loose on the wide world of London an unfortunate creature, whose actions it was my duty, and every man's duty, mercifully to control?' (The Story begun by Walter Hartright, V). If Walter's response to Anne's behaviour is ambivalent or confused then so too is his questioning of his actions in assisting her to escape from her persecutors or carers. Walter seems to be torn between two conflicting duties— the duty to assist the victim of wrongful imprisonment, and the duty (which he shares with 'every man') to control the unruly female. In the second case it is unclear whether it is the duty of every man to control unruly women in order to protect them from the wicked world or, rather, to protect the wide world of London from such women.

Laura's wrongful confinement initially appears to raise quite different issues, and seems to be more closely connected to Gothic plots—and the fears which they embody—about the false imprisonment of sane people in lunatic asylums by relatives who wish to appropriate their money or property. However, on reconsideration, Laura's wrongful confinement raises some of the same questions as Anne's. One of the reasons that Laura is so easily substitutable for Anne is that some of the symptoms of madness that they both display are also symptoms of their feminine passivity, infantilization, and powerlessness, as well as their shared mistreatment by Sir Percival. Whether inside or outside the asylum, Laura might be described in the same way in which Walter describes Anne: 'there was nothing wild, nothing immodest in her manner: it was quiet and self-controlled, a little melancholy and a little touched by suspicion' (The Story begun by Walter Hartright, IV)—in both cases this manner is perfectly understandable in light of their circumstances. The confinement of both women in an asylum raises questions about definitions of madness at a time when there was increasing debate about the 'problematic borderlands of insanity',[8] and when the control of odd or deviant behaviours was becoming increasingly specialized and professionalized. These questions, and the related question of the grounds on which confinement could be justified, were being investigated by the Parliamentary Select Committee Inquiry into the Treatment of Lunatics and Their Property that reported in 1859–60, just as *The Woman in White* was being serialized in Dickens's *All the Year Round*. During the serial run of *The Woman in White, All the Year Round* also ran several articles and stories concerning the treatment of insanity and wrongful confinement. It returned to the subject in 1862 in an article entitled 'M.D. and MAD' which discussed the reports of the Commissioners of Lunacy in 1862.

[W]e do not ... attribute to any ... of these medical gentlemen, a conscious action under mercenary motives. The public danger arising from their influence would be infinitely insignificant if the fact were so. They are highly trained men, who have honestly devoted themselves to a special study of the most difficult questions that can occur to a physician. There is no clear dividing-line between sickness and health of mind; unsoundness of mind is, no doubt as various and common as unsoundness of body. . . .

. . . In questions that concern the mind, the less heed we pay to the theorist, and the more distinctly we require none but the sort of evidence patent to the natural sense of ordinary men in determining what the citizen shall suffer the privations, or what criminal shall enjoy the privileges of unsoundness of mind, the better it will be for us. Let us account no man a lunatic whom it requires a mad-doctor to prove insane.[9]

Collins also took up the theme of the mad-doctor in the career of Doctor Downward in *Armadale*. As this novel nears its denouement, Downward, who has hitherto advertised himself as a doctor specializing in women's complaints (see above), reinvents himself as 'Doctor Le Doux, of the Sanatorium, Fairweather Vale, Hampstead' (Book the Fourth, Chapter III). Le Doux is Collins's parody of the modern mad-doctor and his Sanatorium, which is located in a large house in a half-developed suburb, is a parody of a private asylum for the nervous, which is closely based on aspects of John Connolly's *The Treatment of the Insane Without Mechanical Restraints* (1856).[10] The discarded objects of the old restraint system, 'Horrible objects in brass and leather and glass', occupy one wall of Le Doux's private room. Another bears 'a collection of photographic portraits of men and women, enclosed in two large frames', one set illustrating 'the effects of nervous suffering as seen in the face', the other exhibiting 'the ravages of insanity from the same point of view', whilst between the two was 'an elegantly-illuminated scroll' with the inscription 'Prevention is better than Cure'. The unctuous Le Doux decodes the room for Lydia Gwilt:

there is my System mutely addressing you just above your head, under a form of exposition which I venture to describe as frankness itself. This is no madhouse, my dear lady. Let other men treat insanity as they like—*I* stop it! No patients in the house as yet. But we live in an age when nervous derangement (parent of insanity) is steadily on the increase; and in due time the sufferers will come (Book the Fourth, Chapter III)

Le Doux's system is based on moral management along domestic lines, using 'carriage-exercise and horse-exercise', cheerful drawing-room gatherings, and activities which are designed to 'elevate' and improve the patient. He actively markets his Sanatorium as a domestic sanctuary for those suffering from 'domestic anxiety', 'shattered nerves', and 'nervous derangement', a place of quiet from which all the irritations of everyday life are removed; 'On those plain grounds my System is based. I assert the medical treatment of nervous suffering to be entirely subsidiary to the moral treatment of it. That moral treatment of it, you find here. . . . sedulously pursued throughout the day, [it] follows the sufferer into his room at night; and soothes, helps, and cures him, without his own knowledge' (Book the Last, Chapter III).

However, for all its superficial modernity, and for all Le Doux's caution about the possible intervention of the Lunacy Commissioners if they get to hear of any irregularities even in an unlicensed establishment such as his own, this Sanatorium is used by Collins as the site of a melodramatic plot involving wrongful incarceration and attempted murder. Le Doux agrees to be party to Lydia's plot to lure Allan Armadale to his sanatorium so that she can kill him. With Le Doux's connivance, Lydia plans to murder Allan in one of the closed rooms which has been specially adapted for particularly difficult patients. The doors and windows of this room can only be opened from the outside, and fresh air (or any other substance) can be circulated through it by means of a pipe in the wall. In the end, of course, it is Lydia who is (so to speak) buried alive in the Asylum—as are so many of her real female contemporaries and also Braddon's Lady Audley—when this room becomes the site of her melodramatic suicide.

Collins returned to debates about asylum conditions and different systems of treating the insane in his late novel *Jezebel's Daughter*. The action of this novel begins in 1828, but the events are narrated some fifty years after they have occurred. It begins by reviewing the career of the recently deceased Mr Wagner, 'a man who thought for himself . . . [who] had ideas of his duty to his poor and afflicted fellow-creatures' which in the 1820s 'were considered nothing less than revolutionary', but in 'these days [the late 1870s], when his opinions have been sanctioned by Acts of parliament, with the general approval of the nation', he is more likely to be considered as a ' "Moderate Liberal" . . . a discreetly deliberate man in the march of modern progress' (Part 1, Chapter 2). One of the radical causes that Wagner espoused was that of asylum reform. As a governor of the Bethlehem Hospital (Bedlam) he had opposed (as his widow puts it) 'the torturing of the poor mad patients by whips and chains, and had proposed an experiment, at his own risk and expense', to try 'the effect of patience and kindness in the treatment of mad people' (Part 1, Chapter 3). His widow's determination to continue his work by seeking out the 'poor chained creature' whom he had selected for his benign experiment takes the reader to an unreformed asylum, and along 'dreary stone passages' in which are heard 'cries of rage and pain . . . varied by yelling laughter, more terrible even than the cries' (Part 1, Chapter 4). The object of Mrs Wagner's attention is Jack Straw, who is known as the 'lucky lunatic' on the grounds that he has gained access to a royal institution usually reserved for 'lunatics of the educated class', by virtue of having been discovered in the street by a royal personage whose carriage had run over him (Part 1, Chapter 4). This fellow is so lucky that he has had 'irons specially invented to control him' and a new—and many-lashed—whip purchased especially to keep him in order. There follows an asylum scene that would not have been out of place in one of Dickens's early novels.

We found ourselves in a narrow, lofty prison, like an apartment in a tower. High up, in one corner, the grim stone walls were pierced by a grated opening, which let in air and light. Seated on the floor . . . we saw the 'lucky lunatic' at work [plaiting straw] . . . A heavy chain held him to the wall. It was not only fastened round his waist, it also fettered his legs between the knees and the ankle. . . . [I]t was long enough to allow him a range of crippled movement, within a circle of five or six feet . . . above his head . . . hung a small chain evidently intended to confine his hands at the wrists. . . . His ragged dress barely covered his emaciated form. (Part 1, Chapter 4)

In a move which appears to underline the validity of Wagner's beliefs, the narrator shifts his focus from the pathetic, childlike lunatic with his 'vacantly-patient brown eyes' and 'nervously sensitive lips', to the whip which his wandering eyes detect in the hand of the asylum assistant: 'In an instant the whole expression of the madman's face changed. Ferocious hatred glittered in his eyes; his lips suddenly retracted, showed his teeth like the teeth of a wild beast' (Part 1, Chapter 4). The implication is clear—the restraint method produces the beast rather than contains him. The rest of the complicated plot is designed, among other things, to vindicate Wagner's belief and bring his experiment to a successful conclusion. Released from his restraints and brought up by Wagner's widow, Jack Straw survives as 'the most popular person in the neighbourhood; a happy, harmless creature' (Postscript, 9).

Race, Foreigners, and Empire

If Collins satirized conventional and illiberal conceptualizations of the madman as savage, he also explored—even if he did not always avoid—stereotypical representations of race. In *Armadale*, one of the first descriptions of Ozias Midwinter, the son of a 'negro' mother and a white British father, makes him appear like a madman. Ozias (who has recently recovered from a brain fever) is said to be 'a startling object to contemplate'. With his 'shaven head, tied up in an old yellow silk handkerchief; his tawny, haggard cheeks; his bright brown eyes, preternaturally large and wild; his rough black beard; his long supple sinewy fingers . . . [which] looked like claws'. It is a combination of physical characteristics which evokes stereotypical representations of the savage, the gipsy and the Jew, and it has the effect of making the 'healthy Anglo-Saxon flesh' of Mr Brock creep. Midwinter, who serves among other things as a kind of foreign double to the blond English Allan Armadale, is ultimately integrated into English society where a great future is predicted for him (Epilogue, Chapter II). On the other hand, Ezra Jennings—Collins's other most notable mixed race character—disappears entirely from view after he has performed his vital role in solving the mystery of the disappearance of the Moonstone: he dies from a longstanding wasting illness and insists on his few personal papers being buried with him in an unmarked grave. The first detailed description of Jennings, like the initial description of Midwinter, represents him as both a tortured soul and a racial melting pot.

His complexion was of a gipsy darkness; his fleshless cheeks had fallen into deep hollows, over which the bone projected like a penthouse. His nose presented the fine shape and modelling so often found among the ancient people of the East, so seldom visible among the newer races of the West. . . . From this strange face, eyes, stranger still . . . dreamy and mournful, and deeply sunk in their orbits . . . took your attention captive at their will. Add to this a quantity of thick closely-curling hair, which, by some freak of Nature, had lost its colour in the most startlingly partial and capricious manner. (*The Moonstore*, Third Narrative, Chapter IV)

Jennings's remarkable appearance is partly caused by and (perhaps) partly the cause of the mysterious persecution that has led him to wander from place to place in an attempt to escape the effects of a 'vile slander'. His foreignness, and especially his orientalism, is reinforced by his association with opium to which he has become addicted after using it as a painkiller for many years.

Like Midwinter, Jennings represents a kind of colonial return to the heart of Empire. As he explains to Franklin Blake, 'I was born, and partly brought up, in one of our colonies. My father was an Englishman; but my mother . . .' (Third Narrative, Chapter IX). In this respect both *Armadale* and *The Moonstone* are early examples of the 'reverse colonization' narrative, a type of fiction which Stephen Arata has associated with the 'cultural guilt' of the end of the nineteenth century. In their representation of 'the marauding, invasive Other', Arata argues, novels such as Bram Stoker's *Dracula* (1897) 'mirrored back in monstrous forms' Britain's own imperial practices, and thus had 'the potential for powerful critiques of imperialist ideologies'—a potential which, in Arata's analysis, is rarely realized, as, in his view, these narratives tend to displace British imperial guilt onto the 'invasive Other'.[11]

An interest in questions concerning empire and imperialism is evident throughout Collins's career as a novelist. Although at first sight his first published, novel, *Antonina*—an imperial adventure which drew on Edward Gibbon's account of how ancient Rome fell to the invading Goths—appears to have little connection with British imperialism, Collins repeatedly alerts his readers to possible analogies between the two empires. He does this with such phrases as 'in Ancient Rome, as in Modern London . . .' (Chapter XXII), and (as Conrad was to do in *Heart of Darkness*) by ventriloquizing the 'official' defence of the superiority of the motivations and methods of the empire controlled from modern London: the Roman Empire is said to have been built and sustained by 'incessant bloodshed', whereas the British acquired theirs in the pursuit of noble ideas and ideals. In fact, *Antonina* belongs to a particular moment in the history of British imperial expansion, having been written during the years in which Britain expanded its imperial gains in India by annexing the Punjab (1848–9). Collins's Roman novel repeatedly makes analogies between the imperial practices of the Romans and those of the British officers and employees of the East India Company who lived luxuriously on the wealth of the colony and raped and misused its indigenous women.

When Collins abandoned the historical romance after the publication of *Antonina*, he did not abandon his preoccupation with imperial practices, nor with the growth and decline and fall of empires: he merely translated them to a modern setting. In both *Armadale* and *The Moonstone*, the main narrative concerns the disruption of English domestic life by a colonial legacy. In *Armadale*, the violent, sensual, and acquisitive past of their parents in the British West Indies in the 1820s returns to haunt the next generation of Armadales; and in *The Moonstore*, a 'devilish Indian Diamond', the legacy of violent imperial plunder at the storming of Seringapatam in 1799, disrupts the peace of a quiet country house and its apparently blameless residents:

here was our quiet English house suddenly invaded by a devilish Indian Diamond—bringing after it a conspiracy of living rogues, set loose on us by the vengeance of a dead man. . . . Who ever heard the like of it—in the nineteenth century, mind; in an age of progress, and in a country which rejoices in the blessings of the British constitution? (*The Moonstone*, First Period, Chapter V)

Both *Armadale* and *The Moonstone* problematize the relationship between colony and metropole in narratives in which the 'home country' is invaded by Creoles (Ozias Midwinter and Ezra Jennings) or Hindus (the Indians who have travelled to England to reclaim the Moonstone).

The main narrative of *Armadale* is set in 1851, the year in which the Great Exhibition of the Works of Industry of All Nations, another version of imperial plunder, was held in London. However, its concern with violence in the sugar colonies was particularly topical at the time of the novel's appearance in the *Cornhill* between November 1864 and June 1866. The composition and serial publication of *Armadale* overlapped with the American Civil War, in which slavery was one of the points of contention between the North and South. Even more pertinently, the serialization of *Armadale* overlapped with the Jamaica Insurrection (or Eyre Rebellion) of 1865. Jamaica had been in British hands since 1655, and throughout the eighteenth and early nineteenth centuries it was a lucrative source of trade in sugar and in the slaves who were brought from Africa to work on the British-owned plantations. The novel's pre-narrative is set in the 1820s when liberal and evangelical campaigns to free the slaves were well under way, and its Prologue, set in Wildbad in 1832, just predates the 1833 Emancipation Act, which sought to liberate slaves throughout the British West Indies by making them free apprentices. In the 1860s low sugar prices and low wages, combined with continued injustices and ill-treatment by their former masters, led ex-slaves in Jamaica to seek political reforms. When their demands were rebuffed by Governor Eyre, they attacked a court-house in Kingston, and after a bloody confrontation Eyre declared martial law, violently suppressed the uprising, and hanged its leader, George Gordon. Eyre was recalled to England where he was tried for murder, and acquitted. Subsequently his actions were made the sub-ject of a Royal Commission of Inquiry. Eyre's conduct, which was widely discussed in the press during the period of *Armadale*'s serial-ization, polarized British public opinion: Dickens, for example, was a member of the Eyre Defence Committee which sought to exonerate his conduct as the use of justifiable force against the 'inferior' races; John Stuart Mill, on the other hand, belonged to the Jamaica Com-mittee which campaigned for Eyre's conviction. *Armadale* seems to accept colonial guilt by depicting the corruption, cupidity, and vio-lence of the white colonists, but it displaces that guilt into the past, where it is associated with the 'idleness and self-indulgence' of Allan (Wrentmore) Armadale's 'wild' and 'vicious' youth in the Barbados of the 1820s, where he is corrupted by the power which he enjoyed as a slave owner, lording it over 'slaves and half-castes . . . to whom my will was law' (Prologue, Chapter III). Collins's depiction of the older Allan Armadales, and Lydia Gwilt (who has also spent her formative years in Barbados), suggests that he is, as Lillian Nayder has noted, 'more concerned with the corrupting effects of slavery on the plantation owners than with the suffering of the slaves'.[12] Collins's portrayal of these characters also suggests that he displaces some of the burden of colonial guilt onto the 'otherness' of the colonies. The 'civilized' subjects of the colonizing power succumb to the 'primitive' wild otherness of the foreign lands and peoples which are colonized: the colony colonizes the colonizers.

Collins seems more willing to acknowledge the British burden of imperial guilt when he turns to the legacy of British India in *The Moonstone*. Like *Armadale*, *The Moonstone* begins with a Prologue set in the colonial past—Sir John Herncastle's theft of the Moonstone during the storming of Seringapatam in 1799—which shapes the novel's main narrative. In this later novel there is also an Epilogue, which includes Mr Murthwaite's letter to Mr Bruff, dated 1850, which returns the narrative to India and relates an act of restitution, in which the Moonstone is returned to what readers are encouraged to see as its rightful home. In the main narrative of *The Moonstone*, which is set in the period 1848–9, the legacy of Sir John's act of imperial plunder is played out. The peace of the quiet country house eulogized by Gabriel Betteredge—or at least the peace of mind of some of its inhabitants—is disturbed by the lurking presence of the Indians who have travelled to England in order to retrieve the diamond. More seriously disruptive of domestic peace, however, is the second theft of the diamond, which is taken from its new shrine in Rachel's bedroom in an act of violation which is as shocking for the English as was the removal of the Moonstone from the moon god for the Hindus. By this sleight of hand Collins suggests that the Englishman's home is not a castle but a temple, whose sacred jewel is the chaste goddess whom he will win as his wife.

This perspective on the novel's central event is just one example of the many ways in which Collins complicates the usual terms of imperialist discourse. The English characters perceive the Indians as the alien and mysterious other, and they are linked to reverse colonization or invasion scares by the novel's oriental specialist, Murthwaite, who presents them as members of a secret society made up of other Indian immigrants and the worst kind of Englishman:

a very trumpery affair, according to our ideas, I have no doubt . . . [involving] the command of money; the services, when needed, of that shady sort of Englishman, who lives in the byways of foreign life in London . . . [and] the secret sympathy of such few men of their own country, and (formerly, at least) of their own religion, as happen to be employed in ministering to some of the multitudinous wants of this great city. (Second Narrative, Chapter III)

In their conduct, however, the Indians demonstrate the 'English' virtues of patience, stoicism, resolution, and dedication to justice. The English, by contrast, are represented as duplicitous and secretive, and, in the case of Franklin Blake and Ezra Jennings, foreign. After listening to the stories of the India specialist Murthwaite on the fate that might befall her if she were to wear the diamond in India, Rachel 'safe in England, was quite delighted to hear of her danger in India' (First Period, Chapter X)—but the narrative is designed to demonstrate that her sense of English safety is illusory. The novel also offers an ironic running commentary on imperialism through Betteredge's constant references to his book of consolation, Defoe's *Robinson Crusoe*, a textbook of colonization. The sharpest irony is that Betteredge, as a white man, identifies with the colonizing hero of Defoe's narrative, and fails to see that his relationship to Franklin and to Lady Verinder makes him more of a Friday than a Crusoe. Another commentary on the ideologies of imperialism is offered by the solution of the mystery of the diamond's disappearance, and the explanation of Franklin Blake's role in it. Like imperial conquerors or colonizers, Blake has committed an act of appropriation, a 'bad' act, for an unconsciously 'good' reason—the desire to protect Rachel. As Tamar Heller has pointed out, this explanation of Blake's conduct also serves to reinforce the analogy which the novel makes between 'Victorian ideologies of gender and imperialism'.[13]

The 1799 assault on Seringapatam in the Prologue to *The Moonstone* was one of the key moments in the establishment of British India, because the defeat of Tipu (an ally of the French) gave the British an important foothold in the East. Interestingly, Collins's account of the storming of Seringapatam plays down the emphasis on the brutality of the Indians contained in his source (Theodore Hook's life of General David Baird) and seems to owe more to accounts of the lawless behaviour of the British troops more than half a century later, during the Indian Mutiny of 1857–8, when Indian soldiers (mainly Bengali Muslims) serving in the British army rebelled against their British masters and marched to Delhi to join the Mughal emperor. The Mutiny was another defining moment in the history of the British in India. Its immediate cause was the introduction of cartridges which had been greased with cow's or pig's fat—the handling of which was offensive to both Muslims and Hindus. Its underlying cause was the rapid social change introduced by the British. In part, the Mutiny was a reaction against this upheaval of traditional Indian society, and an attempt to return to a former political order. The suppression of the Mutiny after a year of fighting was followed by the break-up of the East India Company, the exile of the deposed emperor and the establishment of the British Raj, and direct rule of the Indian subcontinent by the British.

In many ways *The Moonstone* is a displaced version of the Mutiny novels of the 1860s which Patrick Brantlinger discusses in *Rule of*

Darkness: British Literature and Imperialism, 1830–1914. However, if Collins's novel deals with the Mutiny at one remove, it also takes a somewhat different stance both to the Mutiny and to the Indians from that taken by the Mutiny novelists considered by Brantlinger. 'Victorian accounts of the Mutiny', Brantlinger argues, tend to display a 'racist pattern of blaming the victim' which is 'expressed in terms of an absolute polarization of good and evil, innocence and guilt, justice and injustice, moral restraint and sexual depravity, civilization and barbarism'. Mutiny novels generally mobilize these categories on behalf of calls for 'the total subjugation of India and at times for the wholesale extermination of Indians'.[14] Collins's novel, on the other hand, while not exactly reversing these categories, applies them equally to 'the lawless Mohammedan' Tipu (Prologue, II), and to the 'deplorable excesses' (Prologue, III) of the British soldiers and John Herncastle. There is no suggestion (as there is in the Prologue to *Armadale*) that the British have 'gone native', nor that they have been morally colonized by the colony. Rather, *The Moonstone* identifies the metropole as the location of depravity through Godfrey Ablewhite and his role (and motivation) as the latest thief of the much-stolen diamond. Moreover, through its depiction of the Hindu Brahmins who dedicate their lives to the restitution of the diamond, and also of the response of the British to them, *The Moonstone* examines the racist thinking of the British and explores the ways in which they blame the oppressed people for the crimes of the imperialist oppressor.

The response to the Mutiny and to the indigenous population of India in *The Moonstone* is consistent with Collins's earlier writings on the subject. In 1857 Collins was co-author (with Charles Dickens) of one of the earliest Mutiny fictions, 'The Perils of Certain English Prisoners', which these frequent collaborators wrote for the Christmas number of *Household Words*. Dickens's feelings about the Mutiny were given with alarming clarity in a letter to his friend Angela Burdett Coutts in which he expressed the wish to be Commander in Chief in India in order that he might 'strike that Oriental race with amazement' and 'proclaim to them . . . that I should do my utmost to exterminate the Race upon whom the stain of the late cruelties rested' (Pilgrim, viii. 459). Instead, Dickens set about writing a story to commemorate 'some of the best qualities of the English character that have been shown in India'. Dickens set this story in an

English colony in Central America, on an island where silver from the local mine is stored under the care of the English population. The Mutiny is represented in the form of a pirate raid on the English community. Dickens supplied both the first chapter, which recounted the happy life of the English colonists before the attack, and the last chapter, which related their escape from imprisonment and their vanquishing of their captors. Collins was responsible for the middle chapter, 'The Prison in the Woods', in which he significantly altered the emphasis of Dickens's depiction of the differences between the prisoners and their captors. While Dickens emphasizes the exotic nature of the pirates, Collins casts them in the mould of dandified English soldiers who abuse their subordinates. In so doing, Collins emphasised what many saw as the underlying cause of the Mutiny. In February 1858, a few months after this story appeared, Collins wrote another *Household Words* piece, 'A Sermon for Sepoys', which comments on the mental colonization that accompanied imperial expansion and emphasizes the common ground shared by Western and Eastern religions.

While we are fighting for possession of India, benevolent men of various religious denominations are making their arrangements for taming the human tigers in that country by Christian means. . . . [I]t might, perhaps, not be amiss . . . to begin the attempt to purify their minds by referring them to the excellent moral lessons which they may learn from their own Oriental literature.[15]

There follows an account of an Indian parable about the active versus the contemplative life, whose lesson is that 'the life that is most acceptable to the Supreme Being, is the life that is most acceptable to the human race'. The piece closes with a question: 'Surely not a bad Indian lesson to begin with, when Betrayers and Assassins are the pupils to be taught?' This question raises the issue of whether it is only the Indians who are betrayers and assassins, just as the opening commentary raises questions about English and Christian assumptions about the superiority of their value systems over those of the Indians over whom they are fighting for possession.

The clash between oriental and European value systems was by no means the only ideological battleground in the mid-nineteenth century. Nor were reverse colonization or invasion scares confined to fears about the oriental colony invading the heart of Empire. When

Murthwaite refers in *The Moonstone* to 'that shady sort of English-man, who lives in the byways of foreign life in London', Collins's readers would not simply have associated 'foreign life' with Indians and other colonial subjects. Throughout the nineteenth century London was home to numerous exiles and émigrés associated with a wide range of nationalist and revolutionary movements in various European countries. In *The Woman in White*, the story of the social and romantic progress of a middle-class drawing master and crime and intrigue among the English upper classes is played out against a background in which the reverberations of European events are felt. Walter is introduced into the Limmeridge household through the Italian Professor Pesca, with whom he had struck up a friendship after 'meeting him at certain great houses, where he taught his own language and I taught drawing' (The Story begun by Walter Hartright, II). Formerly employed in the University of Padua, Pesca 'had left Italy for political reasons', like Gabriele Rossetti (father of the painter Dante Gabriel Rossetti and the poet Christina), and was a member of a secret society of revolutionary Italian patriots, which was involved in Italian wars and revolutions of 1848–9—the years in which the events of the novel occur—and 1859–60, the years in which the novel appeared. When pondering the mystery of Count Fosco and speculating on his reluctance to visit his native country Marian's first recourse is to locate him in the wider mysteries of European political intrigue, and to encourage the reader to speculate further on this:

Perhaps, he has been made the victim of some political persecution? At all events, he seems to be patriotically anxious not to lose sight of any of his own countrymen who may happen to be in England. On the evening of his arrival, he asked how far we were from the nearest town, and whether we knew of any Italian gentlemen who might happen to be settled there. He is certainly in correspondence with people on the Continent, for his letters have all sorts of odd stamps on them . . . [and one had] a huge official-looking seal on it. Perhaps he is in correspondence with his government? And yet, that is hardly to be reconciled . . . with my other idea that he might be a political exile. (Second Epoch, The Story continued by Marian Halcombe, II)

In the light of Fosco's subsequent fate it would appear that Marian is describing the fears and the correspondence of a double agent. Fosco's demise, when it occurs, may serve as a kind of wild justice for his involvement in the plot to incarcerate Laura and rob her of her identity and wealth, but his death is, in fact, a punishment for treachery. When his body is removed from the river Seine it bears the sign of the traitor: 'two deep cuts in the shape of the letter T, which entirely obliterated the mark of the Brotherhood'—the brotherhood of Italian nationalists to which Pesca also belonged (The Story concluded by Walter Hartright, II).

CHAPTER 6

PSYCHOLOGY AND SCIENCE IN COLLINS'S NOVELS

'BE pleased then to remember (first) that the actions of human beings are not invariably governed by the laws of pure reason', Collins wrote in the 'Note to the Reader' with which he prefaced the bound edition of *The Law and the Lady*. From first to last, his novels explore the multiplicity of factors which shape or motivate human actions. In fact, most Victorian readers—and especially Collins's readers—would hardly have needed the reminder which he provided in his note. This may seem a surprising assertion to make about a period which saw the expansion and professionalization of science, and the proliferation of scientific methodologies and materialist philosophies and modes of explanation. However, although the scientific revolution of the nineteenth century challenged and undermined religious and other non-rationalistic modes of thought, it did not by any means obliterate them. Moreover, science brought its own mysteries: the 'laws' of evolution seemed to require as much commentary and exegesis as the biblical and theological 'laws' which they sought to replace, and new theories of consciousness and the mind were no less perplexing for being based (as they often were) in physiology. Other new sciences, or pseudo-sciences, coexisted alongside, and sometimes fed into, the developing new sciences of evolutionary biology and mental science and psychology. Phrenology and mesmerism were just two examples of the pseudo-sciences which attracted a great deal of attention in Collins's formative years and in the early years of his writing career.

Mesmerism, Dreams, and the Unconscious in Collins's Writings in the 1850s and 1860s

One of Collins's earliest public engagements with scientific controversy was a series of letters which he wrote for the *Leader* between January and April 1852 under the general title 'Magnetic Evenings at

Home'. These letters were addressed to a sceptical George Henry Lewes, one of the *Leader*'s founding editors, and subsequently author of (among many other books) *The Physiology of Common Life* (1859) and an ambitious work on psychology, *Problems of Life and Mind* (1873–9). Collins's letters report on several demonstrations of mesmerism, animal magnetism, and clairvoyance which he claims to have observed in a variety of domestic settings in Somerset during 1851. The private and domestic setting is important, because in the 1840s demonstrations of mesmerism and hypnotism had become a popular form of public entertainment, and were frequently associated with trickery and quackery. In the opening letter Collins dissociates himself from such charlatan displays, noting:

Had those proceedings been publicly exhibited for hire, I should certainly not have taken the notes of them from which I am now to write. But they were of a private nature; they were shown only from motives of hospitality and kindness. . . . [therefore] I gladly commit my materials to press . . . believing that they will furnish specimens of evidence, which the opponents of Animal Magnetism will find it much easier contemptuously to reject than fairly to confute.[1]

Collins goes on to report the mesmeric feats performed by 'Count——' on a young girl, 'so quiet and natural in her manner' that it was difficult to imagine that she was 'soon to display before us all the mysterious phenomena of magnetic influence . . . [and] open to our view glimpses into the dim, dark regions of the spiritual world'. He also reports the unnamed Count's version of the theory of Animal Magnetism.

My idea about it is briefly this [says the Count]. We consist of three parts—the organic matter (*i.e.*, bodily structure), the vital principle which animates it, and the soul. We feel that the soul has many of its divinest prerogatives suspended in this life, through its connection with the bodily part of us. To find out such a means of acting on the vital principle, without injuring or destroying it, as to render the organic matter perfectly passive, and thereby to weaken, if not suspend, its influence on the soul, is to give back to that soul, for the time, some portion of its inherent and higher nature—its immortal capacity to overstep all mortal boundaries of time and space. . . . [I]n this way I explain the phenomena of what we term *clairvoyance*. As to what constitutes the essence of the influence thus communicable from one individual to another, I believe it to be simply electricity! But I must repeat that I am only a student in the science; that we are all groping in the darkness of a mystery which is still unrevealed. The relation between cause and effect is not yet traced out in Animal Magnetism. With regard to the practical purpose to which it may be directed, I think it might be used as a curative agent in more forms of disease—especially nervous diseases . . .

This foreign Count, who is in some respects an early version of Collins's more famous aristocratic mesmerist Count Fosco, thus announces himself a follower of Anton Mesmer, whose *Mémoire sur la découverte du magnétisme animal* (1779) claimed to offer a cure for both physical and mental or psychological conditions. Mesmer's theory of animal magnetism was based on the concept of a force or flow which was governed by particular laws and which formed 'a mutual influence between the Heavenly Bodies, the Earth, and Animate Bodies'.[2] According to Mesmer, a misdirection in this force or fluid might cause either a physical or a nervous disorder which could be cured by the redirection of the force through trance or somnambulism. Collins makes a brief reference to the curative properties of mesmerism in *No Name* when Noel Vanstone considers whether he might employ mesmerism to deal with the 'neuralgic attack' which Magdalen suffers under the strain of maintaining the illusion of her borrowed identity as 'Susan Bygrave': 'Mesmerism was frequently useful in these cases. Mr Noel Vanstone's father had been the most powerful mesmerist in Europe; and Mr Noel Vanstone was his father's son. Might he not mesmerize?' (*No Name*, The Fourth Scene, Chapter V).

Mesmerism came to prominence in England in the 1830s and 1840s, and was taken up by John Elliotson, Professor of Medicine at University College London, who founded *Zoist: A Journal of Cerebral Physiology and Mesmerism and their Application to Human Welfare* in 1843. Elliotson was also a champion of phrenology, a branch of science developed by Franz Joseph Gall, and popularized in England by George Combe. Phrenology sought to develop a physiology of the brain, and to 'read' people's characteristics and dispositions from the shape of their skulls, and it had a considerable impact on the diagnosis of mental disturbance in the first half of the nineteenth century. Elliotson saw both phrenology and mesmerism as ways of exploring the dim, dark regions of the mental world. However, his own attempts to practice mesmeric therapy on his patients at University College Hospital had led to his resignation from this post after his methods were attacked in the *Lancet* in 1838. James Braid, whose *Neurypynology; or, the Rationale of Nervous Sleep, considered in Relation with Animal Magnetism* appeared in the same year as the first issues of *Zoist* (1843), sought to separate mesmerism (or, to use his term, 'hypnotism') from the more scientifically dubious theories of animal magnetism. Braid also developed the idea of suggestibility—the notion that some people were particularly susceptible to the suggestions of their would-be mesmerizer or hypnotist. Mesmerism, in its guise of hypnotism, subsequently played a significant part in the study and treatment of a range of physical and mental conditions. Most famously, the French scientist Jean-Martin Charcot used hypnotism as a means of studying hysteria, a condition which was thought to be increasing rapidly in the mid- to late nineteenth century. Charcot believed hysteria to be a progressive, incurable and degenerative condition which was usually induced by a traumatic event but which was also rooted in a hereditary weakness in the neurological system. Charcot's students included Sigmund Freud, who took the view that both hypnosis and hysteria were psychological rather than neurological phenomena. Freud's own use of hypnosis in the study of hysteria formed the subject of *Studies on Hysteria* (1893–5), a series of case studies written jointly with Josef Breuer, which became one of the founding texts of modern psychoanalysis.

Collins makes several references to mesmerism and hypnosis in his novels. Ironically, the otherwise firm and resolute Marian Halcombe is a particularly susceptible subject. The ease with which she falls under the influence of Fosco appears to give substance to this Count's claim to have 'experience of the more subtle resources which medical and magnetic science have placed at the disposal of mankind' (*The Woman in White*, The Second Epoch, The Story continued by Marian Halcombe, X). Marian focuses on Fosco's eyes as the source of his magnetic or mesmeric power: 'the most unfathomable gray eyes I ever saw . . . they have at times a cold . . . irresistible glitter in them, which forces me to look at him and yet causes me sensations, when I do look, which I would rather not feel' (ibid., II) Later on in the narrative the suggestible Marian also falls spontaneously into a clairvoyant trance—'a strange condition', neither waking nor sleeping, in which 'my fevered mind broke loose from me . . . and, in a trance, or daydream of my fancy . . . I saw Walter

Hartright' (ibid., VI). Ozias Midwinter in *Armadale* is a similarly suggestible subject, prone to premonitory dreams, and 'mesmerised' by the sexual power of Lydia Gwilt. But it is *The Moonstone* which makes the most significant narrative use of Collins's fascination with the mental processes upon which mesmerism and hypnosis depend, when Ezra Jennings puts Franklin Blake into an opium trance in order to get him to recover a suppressed memory by re-enacting a scene from the past and solve the mystery of the disappearance of the diamond.

One of the fascinations of mesmerism and hypnotism in the nine-teenth century was that they appeared to give access to the dim, dark regions of the human psyche or soul, and—like the 'sciences' of physiognomy and phrenology that they replaced—to offer a way of 'reading the "hidden man" ' and disclosing 'a concealed domain of inner selfhood'.[3] This point was not lost on the novelists of the period, nor on their readers. Critics of sensation fiction often phrased their objections to such novels in terms of the sensation authors' apparent fixation on the idea of a hidden, inner self. A frequent complaint against sensation novelists such as Collins was that they would have their readers believe that their ordinary-looking neighbour carried some dark secret around within him- or herself. In fact, Collins often seems to represent his characters according to a kind of reverse physiognomy: instead of being able to 'read' the truth about a person's disposition in their physical features, Collins's readers discover, in characters such as Godfrey Ablewhite, that dark secrets lurk in the most innocent of faces and in the most respect-able-looking people. As one would expect of a mystery writer, Collins was fascinated by hidden realities, and by the slow working out of the consequences of past actions and events. His novels also explore and make interesting narrative use of the hidden meanings of apparently supernatural events, such as mysterious premonitory dreams and visions. In all of these respects Collins's novels consistently engage with contemporary psychological debates, particularly debates about the relationship between the brain and the mind, and between the unconscious and the conscious mind.

The concept of 'unconscious cerebration' was developed by William Carpenter, Professor of Forensic Medicine at University College London (from 1856), and a leading figure in the theory and practice of mental physiology in the second half of the nineteenth

century. Carpenter first outlined his theory of 'unconscious cerebration' in the fifth edition of his *Human Physiology* (1855), and he went
on to expand it further in *Principles of Mental Physiology* (1874), in
which he wrote about the human capacity for 'spontaneous', 'automatic', or 'unconscious' recall of something we have tried (and
failed) to recall consciously. Building on eighteenth-century ideas of
mental association, Carpenter developed the notion of unconscious
memory, which works by hidden associations: 'as our ideas are linked
in "trains" or "series",' he wrote, 'so . . . an idea which . . . seems to
have faded completely out of *conscious* memory may be reproduced,
as by the touching of a spring, through a *nexus* of suggestions.'[4]
Collins makes repeated use of unconscious memory, hidden mental
associations, and a nexus of suggestions in a range of novels. But it is
The Moonstone that makes the most explicit reference to nineteenth-
century debates about psychology. Both William Carpenter and John
Elliotson are directly quoted by Ezra Jennings to provide scientific
justification for the experiment he proposes to conduct on Franklin
Blake in order to prove Franklin's innocence and to provide a key to
the mystery at the heart of Collins's narrative—the disappearance of
the diamond. Jennings gleans from Dr Candy's delirious ramblings
during his illness (another example of the unconscious at work) that
on the night of the Moonstone's disappearance the doctor had
secretly conducted his own experiment on Franklin by slipping a
small quantity of the opiate laudanum into his drink. Candy's purpose was to triumph over Franklin by demonstrating that he could
cure the younger man's sleeplessness despite the latter's protestations against the effectiveness of or need for drugs in such cases.
Jennings, himself an opium user and thus well acquainted with its
effects, proposes to repeat Dr Candy's experiment in order to re-
create the conditions in which Franklin apparently took the Moonstone from its lodging place in Rachel Verinder's bedroom. 'Science
sanctions my proposal, fanciful as it may seem', Jennings observes,
and he goes on to cite 'no less a person than Dr Carpenter' as the
authority for 'the physiological principle on which I am acting'.
Jennings presents Franklin with a slip of paper inscribed with these
words from Carpenter's work:

There seems much ground for the belief, that *every* sensory impression
which has once been recognised by the perceptive consciousness, is
registered (so to speak) in the brain, and may be reproduced at some

subsequent time, although there may be no consciousness of its existence in the mind during the whole intermediate period. (*The Moonstone*, Second Period, Third Narrative, Chapter X)

Jennings also refers Franklin to 'Dr Elliotson's *Human Physiology*' and, in particular, to its citation of the case, discussed by the phrenologist George Combe, of an Irish warehouse porter who had mislaid a parcel when drunk and when sober had no recollection of what had happened to it. However, when he was drunk again he was able to return to the house where he had left it.

The two doctors upon whom Jennings (and Collins) draws, would have been reasonably well-known to middle-class readers in the 1860s as representing two very different aspects of nineteenth-century psychology: Carpenter was a respectable and respected representative of a modern mainstream physiological psychology while Elliotson had become a more marginal figure associated with the quackery of mesmerism. What they shared, however, was a common belief in the existence of the unconscious, and a belief that the mind will retain traces of whatever it has taken in, even material which has completely disappeared from the conscious memory. They would also have shared the belief that what cannot be recalled consciously can be reproduced through suggestion and association.

Collins uses contemporary scientific and psychological theories to explain *how* Franklin took the diamond and *what* he did with it. He also uses such theories to provide an explanation of *why* he did it. The answer to the question of what makes Franklin Blake a thief is important both for his own self-conception and for his role as a fictional hero whose fate is to outgrow his youthful fancies and settle down to life as the master of 'our quiet country house' and the husband of Rachel Verinder. Referring to Thomas De Quincey's *Confessions of an English Opium Eater* as well as to Carpenter's theorization of the unconscious as a collection of 'automatic' reflexes beyond the immediate control of the will, Jennings explains Franklin's turning thief as follows:

The action of opium is comprised, in the majority of cases, in two influences—a stimulating influence first, and a sedative influence afterwards. Under the stimulating influence, the latest and most vivid impressions left on your mind—namely, the impressions relating to the Diamond—would be likely, in your morbidly sensitive nervous condition, to become intensified in your brain, and would subordinate to themselves your judgment and your will—exactly as [in] an ordinary dream . . . Little by little, under this action, any apprehensions about the safety of the Diamond which you might have felt during the day would be liable to develop themselves from the state of doubt to the state of certainty—would impel you into practical action to preserve the jewel—would direct your steps, with that motive in view, into the room which you entered—and would guide your hand . . . until you had found the drawer which held the stone. In the spiritualised intoxication of opium, you would do all that. Later, as the sedative action began to gain on the stimulant action, you would slowly become inert and stupefied . . . fall into a deep sleep . . . [and] wake up . . . absolutely ignorant of what you had done in the night. (Second Period, Third Narrative, Chapter X)

Jennings's account of the effects of the opiate on Franklin's unconscious mind not only indicates why Franklin cannot remember taking the diamond (like the drunken Irish porter in Combe's story of the missing parcel), but it also suggests that when he took the stone he was, at one and the same time, not himself and most himself. He was not himself because 'under the influence' of laudanum he was not responsible for his own actions, but at the same time the theft was an expression of the hidden, unconscious self that was anxious to protect both the diamond and Rachel.

Jennings's experiment is an interesting combination of Carpenter the mental physiologist and Elliotson the mesmerist. In a sort of replay of the magnetic evenings at home, Collins's readers are required to observe a small group of characters in the act of observing Franklin's opium-induced somnambulistic trance—with Bruff, the lawyer, cast in the role of a less intellectual George Henry Lewes, proclaiming that 'it was quite unintelligible to *his* mind, except that it looked like a piece of trickery, akin to the trickery of mesmerism, clairvoyance, and the like' (Second Period, Fourth Narrative). But the experiment also depends on Carpenter's idea of the spring which links the broken trains or series through a nexus of suggestions. Jennings notes that Franklin will not only have to take laudanum, but he will also have to be 'put . . . back again into something assimilating to your nervous condition on the birthday night . . . [and] revive, or nearly revive, the domestic circumstances which surrounded you; and . . . occupy your mind again with the various questions concerning the Diamond' (Second Period, Third Narrative, Chapter X). Jennings's experiment thus depends on creating a series of associations which will unlock Franklin's unconscious memory.

Jennings's explanation of the operations of laudanum on Franklin's mind draws on mid-nineteenth-century theories about the unconscious and about dreams. The opium dream, Jennings asserts, is just like an 'ordinary dream' in the way in which it allows 'the latest and most vivid impressions left on [the] mind' to become 'intensified in [the] brain' and to subordinate the judgement and will. This was one of the kinds of dream work that John Abercrombie identified in his *Inquiries Concerning the Intellectual Powers and the Investigation of Truth* (1830). In dreams, Abercrombie wrote, 'ideas and images of the mind follow one another according to associations over which we have no control'.[5] Dreams are a form of memory: recent impressions, events, and emotions become mixed up with each other and with impressions, events, and emotions from the past; 'trains of images brought up by association with bodily sensations'; 'the revival of old associations, repeating things which had entirely passed out of mind and which seem to have been forgotten'.[6] According to the phrenologist Robert Macnish, whose influential study *The Philosophy of Sleep* appeared in the same year as Abercrombie's *Inquiry*, dreams are a 'state of partial slumber' in which the dreamer reworks the recent past, and does so in a way which is determined by his or her own character.[7] Another aspect of dreams that fascinated nineteenth-century psychologists was the uncanny way in which their combining and reworking of past and present emotions and events could often appear prophetic. Nineteenth-century dream theory thus naturalized the apparently supernatural.

Like many sensation novelists (indeed, like many nineteenth-century novelists), Collins made frequent use of and reference to prophetic or premonitory dreams. Perhaps the most prominent example of this is the dream which lies at the heart of the narrative of *Armadale*. This is the 'ugly dream' which Allan Armadale experiences (and whose disturbing effects on Allan's sleeping body are witnessed by Midwinter) in a chapter entitled 'The Shadow of the Past'. This dream is described and variously interpreted in the following chapter, 'The Shadow of the Future'. In this chapter, the contents of Allan's dream are revealed to the reader and to Mr Hawbury, the local doctor, as a series of scenes transcribed in Midwinter's notebook. Armadale, Midwinter, and Hawbury each interpret the dream according to their personal disposition or inclination or, in Hawbury's case, according to their professional training. The bluff young Armadale initially attributes the dream to indigestion, but is subsequently persuaded by the medical man Hawbury's reading of the dream which traces each of its elements back to its causes in 'something that [Allan] has said or thought, or seen or done, in the four-and-twenty hours, or less, which preceded his falling asleep' (*Armadale*, Book the First, Chapter V). Hawbury takes the 'essentially practical point of view' and espouses the theory of dreams 'accepted by the great mass of [his] profession' (such as Abercrombie and Macnish):

A Dream is the reproduction, in the sleeping state of the brain, of images and impressions produced on it in the waking state; and this reproduction is more or less involved, imperfect, or contradictory, as the action of certain faculties in the dreamer is controlled more or less completely, by the influence of sleep.

Despite an initial willingness to escape into the comfort of Hawbury's practical explanation, the nervously susceptible Midwinter retains his 'terrible conviction of the supernatural origin of the dream' and feels condemned to 'wait till the living originals [of the shadows in the dream] stand revealed in the future'.

Collins's narrative self-consciously manipulates both the supernatural and the psychological interpretations of Allan's dream. When read retrospectively, in the context of the frame narrative of Allan's father's history, the elements of the dream can be traced back much further than the twenty-four hours before Allan fell asleep. They can be traced back to his family history and his own psychological history. The dream is also prospective or prophetic, insofar as it prefigures scenes played out in later stages of the narrative in ways which are variously interpretable as coincidence or providence, the enactment of a family curse, or the working out and working through of social and psychological history in complex ways that go beyond the realms of Victorian dream theory.

Midwinter's supernatural interpretation of Allan's dream involves reading that dream as a prophetic moral allegory. Such a reading is just one of the possibilities which Collins offers in his multi-layered use of the dream of two women which the narrator and chief protagonist of *Basil* has on the night after his first meeting with Margaret

Sherwin. As with *Armadale*'s dream, Collins uses Basil's dream both as a vehicle for sensational effect and as a means of building narrative tension. In this case he also uses the dream as a way of providing another perspective on the 'unreliable' first-person narrator who offers a vivid description of a dream in which he gives himself up to the embraces of an alluring, hot-breathed, dark woman (whom the reader has no problem in identifying immediately as Margaret), who emerges from the 'dark secret depths' of a wood, rather than following the beckoning of another woman (clearly his sister Clara) who is clad in a 'white . . . pure, and glistening' robe and who descends from the brightly illumined, clear and cold hills. Basil offers various interpretations of his own dream ranging from an immediate superstitious reading to a retrospective reading which combines moral allegory with psychology. The initial, superstitious, response to the dream is quickly dismissed by the dreamer:

Was it a warning of coming events, foreshadowed in the wild visions of sleep? But to what purpose could this dream, or indeed any dream, tend? Why had it remained incomplete, failing to show me the visionary consequences of visionary actions? What superstition to ask! What a waste of attention to bestow it on such a trifle as a dream! (*Basil*, Part I, VIII)

Another perspective is offered by the sadder but wiser Basil who narrates his own story, and who presents himself as knowing 'now' (as he narrates his story) what he 'knew not then' as he experienced its events. What the narrating Basil 'knows' is that the dream was at once a moral allegory, a kind of moral choice, and an expression of his unconscious desires. Basil has learned to see the dream as the acting out in his psyche of a battle between two different kinds of femininity, between flesh and spirit, between sexuality and family:

[I]t was easy enough [then] for me to dismiss as ridiculous from my mind, or rather from my conscience, the tendency to see in the two shadowy forms of my dream, the types of two real living beings, whose names almost trembled into utterance on my lips; but I could not also dismiss from my heart the love-images which that dream had set up there for the worship of the senses. (Part I, VIII)

Collins presents Basil's dream not only as a kind of shadow play which reveals his unconscious desires to him, but also as a form of experience which changes him. The dream is also both a sign of

Basil's derangement and an event which further deranges him. In *Basil* as in many of Collins's later novels the dream is used to mark the faultline between normal and abnormal mental states. Basil's dream of the dark and fair women is the first stage of a process which ends in behaviour that is interpreted as 'MAD!' (Part II, VII), and to the brain fever, delirium, and hallucinations which are so vividly described at the beginning of Part III of the novel. Basil's 'dream-vision[s]' read like something from Coleridge's 'Kubla Khan' or 'The Pains of Opium' in Thomas De Quincey's *Confessions of an English Opium Eater*:

Away! to a City of Palaces, to measureless halls, and arches, and domes, soaring one above another, till their flashing ruby summits are lost in the burning void . . . Far down the corridors rise visions of flying phantoms . . . their raving voices clanging like the hammers of a thousand forges . . . then an apparition of . . . two monsters stretching forth their gnarled yellow talons . . . the fiend-souls made visible in fiend-shapes—Margaret and Mannion! . . . We stood on a wilderness . . . Outspread over the noisome ground lay the ruins of a house, rooted up and overthrown to its foundations. The demon figures . . . drew me slowly forward to the fallen stones, and pointed to two dead bodies lying among them.
    My father!—my sister! (Part III, I)

Here Basil replays his own history as persecution, aberration, and betrayal and also confronts his own guilt. Collins, on the other hand, replays his protagonist's history as a nightmare from which he finally awakes. This latter pattern is repeated in many of Collins's novels, in plots in which mid-Victorian England is transformed into a dreamlike world whose surreal twists and confusions his characters must negotiate.

'It was like a dream', writes Walter Hartright of his first strange meeting with the woman in white which disrupts his sense of self and initiates the train of events which turns his world upside down. 'It was like a dream. Was I Walter Hartright? Was this the well-known, uneventful road, where holiday people strolled on Sundays? Had I really left, little more than an hour since, the quiet, decent, conventionally-domestic atmosphere of my mother's cottage?' (*The Woman in White*, The Story begun by Walter Hartright, IV). The Walter who narrates his own state of confusion has already begun to represent himself as a somnambulistic subject who walks on Hampstead Heath as if in a trance, and who seems to conjure the woman in white from his own imaginings: she first appears just as he was 'idly wondering . . . what the Cumberland young ladies would look like—when, in one moment, every drop of blood in my body was brought to a stop by the touch of a hand laid lightly and suddenly on my shoulder'. Walter's narrative not only conveys his own sense of disorientation, but it is also the means of disorientating the novel's readers, and propelling them from their own 'quiet, decent, conventionally-domestic atmosphere' to a strange, dreamlike world in which the 'ordinary rules of evidence' are replaced by an associative logic, albeit one which Walter suspects might be delusional. Thus when Marian Halcombe informs him that they are about to be visited by Laura's fiancé, Sir Percival Glyde, Walter immediately links this baronet with Anne Catherick's 'suspicious question about the men of the rank of baronet whom I might happen to know', but notes:

Judging by the ordinary rules of evidence, I had not the shadow of a reason, thus far, for connecting Sir Percival Glyde with the suspicious words of inquiry . . . [of] the woman in white. And yet, I did connect him with them. Was it because he had now become associated in my mind with Miss Fairlie; Miss Fairlie being, in her turn, associated with Anne Catherick, since . . . I had discovered the ominous likeness between them? Had the events of the morning so unnerved me already that I was at the mercy of any delusion which . . . common coincidences might suggest to my imagination? (The Story begun by Walter Hartright, XI)

Collins does not simply create a delusional or dreamlike world in *The Woman in White*, but, as in *Basil* and *Armadale*, he also makes use of premonitory dreams. However, unlike *Basil* and *Armadale*, in *The Woman in White* his dreamers are female. The first of these female dreamers is Anne Catherick, whose dream of Laura's marriage to Sir Percival is narrated in her anonymous letter to Laura—a letter in which she claims scriptural authority for her dream: 'See what Scripture says about dreams and their fulfilment (Genesis xl. 8, xl. 25; Daniel iv. 18–25)' (The Story begun by Walter Hartright, XI). Then there is Marian's 'trance, or daydream of my fancy'—a 'strange condition' neither waking nor sleeping—in which her 'fevered mind broke loose' from her 'weary body' and she has a vision of Walter Hartright. Marian's trance occurs at Blackwater Park, during Walter's sojourn in South America, and it consists of four visions of Walter in each of which Marian addresses him or he communicates with her.

First, Marian sees Walter lying on the steps of a ruined temple surrounded by a group of other men, 'colossal tropical trees', and 'hideous stone idols', and wreathed in a threatening mist bearing disease and pestilence. Marian begs Walter to escape from the dangers of the jungle and return to keep his promise to Laura and herself. Walter, in turn, affirms that the pestilence will spare him and he will return to fulfil the destiny implicit in his first meeting with the woman in white—to be the 'instrument of a Design that is yet unseen'. In the second vision, Walter is in the forest with fewer companions and surrounded by 'dark, dwarfish men' lurking 'murderously among the trees, with bows in their hands', and in the third he is marooned in a wrecked ship. In both of these visions Walter reassures Marian that he will be spared the dangers which are about to befall his dwindling band of companions in order that he may take another step 'on the dark road' of his destiny. In the final vision Walter kneels beside a tomb of white marble as 'the shadow of a veiled woman rose out of the grave beneath, and waited by his side', proclaiming 'Death takes the good, the beautiful, and the young— and spares *me*. The Pestilence that wastes . . . the Grave that closes over Love and Hope, are steps of my journey, and take me nearer and nearer to the End' (The Second Epoch, The Story continued by Marian Halcombe, VI).

The dreams of both Anne and Marian function simultaneously as supernatural prophecy, as clairvoyance, and as psychological revelations which disclose the hidden fears and longings of the dreamers. Collins uses Anne's dream-letter and Marian's trance as ways of developing narrative tension and he also fully exploits their sensational potential.

The Sensation Novel and Nineteenth-Century Medical and Psychological Theories

Sensation was at the heart of Associationism, and Associationism was the philosophical foundation of much psychological theory in the mid-nineteenth century. The roots of Associationism lay in the philosophy of John Locke and in the psychological theories of his eighteenth-century contemporary David Hartley. Put simply, Associationism developed a model of the mind as a receiver and translator of sensations. The mind was conceived of as a blank sheet (or, as Locke put it, a *tabula rasa*) which received sensations, translated them into *ideas* of sensations, and then linked them together according to principles of similarity, proximity, or causality. In other words, the mind worked by associating or bringing together sensations, ideas, and events that seemed similar to each other, were close together in time or space, or which seemed to be connected as cause and effect. Most nineteenth-century Associationists saw this process of linking or association as having a physiological basis in the brain and neurological system. Alexander Bain, for example, expressed this process in terms of neural pathways or currents.

Collins offers a particularly vivid example of Associationism through sensation in his depiction of the way in which Walter Hartright comes to link Laura Fairlie and Anne Catherick together in his mind, long before he learns of any other kind of link between them. Walter's first meeting with Laura (like his first meeting with Anne) is described in terms of sensation:

Among the sensations that crowded on me, when my eyes first looked upon her . . . there was one that troubled and perplexed me; one that seemed strangely inconsistent and unaccountably out of place in Miss Fairlie's presence.

Mingling with the vivid impression produced by the charm of her fair face . . . was another impression, which, in a shadowy way, suggested to me the idea of something wanting. At one time it seemed like something wanting in *her*; at another, like something wanting in myself, which hindered me from understanding her as I ought. (*The Woman in White*, The Story begun by Walter Hartright, VIII)

A few pages and a few hours later Walter's account of his sensations sets off a secondary process of association, which causes the reader to begin to link Walter's sensations—even before he does—with events narrated earlier. As Marian is reading out a passage about Anne Catherick from a letter written by the late Mrs Fairlie, Walter 'start[s] up', 'chilled . . . again' with a 'thrill of the same feeling which ran through me when the touch was laid upon my shoulder on the lonely high-road'. The thrill of the same feeling is caused by the appearance of Laura—which Walter experiences almost as an apparition:

a white figure, alone in the moonlight . . . the living image, at that distance and under those circumstances, of the woman in white! The doubt which had troubled my mind for hours and hours past, flashed into conviction in an instant. That 'something wanting' was my own recognition of the ominous likeness between the fugitive from the asylum and my pupil at Limmeridge House.

Walter's sensational and mental association of Laura and Anne prefigures the narrative revelation of their familial association and their coincidental (or uncanny, depending on the point of view) link to Sir Percival Glyde. These different but connected processes of association also set up other associative possibilities for the reader. Thus, Ann Cvetkovich reads both Walter's and the text's sensational association of Laura and Anne as an example of a particular 'politics of affect' which enables Walter (and Collins) to represent his transformation into a hero and his rise up the social scale 'as though it were the product of chance occurrences, uncanny repetitions, and fated events' rather than a series of social negotiations.[8]

In Collins's narrative, Anne Catherick and Laura are not simply associated in the sensations of Walter and the reader, but they are also associated by heredity. Anne and Laura look alike because they are half-sisters who share the same father, and they share something of his frailty. Sir Percival seeks to exploit their physical resemblance in his plot to obtain control of Laura's fortune by substituting the dead Anne for her living half-sister, who in her turn, is to take 'mad' Anne Catherick's place in the asylum. When Laura claims that she has been wrongfully confined and that she is, in fact, Lady Glyde, her protestations are treated as a symptom of her deranged condition. The association between Laura and Anne, and in particular the physical likeness they inherit from their father, is reinforced by Laura's ordeal at the hands of Sir Percival and her incarceration in the asylum. As a result of being treated like a madwoman, Laura comes to look more like a madwoman. As Walter notes: 'the fatal resemblance which I had once seen and shuddered at seeing, in idea only, was now a real and living resemblance which asserted itself before my own eyes' (The Third Epoch, The Story continued by Walter Hartright, III).

Madness, and the social construction and treatment of madness, features prominently and frequently in Collins's novels as it does in the work of many sensation novelists. This fascination with madness and extreme emotional states was much discussed by reviewers, as for example in an essay on 'Madness in Novels' which appeared in the *Spectator* in 1866. This essay presents the rise of madness in the novel in the 1860s as a fictional convention that allows an author either to dispense with probability or to transcend the limitations of a prosaic and materialistic modern age. 'The nineteenth century believes in love and jealousy, and in a feeble way, even in hate,' the author of the essay wrote, 'but it is aware that the mental concentrativeness out of which these passions spring is in this age rare.' Madness was the device that sensation novelists used to 'intensify' such qualities or propensities as courage, hate, jealousy, or wickedness.[9] Most sensation writers, in their varying ways, made use of contemporary medical discourses and psychological theories, and in their turn, reviewers of their work employed these theories to describe and account for sensation fiction and its effects on the reader. The sensation novel, as Henry Mansel famously expressed it in his review in the *Quarterly Review* in 1863, worked by 'preaching to the nerves', with the sole aim of producing 'excitement':

And as excitement, even when harmless in kind, cannot be continually reproduced without becoming morbid in degree, works of this class manifest themselves as belonging, some more, some less, but all to some extent, to the morbid phenomenon of literature, indications of a widespread corruption, of which they are in part both the effect and the cause; called into existence to supply the cravings of a diseased appetite, and contributing themselves to foster the disease, and to stimulate the want that they supply.[10]

For critics such as Mansel, sensation fiction did not simply work on the nerves of the individual reader, but it was also a shared mania, a collective nervous disorder, or a 'morbid addiction' to which the middle classes had succumbed. In short, in the accounts of its detractors in the periodical press (newspaper reviewers tended to be less censorious about the genre) the sensation novel was represented as both a symptom and a cause of individual and cultural degeneration.

Collins and the Discourses of Degeneration

Collins's sensation novels—indeed his fiction more generally—were not, *pace* Mansel, simply morbid symptoms which were both produced by and provided evidence of the depravity and degeneracy of modern mass culture and modern urban-industrial society. On the contrary Collins's fiction was often fairly directly concerned with a range of issues and ideas in biology, psychology, and social theory that can be subsumed together under the general heading of degeneration. By the mid-nineteenth century degeneration was regarded as both a distinctively modern condition and as an explanation of insanity. From the late 1850s and 1860s onwards there was a perception and concern that the incidence of insanity and mental and physical disorders of various kinds was growing apace with modernity, exacerbated by the speed and pressure of modern urban life. In 1859 George Robinson linked the growth of insanity to social progress, noting that in looking for the causes of moral insanity: 'we shall discover ample evidence of its frequent origin in the vices of a spurious and hollow civilisation'.[11] Such vices (according to commentators like Robinson) included the ceaseless striving after social elevation, a love of display, and foreign (especially French) influence. Another commentator (in the *Edinburgh Review*) linked the growth of 'brain disorders' to increased strain in commercial and public life, and in particular to the 'intense competition which exists between the liberal professions . . . the excitement accompanying the large monetary transactions which distinguish the trading of the present day . . . the gambling nature of many of its operations, and the extreme tension to which all classes . . . are subjected in the unceasing struggle for position and even life'.[12]

The mid-nineteenth-century discourse on degeneration was made up of oppositions and contradictions. On the one hand, degeneration was said to be the product and symptom of the over-refinement of modern civilization: Collins's nervous, effeminate, and hypochondriacal bachelors Frederick Fairlie and Noel Vanstone are examples of this. Yet, on the other hand, degeneration was also associated with atavism or throwbacks to a more primitive biological and social phase of existence, as, for example in the upper-class barbarism of Geoffrey Delamayn in whom the 'savage element in humanity . . . show[ed] itself furtively in his eyes; . . . [and] utter[ed] itself furtively in his voice' (*Man and Wife*, Chapter IV). Degeneration was associated with moral insanity and with a criminality which was either caused or exacerbated by modern social conditions, but it was also thought to be an inherited trait (or set of traits), passed on from parents to children. Collins repeatedly refers to matters of hereditary transmission in his fiction. Examples of this include Mannion's inheritance of his father's villainy, and possibly worse: 'there has been madness in his family or his brain has suffered from his internal injuries', notes the doctor who deals with him after his fall, and who pronounces him 'morally . . . a dangerous monomaniac' although 'legally . . . quite fit to be at large' (*Basil*, Part III, VII). Another example is the protagonist of 'Mad Monkton' who is obsessed with the family madness which he fears he is biologically doomed to inherit. On the other hand, in *Armadale* both Allan Armadale and Ozias Midwinter contrive to escape the moral degeneracy of their biological destinies and the enmity to which their family histories have appeared to condemn them. Midwinter, however, does so only as a result of painfully confronting his fears and fantasies about his origins and after an almost intolerable struggle with his 'nerves'.

No Name, another novel deeply concerned with family history, directs its readers' attention to degeneration as a function of hereditary transmission, the thinning out or wearing down of the natural characteristics of the parent as they are passed on to the next generation. Thus, Norah Vanstone inherits 'the dark majestic quality of her mother's beauty' but her features are less delicate, there is 'less refinement and depth of feeling in her expression', and she is shorter. Underlining his point about the degenerative operations of hereditary transmission, the narrator links it to the idea of degeneration as a distinctive pathology of modern society:

If we dare to look closely enough, may we not observe, that the moral force of character and the higher intellectual capacities in parents seem often to wear out mysteriously in the course of transmission to children? In these days of insidious nervous exhaustion and subtly-spreading nervous malady, is it not possible that the same rule may apply, less rarely than we are willing to admit, to the bodily gifts as well? (*No Name*, The First Scene, Chapter I)

The narrative which Collins constructs for this thinned-down version of her mother's biological stock raises questions about social evolution and adaptation. For the pale and enervated Norah nevertheless proves herself fit to survive and become the wife of the heir to her father's name and fortune. On the other hand, her ebullient sister Magdalen is 'one of those strange caprices of Nature, which science leaves still unexplained' (The First Scene, Chapter I), and bears no resemblance to either parent. Magdalen's appearance is not only a kind of denial of her inheritance, but it also has a restless and oppositional dynamic which is all its own. Her features are 'self-contradictory' and mobile, and they also contradict gender norms—she is too tall and her mouth is 'too large and firm . . . for her sex and age'. There is no modern 'nervous exhaustion' here, all is rude health and vitality: 'all sprang alike from the same source; from the overflowing physical health which strengthened every muscle, braced every nerve, and set the warm young blood tingling through her veins like the blood of a growing child' (The First Scene, Chapter I). Magdalen is thus one of nature's fittest, but she does not easily fit into the habitat which mid-Victorian society has shaped for a middle-class woman. Indeed, Magdalen survives as a social being only after suffering a complete physical and mental breakdown and by being nursed back to health by the manly Mr Kirke.

If degeneration was the dark side of progress, it is precisely this aspect of progress which was the focus of several of Collins's late novels with a purpose. *Man and Wife*, for example, juxtaposes the degeneration of the urban working class (in the shape of Hester Dethridge's drunken and violent husband), with the inculcated superficial 'fitness' which masks the physical and moral atrophy of the public school educated Geoffrey Delamayn. Indeed, Collins's 1870 Preface makes a direct connection between the medical and moral results of 'the present rage for muscular exercises' among 'the rising generation of Englishmen', and the 'violence and outrage' of ' "Roughs" '. Urban degeneration is dealt with even more directly and more polemically in *The New Magdalen*. For example, in this narratorial intervention on a pauper child:

the daughter of the London streets! The pet creation of the laws of political economy! The scourge and terrible product of a worn out system of government and of a civilization rotten to its core! Cleaned for the first time in her life, dressed in clothes instead of rags for the first time in her life. (*The New Magdalen*, Chapter 39)

Here it is not the dirty and puny pauper child who is degenerate, but the 'rotten' civilization which constructs and accepts the 'laws of political economy' and a 'worn out system of government'. The laws of political economy and the social Darwinist notion of competitive individualism which explain class difference in terms of the degeneration of the urban poor are further explored a few years later in *The Fallen Leaves*, one of Collins's less successful later novels, which focuses on the randomness of social exclusion by telling the stories of 'people who have drawn blanks in the lottery of life . . . the friendless and the lonely, the wounded and the lost' (*The Fallen Leaves*, Book the First, Chapter III). One such helpless and unfriended creature is the young prostitute 'Simple Sally', whose fall into prostitution is the result not of inherent degeneration, but of life chances which have been shaped by the ambitions of her father, John Farnaby, who, having seduced her mother (his employer's daughter) in order to force her to marry him, abandons their child to a baby-farmer. Sally's story is, in part, a story about nature versus nurture and heredity versus environment, and it is a story whose terms are slightly slippery. Brought up among such creatures as her drunken stepfather, 'one of the swarming beasts of low London . . . the living disgrace of English civilization' (Book the Sixth, Chapter I), the child of the streets none the less retains an 'artlessly virginal and innocent' appearance, and 'looked as though she had passed through the contamination of the streets without being touched by it' (Book the Sixth, Chapter I).

Questions of heredity and environment are also at the centre of *The Legacy of Cain* (1889), a speculative fiction on the inheritance and transmission of degenerative tendencies. The legacy which is explored in this narrative is the legacy of inherited evil, an issue which is debated in the novel's Prologue—set in a prison—in which a doctor, a clergyman, and the prison governor discuss the moral and medical implications of the case of a woman who has been found guilty of the brutal murder of her husband. The doctor believes in heredity and espouses a degenerationist view, maintaining that he has 'often found vices and diseases descending more frequently to children than virtue and health' (*The Legacy of Cain*, First Period, Chapter VI). On the other hand, the clergyman, the Reverend Abel Gracedieu, believes in the influence of environment on character and in the shaping power of upbringing and moral management. In order to demonstrate the validity of his hypothesis, Gracedieu adopts the murderess's daughter and brings her up with his own daughter without letting either know which of them is his natural child. In the ensuing narrative both the doctor and the clergyman prove to be right, although in unexpected ways. The narrative of the two girls is recovered and reconstructed by the prison governor and is told, in part, through the juxtaposition of their diaries. These journals and the unfolding drama of the narrative reveal that the murderess's daughter does indeed inherit something of her mother's 'evil genius', but this aspect of her inheritance only comes to the surface as a result of extreme pressure and provocation and she is able to control it, thus proving the clergyman right and escaping what the doctor had seen as her destiny. The doctor's view is given some substance by the fate of the clergyman's natural daughter, who is imprisoned for attempted murder, having inherited the morbid tendencies of her own dead mother. However, in an interesting twist, this woman also proves herself her father's daughter by emigrating to America (after serving two years in prison) and becoming the leader of a female religious cult.

Science and Scientists

The plot of *The Legacy of Cain* involves a sort of experiment with human lives by a clergyman. In a number of other novels in the late 1870s and 1880s Collins turned his attention to questions of scientific experimentation, and in particular to the role and power of the scientist and the morality of experimenting on human and animal lives. The first of these novels was *Jezebel's Daughter* (discussed in Chapter 5), which takes the form of a reconstruction in 1878 of a series of events which occurred in Germany and London some fifty years earlier. This novel contrasts the very different inheritances of two widows. The first of these, Mrs Wagner, is the widow of the senior partner in a firm of merchants, Wagner, Keller, and Engelman, who takes up her husband's position running the London office and plans to employ women clerks. Mrs Wagner also takes up her husband's interest in the lunacy reform movement and, having read the copy of Samuel Tuke's *A Description of the Retreat*[13] which she has found among her husband's books she continues his work by rescuing Jack Straw from Bedlam, an old-fashioned asylum which uses the restraint system. The other widow, Madame Fontaine, had been married to an experimental chemist from whom she has obtained a collection of poisons and their antidotes which he had intended should be destroyed on his death, but which she seeks to use as her own means to power. The two widows are connected by Madame Fontaine's designs on the son of one of the partners in Wagner, Keller, and Engelman (Fritz Keller, whose father seeks to prevent his marriage to Madame Fontaine's daughter Minna), and, more importantly by Jack Straw, whose mental impairment is the result of an accident in her husband's laboratory. Madame Fontaine is an example of the bad or mad mother whose 'natural' desire to advance the interests of her own daughter becomes excessive and thus a perversion of nature. Her malign use of her husband's work on poisons and anti-toxins is also an example of a perversion of science—a theme which Collins was to explore more fully in *Heart and Science* (1882–3)

Subtitled 'A Story of the Present Time', *Heart and Science* is both a contribution to a particular scientific controversy of the day and a novel which takes issue with the pretensions of modern science more generally. The particular scientific controversy was the vigorous debate about vivisection, or experiments on live animals, which raged in the law courts, in Parliament and in the newspaper and periodical press from the mid-1870s to the mid-1880s. The controversy began in earnest when a case was brought by the Royal Society for the Prevention of Cruelty to Animals against the French physiologist Eugène Mangan, who had injected a live dog with absinthe at the annual meeting of the British Medical Association. The failure of the case against Mangan led anti-vivisectionists to campaign for new legislation. This campaign also spawned numerous articles (for and against) in periodicals such as the *Spectator*, *Macmillan's Magazine*, the *Contemporary Review*, the *Nineteenth Century*, the *Cornhill*, and *Punch*. A Royal Commission was established to look into the pros and cons of vivisection. Numerous literary figures joined the fray, writing and speaking out against what they saw as a cruel and unjustifiable practice, including Christina Rossetti, Robert Browning, John Ruskin, Lewis Carroll, Alfred Lord Tennyson, and George Bernard Shaw. On the other side, scientists such as Charles Darwin and Thomas Henry Huxley wrote stressing the importance of vivisection for medical and scientific progress. The Cruelty to Animals Act, which introduced a measure of regulation into animal experiments, was passed in 1876. In 1881, shortly before Collins began work on *Heart and Science*, and after a few years of much less widely publicized campaigning, vivisection came into prominence again, when the International Medical Congress (which was meeting in London) declared that experimentation on live animals was 'indispensable' to the future of medical research. This was also the

year of the much-publicized case against David Ferrier, the author of
The Localization of Cerebral Disease (1878), who was accused of
conducting animal experiments without the correct licence. Ferrier's
acquittal after the briefest of trials led to a further war of words in
the press, in which Frances Power Cobbe (a long-time campaigner
against the inequities of women's legal position) wrote powerfully on
the anti-vivisectionist case. Some pro-vivisectionists responded with
attacks on unfeminine and spinster anti-vivisectionists. *Heart and
Science* was Collins's attempt 'to add my small contribution in aid of
this good cause'.[14]

As well as being a specific attack on vivisection, *Heart and
Science*, as Collins indicated in his Preface to the first edition of the
novel, also shares Sir Walter Scott's scepticism about 'the extreme
degree of improvement to be derived from the advancement of
Science; for every study of that nature tends, when pushed to a
certain extent, to harden the heart'. In Collins's novel, the practice
of vivisection is, in one sense, simply a particular instance of the
general tendency of modern experimental science to oppose itself to
feeling and to harden the human heart. In fact, the novel does not, in
the end, offer a simple opposition between 'heart' and 'science',
rather it offers a more complex exploration of good science, which
works in harmony with nature and for the good of others, and bad
science, which sets itself up over nature, becomes detached from
human culture, and works only (or mainly) to satisfy the curiosity of
the individual scientist and to further his or her personal ambitions.
The novel's two chief examples of the dehumanizing tendencies of
modern science are Mrs Galilee and Dr Benjulia. Mrs Galilee, an
extremely unsympathetic picture of a defeminized bluestocking,
neglects her children in favour of her scientific committees, and
cares more for 'the Diathermancy of Ebonite' and Thomson's theory of atoms than for her husband and family. She has no interest in
painting or poetry and is interested in music only as a means of
testing the acoustics of the concert hall. In Mrs Galilee's mental
universe, flowers exist merely to be collected and dissected and the
purpose of children is simply to perpetuate the future of scientific
study. Mrs Galilee seeks to prevent the marriage between her son
from her first marriage, Ovid Vere (the novel's good scientist), and
her niece Carmina Graywell, in order that she may retain control of
Carmina's inheritance to solve the financial problems caused by her

spending on her numerous scientific committees. As a consequence of her machinations against Carmina and Ovid—and of their failure—Mrs Galilee becomes completely alienated from her family and suffers a nervous breakdown. She recovers from the breakdown but she remains within a self-enclosed world in which she fails to appreciate the extent of her isolation from her family and the damage that she has done. She ends the novel proclaiming her satisfaction at having hosted what she feels has been a very successful scientific *conversazione* (an evening of scientific discussion): 'At last, I'm a happy woman!'

The novel's other bad scientist, Dr Nathan Benjulia, brings together the novel's general and particular preoccupations. Like Mary Shelley's Victor Frankenstein before him and Robert Louis Stevenson's Dr Jekyll who came a few years later, Benjulia is a classic example of the driven scientist for whom scientific knowledge is both its own justification and the justification of any practice which will yield such knowledge. Thus, when Carmina becomes ill as a result of the nervous shocks induced by Mrs Galilee's plotting against her, Benjulia, a specialist in diseases of the brain and nervous system, watches her condition get worse—out of scientific interest—instead of intervening to treat it. The extent of Benjulia's possession by his amoral passion for science is dramatically revealed in an outburst to his brother in Chapter XXXII:

Knowledge sanctifies cruelty . . . In that sacred cause, if I could steal a living man without being found out, I would tie him on my table, and grasp my grand discovery in days, instead of months . . . Have I no feeling, as you call it? My last experiments on a monkey horrified me. His cries of suffering, his gestures of entreaty were like the cries and gestures of a child. I would have given the world to put him out of his misery. But I went on. In the glorious cause I went on. . . . I suffered—I resisted—I went on. All for Knowledge! all for Knowledge!

Feeling is like a foreign language to Benjulia. It is like a language that he knows about but which his scientific passion has prevented him from internalizing and using appropriately. Benjulia is all the more convincing for not being simply an inherently evil monster. Indeed, in a letter to Frances Power Cobbe, who advised him on the anti-vivisectionist context for the novel, Collins was at pains to point out that Benjulia's moral coarseness is as much the product of his scientific work as its enabling condition:

In tracing the moral influence of those [detestable] cruelties [of the labora-tory] on the nature of the man who practises them, and the result as to his social relations with the persons about him, I shall be careful to present him to the reader as a man not infinitely wicked and cruel, and to show the efforts made by his better instincts to resist the inevitable hardening of the heart, the fatal stupefying of all the finer sensibilities, produced by the deliberately merciless occupations of his life.[15]

In that part of the Preface to *Heart and Science* which is addressed to 'Readers in General' Collins was also at pains to emphasize that his contribution to the anti-vivisection debate was made primarily in terms of the coarsening moral and emotional effects of vivisection on those who practised it rather than of the physical effects on the animals on whom it was practised.

From first to last, you are purposely left in ignorance of the hideous secrets of Vivisection. The outside of the laboratory is a necessary object in my landscape—but I never once open the door and invite you to look in. I trace, in one of my characters, the result of the habitual practice of cruelty . . . in fatally deteriorating the nature of man—and I leave the picture to speak for itself.

As well as using the delineation of character to demonstrate the harmful (one might almost say the degenerative) effects 'of the habitual practice of cruelty', Collins also uses dramatized argument and plot to make the case against experiments on animals. Chapter XXII provides a good example of the use of dramatized argument, in the dialogue between Benjulia and his brother Lemuel, who has recently joined an anti-vivisectionist society. Collins uses Lemuel to elucidate the central issues of the anti-vivisectionist position whilst the moral and rhetorical weakness of the vivisectionist position is represented in Benjulia's initial failure to counter his brother's argument and in his subsequent eruption in a fit of rage. The defeat of Benjulia's position is also dramatized in a plot development at the end of the novel, when Ovid Vere returns from his exile in Canada armed with a scientific manuscript on brain diseases written by an anti-vivisectionist, which he uses as the basis of a new and successful treatment of Carmina. Persuaded by the manuscript and the evi-dence of Carmina's treatment of the futility of his position, Benjulia releases his laboratory animals and kills himself.

In 1883 the *Academy* pronounced *Heart and Science* 'thoroughly readable and enthralling from its first page to its last'.[16] Whatever their view of the quality of Collins's polemic several other reviewers also commented favourably on his storytelling ability. However, the critical reputation of this late novel-with-a-purpose has been dogged by Swinburne's dismissal of it (in his obituary of Collins) as a 'childish and harmless onslaught on scientific research attempted if not achieved by [a] simple-minded and innocent author'.[17] For most of the twentieth century *Heart and Science* was one of the less widely read of Collins's novels, but in the last ten years it has enjoyed something of a renaissance. In her 1991 biography, Catherine Peters remarks that she senses a return of Collins's 'old energy' in *Heart and Science*.[18] Several new editions have recently appeared, so twenty-first-century readers will be able to decide whether they agree with Steve Farmer (editor of the Broadview edition) that this novel is both readable and thought-provoking, and has more in common with Collins's novels of the 1860s than has previously been acknowledged.

CHAPTER 7

RECONTEXTUALIZING COLLINS
THE AFTERLIFE OF COLLINS'S NOVELS

PERHAPS more than any other novelist in the nineteenth century, or since, Collins was an author who recontextualized his own fiction by adapting his novels for the stage, either at the time of their first appearance (see Chapter 3), or as a way of reviving interest in them or capitalizing on their success—or merely recycling the material—some time after their first publication. Thus, at the end of his most successful decade as a novelist Collins extensively rewrote the novel that had made his name for the London stage. Collins's own adaptation of *The Woman in White* opened at the Olympic Theatre in October 1871 and was an immediate success with both audiences and critics. For the stage version Collins dropped the dramatic scene in which Hartright meets Anne Catherick on the road to Hampstead—evidence, as the reviewer for *The Times* noted of the many changes that Collins made, that he had 'firmly grasped the rarely appreciated truth, that situations which appear dramatic to the reader, are not necessarily dramatic when brought to the ordeal of the footlights'.[1]

In adapting *The Woman in White* and later *The Moonstone* Collins also demonstrated that he had firmly grasped the fact that situations that are mysterious and dramatic for the first readers of a mystery novel are considerably less so for a theatre audience which is already very familiar with the plot of that novel. Collins addressed this problem by removing much of the mystery that was such an important part of the novel's plot and, instead, generated dramatic tension by using the dramatic irony which results from the audience's superior knowledge of the characters' situations. Thus, in the stage version of *The Woman in White* the family relationship between Anne and Laura is revealed early on (in a scene not found in the original novel), and the substitution plot is made very obvious to the audience. Collins clearly felt that his complex fictional plots had to be severely compressed and his extensive cast of characters considerably reduced for successful translation to the Victorian stage. He explained his methods in the programme for the Olympic Theatre production of *The Woman in White*:

[The dramatist] has not hesitated, while preserving the original story in substance, materially to alter it in form. Scenes which he dismissed, when writing as a novelist, in a few lines, he has developed, when writing as a dramatist, into situations which more than once occupy an entire act. On the other hand, passages carefully elaborated in the book have been in some cases abridged and in others omitted altogether, as unsuitable to the play. This method of treatment has necessarily resulted in much that is entirely new in the invention of incident and in the development of character, being the presentation of the story of the novel in a purely dramatic form.[2]

Collins opted for a similar kind of compression in the stage version of *Man and Wife* which was performed by Squire and Marie Bancroft at London's Prince of Wales Theatre in 1873. The fascinating sub-plot concerning Hester Dethridge is not included in the stage version, which has only four settings, one for each act: 'The Summer House at Windygates', 'The Inn at Craig Fernie', 'The Library', and 'The Picture Gallery'. However, *Armadale* was the novel which Collins most radically altered in translating it from page to stage. He wrote a play entitled *Armadale* in 1866, which was published in an edition of only twenty-five copies (by Smith, Elder), largely to protect his own copyright in stage adaptations of his novel. The play *Armadale* was quite different from the novel on which it was based. Set 'in our own time', whereas the novel is set in 1851, the play compresses the action into three acts. The first, set in the park at Thorpe-Ambrose during a 'fancy fair' to raise funds for a local infirmary, brings together Dr Downward, Mrs Oldershaw, and Lydia Gwilt (who now conspire to ensnare Allan Armadale in a marriage trap), Allan and Neelie Milroy (who plan an elopement), and Ozias Midwinter, whose confession of his love for Lydia gives her the idea for the marriage plot. Act Two presents Lydia in her London lodgings masquerading as the widow of Allan Armadale (who has ostensibly perished at sea), only to find her plot disrupted by Allan's return. The act closes with Ozias's reappearance and Lydia's decalaration that 'I am *not* your wife'. The final act takes place in Downward's sanatorium. Its events are closely based on the sanatorium scene in the novel, but it is dramatically dominated by Lydia's soliloquizing in the manner of Lady Macbeth. *Armadale* was

Cartoon of Wilkie Collins, 'The Novelist who invented Sensation', *Vanity Fair*, 1872

Caricature of Collins with Frederick Walker's poster for the stage version of *The Woman in White*, by F. W. Waddy

never staged, but Collins worked on another adaptation with his French friend François Regnier, and an English version partly based on this collaboration was performed as *Miss Gwilt* at the Alexandra Theatre in Liverpool in December 1875 and London's Globe Theatre in April 1876. This drama in five acts was more melo-dramatic than the three-act version, had shorter speeches, more characters and stage action, and more varied settings—the third act is set in Naples. *Miss Gwilt* also gave a far more sympathetic por-trayal of Lydia than either the earlier dramatization or the original novel, and it recast Dr Downward as the main villain of the piece.

Collins also made drastic changes to *The Moonstone* when, in an attempt to capitalize on his theatrical successes of the 1870s, he came to adapt this novel for performance as a drama in three acts at the (by then) Royal Olympic Theatre in 1877. First he reduced the period and scope of the action from five years in various settings to twenty-four hours 'in the present time', and a single setting: the inner hall of Rachel Verinder's country house in Kent. Second, knowing that his story would be familiar to most members of the audience, he allowed them to witness Franklin's theft of the diamond at the end of Act One and used the remaining two acts to unfold the explanation of what they had witnessed. He also made extensive changes to the characters. The Indians, Murthwaite, Rosanna Spearman, Limping Lucy Yolland, Ezra Jennings, and the London characters are all dropped, Godfrey Ablewhite's role is considerably reduced and his reasons for committing the theft are merely hinted at, Betteredge becomes a comic buffoon, and Miss Clack is given a more prominent role than she has in the novel, joining Betteredge in comical asides and slapstick routines. The resulting drama only ran for nine weeks and received rather mixed reviews. The *Athenaeum* was not alone in its opinion that it was obvious from the outset that 'a work so ambi-tious in aim, and so composite in nature, could not without some sacrifice of character and story be brought within the compass of a play', and that there must have been 'some means of obtaining the desired result at a sacrifice less damaging than that of the whole character and conception of the novel'.[3]

As well as adapting his novels for the stage, Collins, following the example of Dickens, also adapted his fiction for the public readings he gave in England, the United States, and Canada in the early 1870s (see Chapter 3). The centrepiece of his North American tour in the autumn and spring of 1873–4 was 'The Dream Woman', a supernatural tale which he had originally written for the Christmas 1855 number of *Household Words*. This story, which was later included in *The Queen of Hearts* as 'Brother Morgan's Story of the Dream Woman', relates the strange history of Isaac Scatchard, an ostler, who wakes on the night of his birthday to see an apparition about to stab him. Seven years later he marries a woman who, according to his disapproving mother, bears an uncanny resemblance to his description of the dream woman. Following their marriage Isaac's wife takes to drink and fulfils his mother's fears and partially fulfils the prophecy of the dream by attacking him on the night of his birthday. She subsequently disappears, but the fear that she will return to complete her deadly purpose haunts Isaac for the rest of his life and prevents him from sleeping. In preparing this story for public reading Collins expanded significantly on his original, adding a great deal of descriptive and circumstantial detail, and in the process removing some of its mystery, its suggestion of the uncanny, and the slightly threatening openness of its ending. The reading version, which took some two hours to perform, is a more sensational tale in which the dream woman is a fallen woman who succeeds in her deadly intent. It clearly offended some of Collins's audience and the local press when he read it in Philadelphia in October 1873: 'It was not pleasant to hear a famous Englishman describing, before several hundred pure girls, how one wretched, fallen woman, after mysteriously killing her man, had captivated two more, and stabbed another to death in a drunken frenzy.'[4]

Collins on Film and Television

Two decades after his death Collins's novels were adapted for the new medium of silent moving pictures that began to replace the melodramatic theatre in the early twentieth century. Collins's popularity with the makers of melodramatic silent movies is perhaps unsurprising given his own associations with the stage melodrama—as actor, playwright, and borrower of its conventions. As well as silent screen adaptations of *The Woman in White* and *The Moonstone* (see below), there was a silent version of *The Dead Secret* (directed by Stanner E. V. Taylor) in 1913, and no less than four different versions of *The New Magdalen* between 1910 and 1914. This flurry of interest in one of Collins's less successful later novels is intriguing. This novel had sold much better in the United States than it had in England when it first appeared. Despite some disapproving comments on its morality, the stage version of *The New Magdalen* had been one of the most frequently performed of Collins's plays in England. The stage version was less of a success in America, but it was still being performed in 1882, when Oscar Wilde saw a stunning performance by Clara Morris as Mercy Merrick. *The New Magdalen*'s portrayal of a female victim struggling against both unjust social exclusion and her own selfish instincts struck a chord with the debates about the nature and social role of women generated by the turn-of-the-century women's movement. No doubt its popularity with makers of silent movies also derived, in part, from the opportunities it provided for actresses to show off their range in the title role.

Later in the twentieth century several of Collins's novels and stories were adapted for cinema, and, more frequently, for radio (either as readings or in dramatized form), and for television, first as genre pieces, and then as nineteenth-century classics. Unsurprisingly, *The Woman in White* and *The Moonstone*, his two most enduringly popular novels, have been the most frequently adapted for all three media. However, on the whole Collins has not been well served by cinema, and there are no great or controversial screen adaptations of his work to compare with David Lean's *Great Expectations* or Roman Polanski's *Tess*. Perhaps the most successful cinematic 'adaptations' of Collins's fiction have been the indirect ones, in which his plot situations, character types, dream scenes, and his creation of atmosphere and suspense have influenced the development of the psychological thriller by directors such as Alfred Hitchcock. Individual novels by Collins have transferred more successfully to the small screen. Indeed, more than one television critic has observed that *The Woman in White* and *The Moonstone* reveal Collins as a prototype television script-writer. These two novels are also the progenitors of two of the genres that became the staples of the small screen in the twentieth century—the thriller and the detective yarn.

Of all of Collins's novels, it is *The Woman in White* that has been the most frequently and variously reproduced. Its basic plot—reread as a story of damsels in distress, their imprisonment and persecution by sinister aristocrats, and their rescue by a modest but noble young hero—lent itself well to the melodramatic treatment of the silent cinema, and gave rise to three productions in this medium, in 1912, 1913, and 1929. Something of the style of the 1912 version (produced by the Tannhauser Film Corporation) can be inferred from the breathless account which appeared in *Bioscope* on 18 January 1913:

The scene opens with the escape from the asylum of Ann Catherine [*sic*], 'The Woman in White,' who secures a hiding place in the house of an old friend in the village. At the same time at the 'big house' . . . Laura Fairlie, the squire's daughter and heiress, is waiting for the arrival of Walter Hartright, her new drawing master. Hartright meets the 'Woman in White, and her appearance leads him to misdirect the keeper when, later, they ask him in what direction the lunatic has gone. Walter falls in love with his pupil, and learns that she shares his feeling, but a letter brings the lovers to a realization of the hopelessness of their dream. Sir Percival Glyde, the fiancé of Laura, announces an approaching visit . . . Laura parts from Walter, who seeks forgetfulness in foreign travel. . . . [Following the marriage of Sir Percival and Laura] Ann confronts Sir Percival with the words, 'I am not mad, and you are not Sir Percival,' but his passion frightens her and she falls insensible . . .[5]

Bioscope goes on to relate how, struck by Anne's resemblance to Laura, Sir Percival drugs his wife and leaves her prone body outside the gates of the lunatic asylum, where she is discovered and assumed to be the escaped Anne. In fact, Anne has died of shock at Sir Percival's outburst—'but not before she has scribbled a message in her own blood inside a book' at the Glydes' house. In this film Walter and Laura are reunited as they are in the novel, but, in another departure from Collins's story, they go together to confront Sir Percival, who denies that Laura is his wife. The denouement is brought about when a servant discovers the book in which Anne had written her dying message, which reveals that the proof that Sir Percival is not who he claims to be is to be found in the register of the old church. Laura and Walter hurry to the church, but Sir Percival is before them, intent on destroying the papers. An overturned lamp sets the building alight and Sir Percival dies after confessing the truth, leaving Laura and Walter united at last. Perhaps the most remarkable feature of this film version is its complete removal from the plot of two of the main characters in Collins's original, Marian and Fosco—an even more surprising omission than Collins's own cutting of Rosanna Spearman and Ezra Jennings from his stage adaptation of *The Moonstone*.

The second of the silent movie versions of *The Woman in White* (another American production by Gem), also leaves Marian out of the picture but gives a prominent place to Fosco, who is forced to leave Italy after betraying his fellow conspirators, and, together with his wife, takes charge of a young heiress. A drawing master falls in love with Fosco's charge but such a marriage does not suit the Count and he marries her off to Sir Percival Glyde. When she refuses to pay his debts, her new husband (assisted by his accomplice Fosco), first incarcerates Lady Glyde in a lunatic asylum under another identity, and then replaces her in his household with the woman in white—a sick girl who resembles Lady Glyde. The sick girl dies and is buried as Lady Glyde. Lady Glyde herself escapes from the asylum and is reunited with her drawing master. Confronted with his crime, Sir Percival accidentally upsets a lamp and dies, but not before being forgiven by his wife, who subsequently marries Hartright. Fosco meanwhile is assassinated, having been tracked down by his Italian co-conspirators.

The first British silent film version of *The Woman in White* was directed by Herbert Wilcox in 1929. This movie certainly conveys the air of strangeness and mystery that marks the original story, and it also sticks much more closely to the original than do its shorter American predecessors. Wilcox's most significant departure from Collins's text is his treatment of Fosco's death—which he presents as a suicide. George King's *Crimes at the Dark House* (1939) took far greater liberties with Collins's novel. In this melodrama, Tod Slaughter, one of the last great barnstormers of the British melodramatic theatre, plays the role of an evil count who (in a very loose adaptation of Collins's plot) enlists the help of an escapee from a lunatic asylum to masquerade as his murdered wife. As Collins's literary reputation began to advance beyond that of merely the Victorian best-seller, critics—if not cinema audiences—became more preoccupied with the issue of the 'faithfulness' of screen adaptations. For example, Peter Godfrey's 1947 Warner Bothers film was castigated for not sticking sufficiently closely to the original and for using American actors (with American accents). On the other hand he was both praised and blamed for the fidelity with which he reproduced Collins's narrative: some reviewers thought he had succeeded in capturing both the atmosphere and the period, whilst others thought that Collins's story was simply too long and complicated to be condensed into a one-and-a-half-hour film. It is worth noting that this film points up some of Collins's ambiguities, and perhaps displays an immediately post-war preference for the feisty woman and interest in the fluidity and multiplicity of relationships, by changing Collins's ending: in this version Laura finds fulfilment through motherhood (having borne Percivel's child) and Walter proclaims his love for Marian.

The Woman in White was first offered to British and American television audiences in 1957 and 1960 respectively. These early television versions were short anthology pieces: the British version was first transmitted as one of the 'Hour of Mystery' dramas by ABC Television, and in the United States Collins's novel was also condensed into just under an hour for the 'Dow Hour of Great Mysteries'. *The Woman in White* was first given the full BBC Sunday classic treatment in a fairly faithful six-part adaptation by Michael Voysey (shown on BBC1 from 2 October until 6 November 1966), with Jennifer Hilary playing both Laura and Anne, Nicholas Pennell as Walter Hartright, Alethea Charlton as Marian, Francis de Wolff as Fosco, and Geoffrey Bayldon 'exquisitely pained as the hypochondriac connoisseur' Frederick Fairlie.[6] The first colour television version of *The Woman in White* appeared on BBC2 in five fifty-five minute episodes running from 14 April until 12 May 1982; it was later shown in the United States on public television's 'mystery' series in 1985. This adaptation (by Ray Jenkins) works hard to find inventive ways of addressing the key problem that faces any writer who seeks to translate *The Woman in White* from the page to the stage or screen: how to negotiate the fact that Collins's narrative is, in fact, a series of narratives, each told by a different character who narrates his or her own version of events as if he or she were in a witness box in a court of law. One of Jenkins's responses to this challenge is to translate some of the individual character's musings into dialogue (this works particularly well in the case of Walter). For his part, the director (John Bruce), makes good use of close-up reaction shots, and recurring motifs (such as the sketch Walter makes of his first meeting with Anne Catherick). Interestingly, the absence of the individual narratives, each with its own distinctive voice and perspective, has the effect of liberating the characters from the perceptual frameworks through which they are mediated to the readers of Collins's text. Thus Laura is freed from the straitjacket of Walter's and Marian's infantilizing narratives about her, and Marian, freed from Walter's mediating perceptions, is presented directly as a beautiful and independent young woman. This representation of Laura (played by Jenny Seagrove) and Marian (played by Diana Quick) undoubtedly owes something to the women's movement of the late 1970s which made the writer, director, and actors alert to Collins's mixed responses to the women's movement of the later 1850s.

The two-part television film directed by Tim Fywell and shown on BBC1 at Christmas 1997 also follows the modern tendency to put Marian at the centre of the narrative and to cast a very attractive actress in the role (in this case Tara Fitzgerald). In this production Marian is the first character the audience sees, and hers is the first voice we hear. It is also Marian whose voice-overs move the narrative along, and thus she replaces Walter as the 'editor' and shaper of the story. This thoroughly modern Marian is not constrained by the petticoat existence about which she complains in Collins's original, but rushes up to London, unchaperoned, to try to discover the truth about Laura's death and Anne's disappearance, and subsequently dashes around the countryside in search of Anne in the company of a man (Walter) to whom she is not married. She resorts to a form of sexual blackmail on two occasions. First, in order to force Walter join her in the search for Anne Catherick, she threatens to throw herself on the mercies of the rough men in the bar where a disgraced Walter (see below) is earning his living by making sketches of the men and their paramours. She also obtains an appointment for a medical examination with the doctor who had first committed Anne to an asylum, and having stripped to her petticoats for the examination, she threatens to accuse him of sexual assault unless he discloses the whereabouts of the asylum in which Anne (actually Laura) has been incarcerated.

David Pirie, who wrote the screenplay for this production, clearly had to be fairly ruthless with Collins's complicated and capacious narrative in order to condense it into a two-hour film. He made important revisions to the end and beginning of Collins's story by cutting all reference to Fosco's demise and transplanting the thrilling Hampstead Heath scene to Cumberland, where Walter's eerie first encounter with the woman in white takes place as he walks from the railway station to Limmeridge House to take up his new post as drawing master. By locating the meeting with Anne in the vicinity of the house where she grew up Pirie also seeks to reduce the Victorian novelist's reliance on an over-abundance of rather extraordinary coincidences. Pirie also reduces the novel's geographical range by confining the action to England: in this version Walter does not go off to learn how to be a man by confronting himself and overcoming the terrors of nature in the jungles of Brazil when he flees Limmeridge, but rather he journeys into the nether world of darkest London.

This very late-twentieth-century adaptation of *The Woman in White* also updates some of the novel's social concerns. The mid-nineteenth-century story of domestic imprisonment and asylum abuse also becomes a story of domestic violence and child abuse. In this version Laura is in physical fear of her husband and she has the bruises to show both Marian and the audience why she is so afraid of him. One of Anne Catherick's secrets (and one of the causes of her derangement) is the fact that Sir Percival had been in the habit of visiting her bed 'as a husband does his wife' when she was a mere child of 12. Here, as in most late-twentieth-century adaptations of Collins, the sexual undertones of the novel are not only brought to the surface but they are also emphasized and additional details are provided. For example, there are a number of sexually charged encounters between the drawing master and his pupil which are voyeuristically observed by Marian. Moreover, in this version Walter does not leave Limmeridge in an act of self-suppression and advised by Marian acting as his moral mentor, but instead is dismissed from the house when a maid accuses him (falsely as it turns out) of trying to make her undress. The maid is later revealed as one of Sir Percival's co-conspirators and also his mistress. James Wilby's Sir Percival adds an air of perverse sexuality, and even sadism to Collins's original characterization, and this is underlined by Laura in a dialogue with Marian—which was added by the screenwriter—in which she confesses that she had not realized that a man could take pleasure in 'the act' even when he hates his wife.

Perhaps responding to the observations of late-twentieth-century literary critics and cultural historians on Collins's fascination with issues of heredity and degeneration, Pirie added to the novel's suggestions of hereditary degeneration by changing the relationship between Marian, Laura, and Anne. In Collins's novel Marian and Laura are half-sisters who share the same sensible, bourgeois mother, and Laura and Anne are half-sisters who share the same effete and morally lax aristocratic father. In Pirie's screenplay all three are half-sisters who share the same father—Mr Fairlie. Much is made of Marian's sense of their father's sexual degeneracy, both as the father of an illegitimate child and as a man who subsequently connives (or so it is implied) at that child's sexual abuse at the hands of Sir Percival. Marian is represented as coming to fear that both she and Laura may have inherited their father's propensity to sexual degeneracy and moral degradation, and the film closes with a shot of Marian clutching Laura and Walter's daughter Anne to her breast as her voice-over expresses the wish that the cycle has come to an end at last. In their search for late-twentieth-century relevance and resonance Pirie and Fywell do not neglect the Gothic and melodramatic elements of Collins's story—Pirie even has Marian and Laura discuss their taste for the Gothic novel in one added scene. The deranged Anne haunting the woods around Limmeridge is extremely melodramatic, as are Marian's dreams of Laura's fate. Excellent camerawork also brings out the filmic nature of Collins's hallucinatory imagination.

The most recent adaptation of *The Woman in White* is also the most unusual, indeed, as far as I know it is unique. In July 2003 at his private arts festival at Sydmonton, his English country home, Sir Andrew Lloyd Webber, composer of the extremely successful musicals *Jesus Christ Superstar*, *Evita*, *Phantom of the Opera*, and *Cats* (based on T. S. Eliot's *Old Possum's Book of Practical Cats*), presented parts of his semi-operatic musical, *The Woman in White*. The Sydmonton presentation, which was directed by Sir Trevor Nunn, was a workshop version of the first act of the show which was to replace Lloyd Webber's *Les Misérables* when it ended its nineteen-year run at London's *Palace* theatre in 2004. The book for this musical, very freely based on Collins's novel, is by Charlotte Jones, a young playwright whose extremely successful 2001 play, *Humble Boy*, updates *Hamlet*. The songs for *The Woman in White* are written by David Zippel, whose previous work includes *City of Angels* (1989), a spoof of 1940s detective movies. The full production opened at the Palace Theatre in September 2004 to mixed reviews, both for the music and the liberties taken with Collins's novel. Many admirers of the book were particularly disappointed to see that although Jones's adaptation followed recent trends in giving the narrative a feminist slant and putting Marian Halcombe at the centre of the action it also transforms Marian from Walter's feisty and resourceful assistant into a love-sick woman pining for his affection. (This shift is underlined by the lyricist who gives Marian the constant refrain 'I close my eyes and still I see his face'). Even more alarming is the spectacle of Marian attempting to seduce Count Fosco, especially as this Count is played for laughs by Michael Crawford who is coiffed with a curly wig and made up to look hugely fat. Fosco is prominent in other ways, and he is given one of the liveliest songs, in which he celebrates his own ability to 'get away with anything'. On the other hand, Laura and Anne are reproduced fairly faithfully as twin victims of their crucially different circumstances, and Walter is presented as a fairly straightforward hero. While it would be unreasonable to expect a musical to replicate the complexity of the novel's innovative narrative method (as Michael Billington pointed out in the *Guardian* on 16 September 2004), Trevor Nunn's production is quite successful in conveying its multiple settings by means of the designer William Dudley's shifting video projections. The use of this early twenty-first-century technology and cinematic technique is sometimes suggestive of the video game and sometimes of the nineteenth-century diorama or sensation drama. The sensation theatre is particularly strongly evoked in the second act when a railway train rushes noisily out of a tunnel which is projected on to the set, and seems about to crash into the front row of the stalls.

As far as I know, there are no plans to stage a musical version of *The Moonstone*. However, one could envisage some splendid song opportunities for the lovelorn Rosanna Spearman, the embittered Limping Lucy, and the garrulous Miss Clack. Moreover, Franklin's opium-induced re-enactment of the theft of the diamond has distinct balletic possibilities. Notwithstanding the absence of a musical version, in most other respects the twentieth-century history of adaptations of *The Moonstone* follows a remarkably similar pattern to that of *The Woman in White*. There were at least three silent versions at the beginning of the century, all entitled *The Moonstone*. The first, an American production of 1909, gave great prominence to the hypnotic trance. Two years later a French production focused on the curse which is visited on those who steal the diamond. A second American production followed in 1915 and apart from changing the surname of the villain from Ablewhite to White it stuck fairly faithfully to Collins's original. The same cannot be said of the next

American version (1934, with sound), which relocated Collins's narrative to the 1930s, renamed some of his characters (all of whom have transatlantic accents), and rearranged his plot, most notably by making the doctor who drugs Franklin the father of the heroine and hence Franklin Blake's prospective father-in-law. In this version Franklin, accompanied by his Hindu servant Yandoo (an invention of the screenwriter), arrives on a dark and stormy night at Vandier Manor, the home of a doctor, Sir John Verinder. Franklin's mission is to deliver the diamond—which, as in the novel has been stolen from an Indian Temple in 1799—to his fiancée Anne Verinder. Anne is warned to lock the diamond away, but instead, places it under her pillow, from where it is stolen as she sleeps. Inspector Cuff of Scotland Yard is called in to investigate, and duly questions in turn Anne (who refuses to say anything), a money-lender, the Indian servant, Betteredge the female housekeeper (an interesting change of sex here), a parlourmaid with a criminal past, Franklin, and his cousin Godfrey Ablewhite (in this version, a dealer in rare books). A delirious Sir John Verinder subsequently reveals that he had drugged Franklin's bedtime glass of milk on the night of the theft, and Cuff arranges for Franklin (without his knowledge) to be given another drugged nightcap. Franklin repeats his sleepwalking actions and reveals that he was intercepted by Godfrey. Cuff speeds off to London to apprehend the thief (Godfrey) as he arrives at the money-lender's with the diamond. It is not Wilkie Collins's *The Moonstone*, as the *Monthly Film Bulletin* noted when the film came out: 'there is enough of the plot left to make it difficult to understand if one does not know the original, but not enough to say that it is the original.'[7]

Television has been rather kinder to *The Moonstone*, with three quite sympathetically adapted BBC versions to date. The first (shot in black-and-white film and shown in seven thirty-minute episodes between Sunday, 21 August and Sunday, 2 October in 1959) was produced by Shaun Sutton, later head of Drama at the BBC and producer of a wide range of material from Shakespeare's plays to *Dr Who*. The screenplay was written by A. R. Rawlinson, whose earlier screen adaptations of nineteenth-century novels and plays included Tom Taylor's 1863 stage melodrama, *The Ticket of Leave Man*, Rider Haggard's novel *King Solomon's Mines*, and Dinah Mulock Craik's *John Halifax, Gentleman*. The Irish-born playwright Hugh Leonard wrote the screenplay for the five-part version of *The*

Moonstone directed by Paddy Russell and shown by the BBC between 16 January and 13 February 1972. This production was strong on period detail and it also worked hard to enmesh the viewer in the intricacies of the puzzle at the centre of the plot. Indeed, at some risk of sacrificing pace, Leonard and Russell took great pains in the opening episode to lay out all of the elements of the plot and to establish the characters. A strong cast included Basil Dignam as Betteredge, Peter Sallis as an irascible Bruff, Robin Ellis as Franklin, Martin Jarvis as Godfrey, Vivien Heilbrun as a strong-minded but capricious Rachel and Anna Cropper as Rosanna.

The most recent BBC television version of *The Moonstone* was shown in two one-hour parts on 29 and 30 December 1996. The screenplay was written by the playwright Kevin Elyot, the author of a stage version of *The Moonstone* first performed in 1990. In his stage play Elyot retained the multiple narrators used in Collins's original, but in the television version he relied heavily on Betteredge (splendidly played by Peter Vaughan) to read out letters which explain the plot, or to pick up and disseminate essential plot information during the course of his duties in the Verinder household. Anthony Sher's Cuff emphasizes (and adds to) the quirks of Collins's detective and in doing so underlines for a late-twentieth-century audience the nineteenth-century origins of the eccentric professional detectives who fill their television screens in series after series. To some extent this production sidelines the aristocratic characters who are ostensibly at the centre of the story. Rachel Verinder (played by Keeley Hawes) and Franklin Blake (Greg Wise) are less interesting than Collins's originals. Rosanna Spearman (Lesley Sharp), on the other hand, is both spiky and complex and her death in the Shivering Sands is done in a brilliantly atmospheric close-up. This production makes good use of visual effects to bring the different worlds of the novel into sharp relief. The film opens with a vivid and colourful scene showing the theft of the diamond in the storming of Seringapatam, and cuts immediately to a very white image of Franklin Blake, who has just awoken from this dream of the assault and who is lying beside his sleeping wife in their bed in a quiet country house whose peace is disturbed by the violent dream. Throughout the film the colourful garden and the warm domestic interiors of the Verinder house are juxtaposed with the stark grey image of the Shivering Sands. The closing shots of the production provide a visual reprise of these different worlds as a strangely dreamlike Indian scene depicting the purification of the Brahmins is followed by a repeat of the scene of Franklin and Rachel sleeping in their bed, and then a long fading shot of the Shivering Sands. One effect of these juxtaposed scenes is to suggest the oriental otherness of the Indians; another is to suggest that empire is a troubling element of the English psyche, a nightmare from which the English paterfamilias struggles to awake.

Although *The Woman in White*, together with *The Moonstone*, have been the most copied and adapted of Collins's novels, the most recent film version of a Collins novel reworks one of his least reproduced novels. Radha Bharadwaj's *Basil* (1997), first shown on the American Movie Classics channel in the United States in November 1998, is, as far as I know, the only film version to date of Collins's first novel of modern life, and, indeed, the only other twentieth-century reworking of *Basil* seems to have been a BBC radio adaptation in 1983. Bharadwaj, who wrote, produced, and directed this film, has added a pre-history to Collins's narrative. Her film opens with a long section on Basil's childhood and early youth that seeks to give its own explanation of Basil's family circumstances, which in Collins's novel are conveyed in a few economical paragraphs. In Bharadwaj's version Basil (played by Christian Slater) does not meet Margaret Sherwin on an omnibus, but instead is introduced to Julia (as Margaret is renamed) by Mannion, whom he has already met in the film's opening section, when he saves Basil from drowning. Bharadwaj points up the resonances of Collins's tale of mid-nineteenth-century modern life with the realities of late-twentieth-century postmodern life by focusing on the novel's preoccupation with money, class, and cross-class relations. At the end of the decade in which the watchword of many was 'greed is good', Julia (played by Claire Forlani) is represented as an avaricious young woman who responds to Basil's courtship of her with disdain and contempt, but nevertheless makes a calculating marriage with the blessing of her mercenary father (played by Derek Jacobi). Mannion and Julia conduct a prolonged secret affair until they are discovered in bed by Basil, who launches a ferocious attack on Mannion, whom he leaves for dead. Basil is rejected by his father and is forced to work for a living. He is subsequently pursued by a vengeful Mannion who has been seriously disfigured by the attack. As in the novel, Mannion

Alan Badel as Count Fosco and Diana Quick as Marian Halcombe in BBC
Television's 1982 adaptation of *The Woman in White*

Peter Vaughan and Anthony Sher in BBC Television's 1996 adaptation of
The Moonstone

explains his actions in terms of his desire to avenge the mistreatment of a member of his own family by one of Basil's relatives. However, Bharadwaj sexualizes the revenge plot by locating Mannion's enmity towards Basil in the sexual misdemeanours of Basil's brother rather than in the soured business relations of his own and Basil's father. In this version, Mannion is motivated by the desire to avenge the death of his sister, who has died as the result of an attempted abortion after being seduced and abandoned by Basil's reprobate brother Ralph.

Another tale of 1852, 'A Terribly Strange Bed' has had several outings as a genre piece. It has appeared in three different versions as a kind of mystery anthology piece for television. In 1949 it was one of the early fifteen-minute episodes in a new American television network series called *Fireside Theatre*. In 1961 it formed the second act of Ida Lupino's 'Trio for Terror', a compendium episode in a series called *Thriller* which was shown on American television. In the early 1970s Collins's story appeared in yet another series of mysteries, when it was directed by Alan Cooke for an Anglo-American television anthology production entitled *Orson Welles Great Mysteries*. This twenty-four-minute colour film, shown in the United States in 1973 and in Britain in July 1974, was adapted by Anthony Fowles and starred Rupert Davies and Colin Baker.

Collins in Print

Collins's shift in status, from a popular nineteenth-century author whose books and stories were thought to be suitable for adaptation for genre or mystery slots on radio or television to a 'classic' author whose novels are given the full-blown BBC classic treatment or served up as a Christmas feast, is mirrored by his explosion back into print in the last quarter of the twentieth century. Although *The Woman in White* and *The Moonstone* have never been out of print since their first publication in the 1860s, by 1985 they were the only two of Collins's novels that were widely available. At the beginning of the twenty-first century things look very different. At the time of writing, *No Name*, *Armadale*, and *The Law and the Lady* have been added to the Penguin Classics Library. The more extensive Oxford World's Classics series currently includes *Armadale*, *Basil*, *The Dead Secret*, *Hide and Seek*, *The Law and the Lady*, *Mad Monckton and Other Stories*, *Man and Wife*, *Poor Miss Finch*, and *No Name*, as well as the single-volume *Miss or Mrs?*, *The Haunted Hotel*, *The Guilty River*. Unlike Penguin and Oxford, Sutton Publishing do not include *The Woman in White* or *The Moonstone* in their list of Collins's works. However, they have made available several titles which have long been out of circulation.[8] These publishers' lists are a sign of both a renewal of interest in Collins's work by the general reader and an increase in his critical status in the last quarter of the twentieth century. Another sign of his critical status was the inclusion of *The Woman in White* and *The Moonstone* in the two hundred and fifty 'major' works of literature that were to be sent out to every secondary school in Britain as part of a joint project by Millennium Commission and Everyman publishers (a further 1,500 sets of the books were to be sent overseas under the auspices of the British Council).

Another way of looking at Collins in print at the turn of the twenty-first century is to consider the ways in which his work has been adapted or recontextualized by later writers. As an extremely successful early exponent of the thriller, mystery, and detective genres, Collins had a very important influence on the development of the novelistic form of the thriller and the detective yarn both in the latter part of the nineteenth century and in the twentieth century. *The Moonstone* effectively established what were to become the main features of a dominant form of the English detective novel for the remainder of the nineteenth and the whole of the twentieth century: it involves a crime committed in a quiet country house at which a number of people have been gathered together by circumstance; it emerges that there is circumstantial evidence against virtually all of these people; the novel's main mystery (the disappearance of the diamond) is solved by gathering together some of the main protagonists and re-enacting the crime; there is a blundering local policeman (or policemen) who actively complicates the mystery through his incompetence; the incompetent local policeman acts as a foil to an eccentric but acute professional, in this case Sergeant Cuff, the eccentric detective with a wry sense of humour and a passion for growing roses, who 'might have been a parson, or an undertaker—or anything else you like, except what he really was' (First Period, Chapter XII). Fictional detectives from Arthur Conan Doyle's Sherlock Holmes to Colin Dexter's Inspector Morse all owe something to Cuff. Collins also formulated what were to become what Dorothy L. Sayers, one of the twentieth-century 'queens of crime', described as the rules of fair play—that 'no vital clue should be concealed, that reader and detective should start from scratch and run neck and neck to the finish'.[9] Another of the rules of the game of the detective novel which Collins perfected was the prolongation of the mystery by distributing the narrative between several narrators—each of whom only knows part of the story—and interleaving these narratives with the text of letters, diaries, and other documents (a technique which is still used to great effect by current best-selling authors such as Minette Walters).

Some contemporary novelists have returned to Collins's work in a more self-consciously referential manner. Sarah Waters is one example of a late-twentieth-century novelist who has both emulated and re-investigated her nineteenth-century predecessors (including Collins) in her reworking of the sensation novel, the ghost story, the tale of mystery and suspense, and the crime novel in *Affinity* (Virago, 1999) and *Fingersmith* (Virago, 2002). Like Collins, Waters focuses on the duplicities and constraints of respectable Victorian society and on the relationship between respectable middle-class society and the other worlds of the working class and the criminal classes. *Affinity* is a kind of ghost story set in and around a London women's prison in the 1870s. It shares Collins's interest both in cross-class (and in this case same-sex) liaisons and in seances and the mesmeric. The form of Waters's novel also owes something to Collins's experiments with narrative technique. Like many of Collins's novels, this tale of mystery and intrigue is told in the form of intertwined narratives— in this case the diaries of the two women at the centre of the novel. Waters's next novel, *Fingersmith*, borrows some of its dark atmosphere as well as some of its plot elements from *The Woman in White*: Richard Rivers, a dashing criminal, poses as a drawing master and gains entry to the home of the effete scholarly uncle of a vulnerable young heiress, Maud Lilly, in order to entrap her into marriage. Like Collins's Frederick Fairlie, Waters's recluse lives surrounded by his treasures, but in this case the treasures are the books and pictures that comprise his extensive collection of pornography, for which—in a well-established Victorian taxonomic tradition—he is preparing an index (with the assistance of his niece). Like Sir Percival Glyde in *The Woman in White*, Rivers is involved in a plot to rid himself of his wife and gain access to a fortune by dumping her in an asylum. Again, Waters borrows Collins's technique of telling the story (or stories) from different points of view—in this case, from the perspectives of the two women at the centre of the novel's plot. If anything, Waters outdoes her Victorian predecessor in the intricacy of her plotting and in the surprise produced by an extremely deft twist of the plot as the narration changes hands for the first time.

The Woman in White has also become caught up in the recent fashion for sequels to, or revisions of, iconic novels of the nineteenth century. James Wilson's *The Dark Clue* (Faber, 2001) does at length what many nineteenth-century readers probably did, at least briefly, in their own imaginations—he speculates on possible developments in the relationship between Collins's Walter Hartright and Marian Halcombe. Wilson begins his novel by unpicking the ending of Collins's narrative. Collins's novel ends by transporting Walter to Limmeridge to join Laura and Marian in a *ménage à trois* dedicated to the care of the heir of Limmeridge—Walter and Laura's firstborn—and any subsequent children they may have. This ending leaves unresolved the tension between Walter, the father of the heir to a family fortune which includes a landed estate, and Walter the aspiring professional who hitherto had been concerned to establish himself in a 'permanent engagement on the illustrated newspaper, to which I was only occasionally attached', and had succeeded in earning a steady income on which the family could live 'simply and quietly' (The Story concluded by Walter Hartright, III). Wilson begins by splitting up the *ménage à trois* with which Collins closes *The Woman in White*, and maroons a pregnant Laura in Limmeridge caring for her children, whilst Walter and Marian are left together in the family's London home. He picks up on Collins's clue that the unconventional and spirited Marian understands Walter better than Laura ever could, and endows Marian with an understanding of the frustrated artist who lies under the skin of the drawing master who married his mistress:

[Y]ou have become restless, and distracted. You paint and draw less than you did . . . you still harbour the faint suspicion that you have somehow become a pensioner, and it is an agony to you . . . Worse still, you feel a certain vacancy at the centre of your life. You have everything that, in the eyes of the world, should make a man happy: a gentle and loving wife, two beautiful children, a fine estate, and the regard of your brother artists. Yet something is lacking: a *cause* capable of stirring your soul, and carrying you beyond the concerns of family and home.[10]

In an effort to assuage Walter's frustration with the role of Victorian paterfamilias and to give him a cause and purpose, Marian arranges for him to become the biographer of the painter J. M. W. Turner. In his quest to understand the mind of the great artist and to penetrate the mysteries and secrets which surround his life Walter leaves the drawing rooms of fashionable London and haunts the capital city's less salubrious regions. In the process Walter and Marian discover something of their own hidden selves and desires. Wilson's narrative, as Collins's is in part, is constructed in the form of diaries and letters. However, the individual narratives which make up Wilson's narrative function rather differently from those which comprise Collins's tale. Collins's Walter Hartright collects and marshals the narratives and diaries of others in order to reveal the truth of events; his purpose is to tell the whole story, a story which, were it not for his efforts, would go untold under the pressure of the 'lubricating influences of oil of gold' (The Story begun by Walter Hartright, I). The story told by Wilson's Hartright, on the other hand, is a twice- (or even thrice-) buried tale. In Wilson's novel Marian and Walter confront their own buried lives as well as the buried life of their biographical quarry, Turner, but they do so only to have Walter re-bury the stories of these buried lives, as indicated in the statement signed WH which prefaces the narrative:

This is a book begun, but not finished.
   I could not finish it.

Many times I have come close to destroying it . . .
   I could not bring myself to do it.

I have therefore given instructions that it should be sealed in a box, which is to remain unopened until I, my wife, Laura, our sister, Marian Halcombe, and all our children are dead . . .

Collins in Criticism

In 1974 the editor of a collection of extracts designed to illustrate the critical reception of Collins's work in the nineteenth century prefaced his volume with a slightly apologetic justification of the claims of his chosen author on the attention of the twentieth-century reader, and more especially, literary critic. Norman Page found it necessary to remind his readers that despite the fact that Collins was one of the most popular and prolific authors of the second half of the nineteenth century 'only two novels have achieved undisputed classic status' and a mere 'handful of others (*Armadale*, for instance, and *No Name*) still retain some kind of currency'. The rest of Collins's substantial output, he adds, is 'forgotten by all except the most dedicated specialists'.[11] In fact, the process of critical sifting, which involved the 'forgetting' or downgrading of most of Collins's substantial output apart from the four big novels of the 1860s, had begun in the last decade of his career and was continued in obituaries and reviews of his achievements following his death in September 1889. For example, some eighteen months before Collins's death, Harry Quilter struck a somewhat obituary tone in an essay for the *Contemporary Review*, entitled 'A Living Story-teller', which he presented as an attempt to rescue from critical neglect 'the last of that group of great novelists whose work will make the fiction of the Victorian era for ever famous'.[12] Despite his continuing popularity with readers, Quilter asserts, and despite his importance as an inimitable storyteller, whose tightly organized plots—at their best—depend 'on the influence exercised by character over circumstance',[13] 'we rarely hear the name of Wilkie Collins mentioned in England nowadays . . . [or] read a word in his praise, or hear of the slightest claim being made on his behalf'.[14] In a long and detailed essay, Quilter reviews Collins's early career—displaying an unusually high regard for the humour of *Hide and Seek* (1854)—as a preparation for the height of his fictional achievement in the four great novels of the 1860s. For Quilter, as for many critics before and after him, *The Woman in White* was a groundbreaking text, 'a book which made a new era in novel-writing' and 'opened up a new view of the art'.[15] The enormous popularity of *The Moonstone* is acknowledged, but Quilter regards this as 'the least important' of Collins's 'four finest novels', and considerably less interesting than *No Name*, which is said to be 'the most fascinating' of all of Collins's fictions.[16] The greatest accolade, however, is reserved for *Armadale*, as 'the most important', indeed 'the greatest' of all Collins's work and the culmination of his powers as a novelist: 'It has all the interest and sustained purpose of *The Woman in White*, while it is drawn on a much larger scale, and shows a much wider knowledge of character . . . but it is more than this. It is . . . a successful attempt, to deal from the imaginative point of view with the doctrines of heredity, both physical and moral'.[17]

Armadale was also ranked as one of Collins's best novels—a ranking it shared with *The Moonstone*—in the obituary article which appeared in the *Athenaeum* just five days after his death. Like most other immediately post-mortem assessors of Collins's achievements the *Athenaeum*'s obituarist also acknowledged the importance of *The Woman in White*, but, rather unusually, this writer also gave honourable mention to some of the later novels, including *Man and Wife* and *The New Magdalen*. More in keeping with what was to become the settled view in the years immediately following Collins's death, *Armadale* was not ranked highly in the obituary in the *Spectator*, which appeared on the same day as the *Athenaeum*'s (28 September 1887). However, the *Spectator*, like the *Athenaeum*, also included *Man and Wife* in its list of Collins's four main achievements—the others are *The Woman in White*, *No Name*, and *The Moonstone*, the latter singled out as 'the one which will live for years'.[18] The poet and critic A. C. Swinburne, writing in the *Fortnightly Review* some four or five weeks later, gave a similar ranking of Collins's novels, which he offered as 'the general opinion—an opinion which seems to me incontestable', namely that *The Woman in White* and *The Moonstone* were the two works of 'indisputable' and 'incomparable ability', with *No Name* 'an only slightly less excellent example of as curious and original a talent'.[19] For Swinburne, *Man and Wife* ranks fourth, even if it is some way behind the first three: 'the first and best of Wilkie Collins's didactic or admonitory novels is so brilliant in exposition of character, so dexterous in construction of incident, so happy in evolution of event, that its place is nearer the better work that preceded it than the poorer work which followed it'.[20] Like most late-nineteenth-century commentators on Collins, Swinburne was very dismissive of most of the later fiction. He denounced *The New Magdalen* as 'silly, false and feeble in its sentimental cleverness', and found *The Fallen Leaves* 'too ludicrously loathsome for comment or endurance'.[21] On the other hand he did not share in the general condemnation of *Heart and Science*, which he pronounced 'less offensive' and 'more amusing' than the latter two, and 'the best— after *Man and Wife*, and a good way after—of all its writer's moral or didactic tales'.[22] Few other commentators in the next few years troubled to discriminate between the novels of Collins's later years, but tended, like Andrew Lang, writing in the *Contemporary Review* in January 1890, to offer a blanket dismissal of 'the flood of later novels, in which he so decidedly fell below his own standard [but which] . . . will be forgotten'.[23]

These late-career and obituary reassessments of Collins's work returned time and again to the questions which had dominated critical discussion of his fiction throughout his publishing life. Was he a literary artist or a mere plot-maker and manufacturer of effects? Was he a consummate and innovative storyteller who had elevated a particular kind of storytelling into a new art form? Did he sacrifice character to plot? Was he capable of creating credible characters, or did he merely manufacture eccentrics, and did it matter? Was he merely a producer of 'light reading' and an enter- tainer who had a facility for mastering certain 'low' literary modes and genres such as melodrama, sensation, mystery, and detection? Could he be taken seriously as a social critic or as a commentator on the human condition? By the end of Collins's career some critics, like Swinburne, were willing to concede that he was 'in his own way a genuine artist', but that 'the crowning merit, the most distinctive quality of his very best work was to be . . . found in the construction of an interesting and perplexing story, well-conceived, well contrived, and well moulded into lifelike and attractive shape'.[24]

The indisputable fact that Collins, in common with many of his contemporaries, wrote a great deal over the course of a very long career was often translated into the critical judgement that he wrote too much and for far too long. His critical reputation also suffered because, again like many of his contemporaries, he was associated with popular or low genres and ephemeral modes of publication (such as weekly or monthly periodicals, or newspapers). Like many of his contemporaries, he also suffered in the general reaction against Victorianism which had begun to set in by the last decade of his career—hence Quilter's attempt to rescue one of 'those authors who have gladdened us in former days'.[25] This reaction against the Victorians became even more pronounced in the twenty or thirty years following Collins's death. He was one of several Victorian authors whose reputations languished at the turn of the nineteenth and twentieth centuries. He received the briefest of mentions in most of the literary histories of the nineteenth century published during this period. George Saintsbury, for example, gives him only one paragraph in *The English Novel* (1913), and he was not included in the 'English Men of Letters' series edited by John Morley (which had been inaugurated in 1878). '[S]igns of a considerable revival of interest in the books of Wilkie Collins' were detected in the American edition of the *Bookman* in August 1912,[26] and he was given fairly full consideration in Walter C. Phillips's *Dickens, Reade, and Collins: Sensation Novelists* (1919)—though Phillips tended to echo the conventional judgement that Collins's novels are dominated by plot and structure and that his characters are 'automata'.[27] Collins also appeared alongside Dickens and Reade as the subject of a fairly unexceptionable chapter in the second volume of Oliver Elton's *A Survey of English Literature, 1830–1880* (1920).

In fact, despite the fact that he received only brief, and often condescending, mention in the standard literary histories of the first two decades of the twentieth century, Collins's novels never lacked readers, and nor did their author lack champions. By the 1920s, however, Collins's reputation certainly began to undergo something of a revival, not least at the hand of T. S. Eliot, in an essay on 'Wilkie Collins and Dickens', which appeared in the *Times Literary Supplement* (4 August 1927), and in his introduction to the 1928 World's Classics edition of *The Moonstone*. In these essays, Eliot made considerable claims for Collins as both a master of melodrama and an extremely skilled exponent of the genre of detective fiction (claims that were echoed by Dorothy L. Sayers in her introduction to *The Omnibus of Crime*, published in New York in 1929). In describing Collins's contribution to the development of the English detective novel, Eliot implicitly rejected a dominant Victorian judgement of Collins as a mere plot machinist or chess player: 'the detective story, as created by Poe, is something as specialised and intellectual as a chess problem; whereas the best English detective fiction [which Collins inaugurated] has relied less on the beauty of the mathematical problem and much more on the intangible human element'.[28] Eliot implicitly took issue with a critical tradition which had devalued a novelist such as Collins on the grounds that his works were merely thrilling or melodramatic, and instead he looked back to (or possibly invented) a Victorian golden age in which there were no false distinctions between 'such terms as "high-brow fiction", "thrillers" and "detective fiction" ', an age which realized that 'melodrama is perennial and that the craving for it is perennial and must be satisfied', an age in which '[t]he best novels *were* thrilling'.[29] Eliot's essay in the *Times Literary Supplement* did much for Collins's reputation by discussing him in the same breath as Dickens (even though he judged him 'a Dickens without genius'[30]), by championing him as the writer who first perfected the art of the English detective novel, and by defending his abilities as a creator of character. More than this, however, Eliot also argued for the importance of *Armadale*, *The Frozen Deep*, *The Haunted Hotel*, and *The New Magdalen*—as classics of melodrama. There is no contemporary novelist, Eliot opined, 'who could not learn something from Collins in the art of interesting and exciting the reader'.[31]

Eliot's essays were symptomatic of a broader revival of interest in Collins in the late 1920s and early 1930s. His fiction was praised (even as his negative influence on Dickens was lamented) in Hugh Walpole's 1929 essay on 'Novelists of the 'Seventies' (in Harley Granville-Barker, ed., *The Eighteen-Seventies*). Walter de la Mare's 1932 essay, 'The Early Novels of Wilkie Collins' (in John Drinkwater, ed., *The Eighteen-Sixties*) presented him as a fine, if inconsistent, craftsman who was on occasion able to write brilliant prose. S. M. Ellis devoted a generally positive chapter to Collins in his 1931 book on *Wilkie Collins, Le Fanu and Others*. He was also the sole subject of a chapter in Malcolm Elwin's *Victorian Wallflowers* (1934), which expressed some surprise at the relative lack of serious attention that Collins had received hitherto. For the most part Elwin discussed Collins in the familiar terms—as a writer who 'lacks distinction', but one who '[a]t his best . . . tells his story simply and well, occasionally gaining a certain grandeur from baldness and brevity' and who even at his worst produced plots 'remarkable for ingenuity in construction'.[32] Elwin's essay is noteworthy for the claims which he makes for Collins's modernity and his influence on the development of the novel in English: 'by rigorously excluding any matter extraneous to the action and independent of the plot, [Collins] introduced an economy of expression upon the lines from which the modern style in fiction has developed.'[33] In the same year Thomas J. Hardy also argued for Collins's modernity in a chapter on 'The Romance of Crime', which placed *The Woman in White* as the first novel 'that made the new scientific outlook and method its own', and claimed that 'Collins was too true an artist, too acute an explorer in the unworked vein of Psychology to be dismissed with a few references to melodrama and clumsy contrivance'.[34]

During the 1940s Collins became the focus of more serious academic attention—especially in the United States—and his life and work were the subject of several Ph.D. theses. This flurry of academic interest resulted in the publication of several books and articles in the 1950s, including Robert Ashley's 'Wilkie Collins Reconsidered' (1950) and his 'Wilkie Collins and the Detective Story' (1951);[35] Bradford Booth's 'Collins and the Art of Fiction' (1951);[36] Kenneth Robinson's *Wilkie Collins: A Biography* (1951), a solid account of Collins's life and work drawing on his (then) uncollected letters; Robert Ashley's volume on Collins for an American series on 'The English Novelists (1952) which attempted to 'rehabilitate Collins the novelist, . . . revitalise Collins the man and to present the known biographical facts';[37] and Nuel Pharr Davis's lively but rather speculative *The Life of Wilkie Collins* (1956). Ashley's book (drawing on his Ph.D. research and the articles he published in *Nineteenth-Century Fiction*) started from the premiss that his author had been 'the victim of more misrepresentation and slipshod scholarship than any other English novelist of comparable stature, chiefly because until recently no one had made him the object of a major investigation', as critics had tended to stumble on Collins 'in the course of investigating someone else, most frequently Dickens'.[38] In his slim but well-informed volume Ashley succeeded in undermining the 'legend that the Collins of the 'seventies and 'eighties was a pitiful but heroic figure laboriously and painfully grinding out "wretched" novels which nobody bothered to read',[39] and in persuading his readers that Collins had a salutary influence on the unruly plotting and shape of the nineteenth-century novel as well as being an unrivalled master of suspense and atmosphere.

Further articles reassessing various aspects of Collins's work appeared in the 1960s, several of them exploring his contribution to the development of the detective novel. One reassessment of Collins's work dating from this period, which proved very influential on rereadings of Collins's fiction in the 1980s and 1990s, was Kathleen Tillotson's concise recontextualization of *The Woman in White* in relation to 'the lighter reading of the eighteen-sixties' in her introduction to the 1969 Riverside edition of this novel. Tillotson takes *The Woman in White*, *Great Expectations*, *East Lynne*, and *Lady*

Audley's Secret—four novels that 'would never now be spoken of in the same critical breath'—and demonstrates why it is important to read them alongside each other as Victorian best-sellers, sensation novels, and (in varying degrees) 'experiments in narrative form, stimulated by the need to sustain a mystery and delay its solution'.[40] Viewed in this light, Collins is revealed not as a mere carpenter of plot, but rather as a writer working at the cutting edge of fictional form, the evolver of 'a new and severer method' for sustaining both mystery and 'the sense of actuality and close involvement'.[41]

It was not until 1970 that Collins's fiction was the subject of a book length *critical* study—William Marshall's short, general introduction in the Twayne Authors series. Marshall, who claimed that his book was the first 'to deal extensively and exclusively with the *literary art* of Wilkie Collins and the part it played in the development of the English novel',[42] presented Collins as a 'minor novelist' who produced five major novels—*The Woman in White, No Name, Armadale, The Moonstone*, and *Man and Wife*. In a chapter entitled 'The World of Wilkie Collins', Marshall also sought to read Collins's fiction in relation to the time in which it was written—albeit in a rather general discussion of Collins's treatment of modern alienation, which concluded that Collins's novels, in fact, make 'very little reference to the intellectual currents of his own time, or even to their cultural ramifications'.[43] On the contrary, much of the most interesting work of the last third of the twentieth century focused on the complexities of the various ways in which Collins's fiction engaged with the social, cultural, and intellectual environment in which he grew up and worked. This trend began in the five-year period following the publication of Marshall's book with the publication of several articles exploring Collins's relationship to the intellectual, psychological, and cultural currents of his own age. Particularly influential were John R. Reed's 'English Imperialism and the Unacknowledged Crime of *The Moonstone*', in *Clio* in 1973, and U. C. Knoepflmacher's 'The Counterworld of Victorian Fiction and *The Woman in White*', which appeared in 1975.[44] In the first of these essays Reed opened up what was to become a very rich seam of argument for Collins studies by claiming that, far from being simply a classic detective tale, *The Moonstone* 'is a novel of serious social criticism, conveying its meaning through unconventional characters and historical allusion'.[45] This essay reads Herncastle's original theft of the diamond in 1799 as an act of individual greed which the novel presents as being 'emblematic of a far greater crime'[46]—the British military conquest and commercial exploitation of India. Collins's representation of English life is seen as exposing the hollowness and moral bankruptcy of the society which is built on such crimes. The hollowness of conventional Victorian society was also the focus of Knoepflmacher's essay, which read *The Woman in White* as a novel that makes no attempt to suppress its fascination with the anarchic counterworld which (it was argued) lay below the ordered, civilized world on which the official morality of the Victorian novel was posited. On the contrary, Knoepflmacher argued, Collins took great relish in presenting outspoken villains, such as Fosco, with his belief in the fragility of moral and social identity and the hypocrisy of respectable society.

Assessing Collins's critical standing in 1974, Norman Page noted that his 'place in general critical esteem is [now] perhaps sufficiently firmly established without inflated claims being made for him of a kind which inevitably produce an eventual reaction'.[47] Since the mid-1970s, however, there has been a sea change in Collins's critical importance and in the kind of critical scrutiny that he has received. Reviewing studies of Wilkie Collins in the last twenty years of the twentieth century for *Dickens Studies Annual* (1999), Lillian Nayder notes that not only has a wide range of Collins's work become 'increasingly well known to general readers' during this period, but also that 'his claim to artistic renown has been secured' and 'virtually all of [his] writings have now become a legitimate subject of academic discussion'.[48]

Collins has undoubtedly gained both greater critical visibility and academic credibility as a result of the refocusing of literary studies and Victorian studies that took place in the last third of the twentieth century. He has certainly benefited from the shift of critical attention to popular culture and to genre fiction such as the sensation novel and the Gothic—often (though not exclusively) prompted by a feminist interest in re-examining forgotten or undervalued genres. Kathleen Tillotson's recontextualizing of Collins's novels of the 1860s in relation to the sensation phenomenon (see above) and Philip Edwards's *Some Mid Victorian Thrillers: The Sensation Novel, its Friends and Foes* (1971) led in the 1980s and 1990s to fuller, more politicized, discussions of Collins's fiction in relation to other sensationalists, for example by Winifred Hughes in *The Maniac in the Cellar: Sensation Novels of the 1860s* (1980), and Lyn Pykett in *The Sensation Novel from 'The Woman in White' to 'The Moonstone'* (1994), both of whom read Collins's novels of the 1860s in relation to the cultural meanings of the sensation novel and the debates surrounding it. Jenny Bourne Taylor's *In the Secret Theatre of Home: Wilkie Collins, Sensation Narrative, and Nineteenth-Century Psychology* (1988) took a longer view of Collins's sensationalism—as extending from *Basil* to *The Legacy of Cain*—and read it in relation to nineteenth-century theories of mind. Taylor's complex and rewarding study is informed by feminist cultural history and theory and also by Michel Foucault's work on both the history of sexuality and of the construction and management of madness. However, as she points out, it seeks to avoid the monolithic nature of much of Foucault's work by focusing on the 'dissonances' in both nineteenth-century theories of the mind and in Collins's novels. To this end, Taylor reads Collins's novels in relation to literary, medical, and psychological theories of sensation in the nineteenth century, focusing particularly closely on contemporary definitions of insanity and the theory and practice of the 'moral management' of psychological deviance or moral insanity. She argues that these theories both derived from and reproduced a contradictory conception of identity, which 'provides the overarching ideological framework for Collins's fiction'.[49] Taylor's Collins is a ' "modern" (even postmodern)' novelist, a disruptive writer who focuses on the instability and social constructedness of identity, and on 'play, doubling and duplicity', in narratives which are 'dialogic and self-reflexive'.[50]

Jonathan Loesberg, on the other hand, in his 1986 essay on 'The Ideology of Narrative Form in Sensation Fiction', interpreted Collins's concern with 'identity and its loss' as symptomatic of a distinctively Victorian anxiety about the threat (or promise) of reform politics to merge or change class identities, and read the contradictions of *The Woman in White* as evidence of that novel's 'politically charged structure'.[51] Nicholas Rance also located Collins's sensation fiction in a political context in *Wilkie Collins and Other Sensation Novelists: Walking the Moral Hospital* (1991), reading Collins's sensation novels as a response to and a satiric exploration of the mid-Victorian doctrine of 'self-help'. Rance is at pains to present Collins as a radical, and to distinguish his brand of sensationalism from the conservative sensationalism of, for example, Ellen Wood. The politics of Collins's novels has come under ever closer scrutiny in the last twenty-five years or so as a result of the growing pre-occupation of cultural historians and critics with the ideological work performed by fiction. On the one hand Collins has been 'recon-textualized' as a subversive or dissident writer, whose novels offered a critique of the class and gender hierarchies of Victorian society; as a proto-feminist whose portrayal of such transgressive, independent women as Marian Halcombe, Magdalen Vanstone, Lydia Gwilt, and Valeria Macallan were part of a more general exposure of the social constraints on women; and as a social critic who exposed the hyp-ocrisies involved in constructing and sustaining Victorian bourgeois respectability. On the other hand, his fiction has been explored (or exposed) as evading or retreating from radical social critique.

Thus, Tamar Heller in *Dead Secrets: Wilkie Collins and the Female Gothic* (1992) explores the way in which (she argues) Collins flirts with the subversive potential of a genre such as female Gothic which (as interpreted by feminist critics) exposes the victimization of women in a patriarchal society, only to distance himself from both the genre and social critique in order to establish his credentials as a male professional. Collins, Heller suggests, appropriates female Gothic as 'a way of being a social critic' and expressing his 'often liberal view on social issues', but ends up by constructing Gothic plots which contain 'the Gothic as a site of subversion and literary marginality'.[52] Alison Milbank came to similar conclusions in *Daughters of the House: Modes of the Gothic in Victorian Fiction*— also published in 1992—arguing that *The Woman in White* and *The Moonstone* are versions of female Gothic in which the plot of female escape is discredited, whilst *No Name* and *Armadale* are more like 'the male Gothic' in which transgressive women are reined in and made to 'collapse into passive conformity' in ways which serve the novelist's 'erotic aims'.[53]

In a period in which postcolonial theory and criticism have come increasingly to the fore, Collins has also been recontextualized in relation to the politics of race and empire. John R. Reed's 1973 positioning of Collins as an anti-imperialist for his critique of colo-nial plunder and violence and his valorization of the morality and culture of the Hindus in *The Moonstone* has been endorsed by several subsequent critics, including Patricia Miller Frick, who argues that this novel contrasts the 'sincerity' and 'persistence' of the Indians with the 'doubt and disorder' of the English middle classes.[54] On the other hand Ashish Roy has questioned *The Moonstone*'s reputation as an anti-imperialist text, arguing that it is a more thorough justification of empire than even *Robinson Crusoe*.[55] Deidre David has also questioned the extent of *The Moonstone*'s critique of British imperialism, suggesting that it is limited to a critique of the earlier, militaristic phase of empire, and that the novel is a kind of defence of a domesticated form of empire which rules by disciplining its subjects; David offers the marginalized and orientalized Ezra Jennings as an example of a colonized, disciplined subject.[56] Other recent critics—including Jaya Mehta and Lillian Nayder—have read *The Moonstone* as a contradictory response to a relatively recent episode of imperial violence, the Indian Mutiny of 1857. In 'English Romance; Indian Violence', Mehta charts the ambiguities of Collins's critique of imperialism in which 'colonial retribution' is rewritten as 'colonial violence', and colonial, racial, and gendered knowledge 'emerges and submerges like clues in the quicksand'.[57] In her 1997 book (which replaces Marshall's volume in the Twayne Authors series) Lillian Nayder reassesses *The Moonstone*'s career as Collins's anti-imperialist text, by demonstrating that various of his novels (including *Antonina*, *Armadale*, and *The New Magdalen*) dramatize imperial crime and punishment in their staging of 'the reverse colonization' of England by the Creoles, Hindus, and others 'who invade the home country'.[58] Nayder suggests that these novels also assuage imperial guilt by naturalizing political and cultural differences.

Critics often base their assessments of Collins's political sympathies on their judgements of the significance and innovativeness of his narrative strategies.[59] Collins's avoidance of a single narrative voice, whether it be that of an omniscient third-person narrator or a privileged first-person narrator, in favour of a dispersal of his narrative across a range of narrators of various classes, each of whom views events from a different and partial perspective, has been variously associated with moral relativism, disruption or subversion of the status quo, and the author's radical politics or his democratic instincts. The late-twentieth-century critical recontextualization of Collins as a rebel with various causes which were pursued with varying degrees of narrative and representational dexterity continues into the twenty-first century, but so too does the questioning of his radical credentials. Perhaps the most influential attacks on the claims that were made for Collins's subversiveness and dissidence in the 1970s and early 1980s were those that came from Foucauldian critics. One particularly influential work in this respect was D. A. Miller's *The Novel and the Police* (1988), which drew on Michel Foucault's *Discipline and Punish* in order to recontextualize Collins as a social disciplinarian or narrative policeman whose two most widely discussed novels work to discipline their readers and reinscribe the Victorian class and gender norms which they appear to question or subvert. Thus, in Miller's reading, *The Woman in White* appears to blur or subvert conventional gender boundaries through its portrayal of womanly men (Hartright) and manly women (Marian), but ultimately, he argues, Collins's plot restores these apparently transgressive or subversive characters to their proper gendered place. This reinscription of gender norms is said to be reinforced by Collins's use of sensation and, in particular, Walter's female nervousness, to elicit a homophobic response from his male readers. Similarly, Miller argues that the apparently subversive narrative method of *The Moonstone* is merely an illusion. This novel's multiple narrators appear to relativize perception and democratize narrative control, but this dialogism (Miller asserts) is actually monological because the novel's several narrators all tell the same story of a highly specific guilt and thus reinforce a single perception of power.

Miller's powerful (if partial) rereading of Collins certainly put his fiction at the centre of important late-twentieth-century debates about the nature of narrative and its role in the ideological work of the novel in the nineteenth century. One thinks, for example, of Ann Cvetkovich's exploration of the ideology of the sensation narrative form of *The Woman in White*, which argues that many of the most sensational moments in the narrative serve to mask the material and social realities of Walter's 'accession to power' (through his marriage to Laura). The narrative is structured, Cvetkovich argues, so as to make it appear as if his rise 'were the product of chance occurrences, uncanny repetitions, and fated events'.[60] However, despite the attempts of critics such as Miller and Cvetkovich to read Collins merely as a social policeman whose narratives both mask and reinforce the operations of social discipline and the existing hierarchies of power, other late-twentieth-century critical recontextualizations of his fiction have continued to produce a version of Collins as a social detective intent on exploring and exposing the various forms of social discipline and the operations of power—in the law and policing, and also in the structures of marriage and the family. Anthea Trodd, for example, sees 'middle-class domesticity [as] . . . the real crime to be discovered' in *Basil*,[61] and Elizabeth Rose Gruner presents *The Moonstone* as a novel which exposes the secrecy, hypocrisy, and criminality of the Victorian family.[62]

In short, Collins criticism at the beginning of the twenty-first century seems to be as voluminous and as contradictory as the novels on which it comments. The publication of two volumes of Collins's selected letters and of his first and previously unpublished novel *Iolani* in 1999 will no doubt lead to further rereadings and recontextualizations of Collins's novels in the next few years. However, whatever Collins's fortunes may be in the changing fads and fashions of literary criticism, the sheer readability of his best novels and the power of his narratives to grip the attention of the reader will ensure that he continues to command a large and wide readership among 'King Public'.

NOTES

CHAPTER 1. The Life of Wilkie Collins

1. Wilkie Collins, *Armadale*, ed. Catherine Peters (Oxford: Oxford University Press, 1989), p. xxxix.
2. 'Our Portrait Gallery: Mr Wilkie Collins', *Men and Women*, 3 (5 Feb. 1887), 281.
3. 'Memorandum Relating to the Life and Writings of Wilkie Collins 1862', *Bentley's Miscellany*, 21 Mar. 1862, 37.
4. 'Reminiscences of a Story-Teller', *Universal Review*, 1 (1888), 182–92, quoted in Catherine Peters, *The King of Inventors: A Life of Wilkie Collins* (London: Secker and Warburg, 1991), 49.
5. L. B. Walford, *Memories of Victorian London* (London: Edward Arnold, 1912), 325.
6. Quoted in William M. Clarke, *The Secret Life of Wilkie Collins* (Stroud: Alan Sutton Publishing, 1999 [1988]), 44.
7. Quoted ibid. 45.
8. Ibid. 46.
9. 'Our Portrait Gallery: Mr Wilkie Collins', *Men and Women*, 3 (5 Feb. 1887), 281.
10. Reprinted in *Little Novels*, 1887. First published as 'The Clergyman's Confession' in the *World*, 4–18 August 1875.
11. Quoted in Clarke, *Secret Life*, 47.
12. The process of qualifying to become a barrister involved being accepted for a pupillage in a legal practice or Chamber, and attending formal dinners at the Inns of Court.
13. See Peters, *King of Inventors*, 69.
14. Concerns about the numbers of 'superfluous' women who were unable to marry or gain employment in Britain led to the encouragement of female emigration, and the establishment of societies to assist women seeking to emigrate.
15. *Spectator*, 11 March 1850, 257.
16. *Athenaeum*, 16 March 1850, 285.
17. *Bentley's Miscellany*, April 1850, 378.
18. Quoted in Andrew Gasson, *Wilkie Collins: An Illustrated Guide* (Oxford: Oxford University Press, 1998), 70. Gasson notes that in fact 'only six pages of the manuscript, part of 'The Narrative of Miss Clack', were dictated.
19. *Pall Mall Budget*, 3 Oct. 1889, 5.

CHAPTER 2. The Social Context

1. Norman McCord, *British History, 1815–1906* (Oxford: Oxford University Press, 1991), 83.
2. Thomas Carlyle, 'Signs of the Times', in *Thomas Carlyle: Selected Writings*, ed. Alan Shelston (Harmondsworth: Penguin, 1971), 64–5.
3. Edward Bulwer Lytton, *England and the English* (Paris: Bandry's European Library, 1834), 318–19, emphasis added. First published 1833.
4. Carlyle, 'Chartism', in *Carlyle: Selected Writings*, ed. Shelston, 151.
5. *Leader*, 17 Jan. 1852, 45.
6. Letter to Pigott, 16 Sept. 1852, quoted in Kirk H. Beetz, 'Wilkie Collins and *The Leader*', *Victorian Periodicals Review*, 151 (1982), 25.
7. Lee Holcombe, 'Victorian Wives and Property: Reform of the Married Women's Property Law, 1857–1882', in M. Vicinus (ed.), *A Widening Sphere: Changing Roles of Victorian Women* (London: Routledge, 1980 [1977]), 4.
8. Ibid.
9. Barbara Leigh Smith (later Bodichon), *A Brief Summary, in Plain Language, of the Most Important Laws Concerning Women, Together With a Few Observations Thereon* (London: J. Chapman, 1854), 4.
10. Martin Wiener, 'Domesticity: A Legal Discipline for Men?', in Martin Hewitt (ed.), *An Age of Equipoise? Reassessing Mid-Victorian Britain* (Aldershot: Ashgate, 2000), 158.
11. *The Life of Frances Power Cobbe By Herself* (1894), quoted in Mary Lyndon Shanley, *Feminism, Marriage, and the Law in Victorian England, 1850–1895* (Princeton: Princeton University Press, 1989), 164.
12. Martin Wiener, *Reconstructing the Criminal: Culture, Law and Policy in England, 1830–1914* (Cambridge: Cambridge University Press, 1990), 67.
13. Ibid. 91.
14. Ibid. 244.
15. Charles Dickens, *Selected Journalism, 1850–1870*, ed. David Pascoe (London: Penguin, 1997), 246.
16. Ibid. 248.
17. Ibid.
18. The doctrine of the separate spheres and the figure of the angel in the house were developed in the early nineteenth century. In *Family Fortunes: Men and Women of the English Middle Class, 1780–1850* (Chicago: University of Chicago Press, 1987), Leonora Davidoff and Catherine Hall link their development to the growing separation of the home and the workplace under capitalism and (increasingly) industrialism. As I note in the current chapter, the doctrine of the separate spheres was breaking down during Collins's lifetime (especially after 1850). Indeed, Amanda Vickery has suggested that even in the first half of the nineteenth century 'separate spheres' was a normative rather than a descriptive doctrine, and that it signalled male anxieties about women's attempts to change their roles as much as it described social realities. See Amanda Vickery, 'Golden Age to Separate Spheres? A Review of the Categories and

Chronology of English Women's History', *Historical Journal*, 36 (1993), 383–414.

19. John Ruskin, 'Of Queens' Gardens', *Sesame and Lilies* [1865], in *The Works of John Ruskin* (London: George Allen, 1880), i. 91–2.
20. Ibid. 91.
21. Wiener in Hewitt (ed.), *Age of Equipoise?*, 155.
22. John Tosh, *A Man's Place: Masculinity and the Middle-Class Home in Victorian England* (New Haven: Yale University Press, 1999), 6.
23. Ibid.
24. Ibid.
25. W. R. Greg, 'Why Are Women Redundant?', *National Review*, 14 (1862), 446.
26. T. H. S. Escott, *England: Her People, Polity, and Pursuits* (1879), reprinted in J. M. Golby (ed.), *Culture and Society in Britain, 1850–1890: A Source Book of Contemporary Writings* (Oxford: Oxford University Press, in association with the Open University Press, 1986), 27.
27. Ibid.
28. Ibid.
29. Ibid. 28. Although Escott is probably correct in dating the gentrification (so to speak) of the master manufacturers and retailers to about 1832, some aspects of his dating of the processes he describes would not be accepted by most modern historians. The gentrification of the great bankers and professionals began in the late eighteenth century (some would put it even earlier).
30. Ibid. 30. For a more recent view of the processes described by Escott, see Harold Perkin, *The Rise of Professional Society: England since 1880* (London: Routledge, 1989).
31. Ibid.
32. Ibid. 30–1.
33. John Kucich, *The Power of Lies: Transgression in Victorian Fiction* (Ithaca, NY: Cornell University Press, 1994), 81 ff.
34. Tosh, *A Man's Place*, 177.
35. Robert Lowe, quoted in Asa Briggs, *Victorian People: A Reassessment of Persons and Themes, 1851–67* (Harmonsworth: Penguin, 1965), 362.
36. Hugh McLeod, *Religion and Society in England, 1850–1914* (London: Macmillan, 1996), 1.
37. Geoffrey Best, *Mid-Victorian Britain, 1851–75* (London: Fontana, 1979 [1971]), 193.
38. Robin Gilmour, *The Victorian Period: The Intellectual and Cultural Context of English Literature, 1830–1890* (London: Longman, 1993), 72.
39. Quoted ibid. 74.
40. The Hennells were a family of Manchester manufacturers. Charles C. Hennell was the author of *An Inquiry Into the Origins of Christianity* (1838). He became acquainted with George Eliot through his sister Caroline, who married Charles Bray, son of a Coventry ribbon manufacturer and author of *Philosophy of Necessity or The Law of Consequences; as Applicable to Mental, Moral and Social Science* (1841).

41. Gilmour, *Victorian Period*, 87.

42. Nuel Pharr Davis, *The Life of Wilkie Collins* (Urbana: University of Illinois Press, 1956), 19, 21–2.

43. Keith Lawrence, 'The Religion of Wilkie Collins; Three Unpublished Documents', *Huntington Library Quarterly*, 52 (1989), 389.

44. Sue Lonoff, *Wilkie Collins and his Victorian Readers* (New York: AMS Press, 1982), 216.

45. Ibid. 218.

46. Lawrence, 'Religion of Wilkie Collins', 393.

47. See Beetz, 'Wilkie Collins and *The Leader*, 20.

48. See P. J. Cain and A. G. Hopkins, *British Imperialism: Innovation and Expansion, 1688–1914* (London: Longman, 1993).

49. Christine Bolt, *Victorian Attitudes to Race* (London: Routledge and Kegan Paul, 1971).

50. Quoted in Susan Meyer, *Imperialism at Home: Race and Victorian Women's Fiction* (Ithaca, NY: Cornell University Press, 1996), 15.

CHAPTER 3. The Literary Context

1. Norman Page (ed.). *Wilkie Collins: The Critical Heritage* (London: Routledge and Kegan Paul, 1974), 1.

2. John Eagles [unsigned] 'A Few Words About Novels—A Dialogue', *Blackwood's*, 64 (1848), 462.

3. David Masson, *British Novelists and their Styles* (1859), from extract reprinted in Edwin Eigner and George Worth (eds.), *Victorian Criticism of the Novel* (Cambridge: Cambridge University Press, 1985), 152.

4. Anthony Trollope, 'On English Prose Fiction as a Rational Amusement', in *Four Lectures*, ed. M. L. Parrish (London: Constable, 1938), 108.

5. 'Penny Novels', *Macmillan's Magazine*, 14 (1866), 97.

6. See Graham Law, *Serializing Fiction in the Victorian Press* (London: Palgrave, 2000), 171.

7. Deborah Wynne, *The Sensation Novel and the Victorian Family Magazine* (Basingstoke: Palgrave, 2001), 100.

8. Quoted in Sue Lonoff, *Wilkie Collins and his Victorian Readers* (New York: AMS Press, 1982), 53.

9. *Graphic*, 30 Jan. 1875, 107.

10. Guinevere Griest, *Mudie's Circulating Library and the Victorian Novel* (Newton Abbot: David and Charles, 1970), 32.

11. Collins, 18 March 1873, quoted in Catherine Peters, *The King of Inventors: A Life of Wilkie Collins* (London: Secker and Warburg, 1991), 340.

12. 'A New Censorship in Literature', reprinted in G. Moore, *Literature at Nurse, or, Circulating Morals*, ed. Pierre Coustillas (Hassocks: Harvester, 1976), 28.

13. H. L. Mansel [unsigned] 'Sensation Novels', *Quarterly Review*, 113 (1863), 485.

14. Collins, quoted in Lonoff, *Wilkie Collins and his Victorian Readers*, 5.

15. George Eliot [unsigned] 'Silly Novels by Lady Novelists', *Westminster Review*, October 1856, reprinted in George Eliot, *Selected Critical Writings*, ed. Rosemary Ashton (Oxford: Oxford University Press, 1992).

16. See Eliot's essay 'The Natural History of German Life' first published (unsigned) in the *Westminster Review* in July 1856, reprinted in Ashton (ed.), *Selected Critical Waitings*.

17. Henry James, unsigned review of *Middlemarch* in *Galaxy*, March 1873, reprinted in David Carroll (ed.), *Middlemarch: The Critical Heritage* (London: Routledge and Kegan Paul, 1971), 359.

18. 'Popular Novels of the Year', *Frazer's Magazine*, 68 (1863), 262.

19. From the prospectus to 'The Sensation Times' in *Punch*, quoted in *Christian Remembrancer*, 46 (1864), 210.

20. Ibid.

21. W. F. Rae, 'Sensation Novelists: Miss Braddon', *North British Review*, 43 (1865), 204.

22. Mansel, 'Sensation Novels', 488–9.

23. Elaine Showalter, 'Family Secrets and Domestic Subversion: Rebellion in the Novels of the Eighteen-Sixties', in A. S. Wohl (ed.), *The Victorian Family: Structure and Stress* (London: Croom Helm, 1978), 104.

24. Henry James, 'Miss Braddon', *Nation*, 9 Nov. 1865, 594.

25. *The Times*, 18 Nov. 1862, 8.

26. *Lucretia; or, The Heroine of the Nineteenth Century. A correspondence, sensational and sentimental. By the Author of 'The Owlet of Owlstone Edge' (F.E.P)* (London: Joseph Masters, 1868), 305.

27. 'Novels', *Blackwood's*, 102 (1867), 274–5.

28. Tamar Heller, *Dead Secrets: Wilkie Collins and the Female Gothic* (New Haven: Yale University Press, 1992), 7.

29. 'Sensation Novels', *Blackwood's*, 91 (May 1862), 564–84.

30. Mary Elizabeth Braddon, *The Doctor's Wife*, ed. Lyn Pykett (Oxford: Oxford University Press, 1998), 11.

31. Ronald Thomas, 'Detection in the Victorian Novel', in Deidre David (ed.), *The Cambridge Companion to the Victorian Novel* (Cambridge: Cambridge University Press, 2001), 169.

32. Walter Benjamin, *Charles Baudelaire: A Lyric Poet in the Era of High Capitalism* (London: Verso, 1973), 43.

33. A. C. Swinburne, 'Wilkie Collins', *Fortnightly Review*, 1 Nov. 1889, reprinted in Page (ed), *Critical Heritage*, 262.

34. Michael Booth, *Theatre in the Victorian Age* (Cambridge: Cambridge University Press, 1991), 151.

35. *Leader*, 30 March 1850, 20.

36. Lonoff, *Wilkie Collins and his Victorian Readers*, 50–1.

37. Edward Marston, *After Work* (London: Heinemann, 1904), 85.

38. Quoted in Robert Ashley, *Wilkie Collins* (London: Barker, 1952), 29.

39. All quotations from Page (ed.), *Critical Heritage*, 6–7.

40. *Leader*, 27 Nov. 1852, 1142.

41. Quoted in Page (ed.), *Critical Heritage*, 7.

42. 'The Progress of Fiction as an Art', *Westminster Review*, 60 (1853), 373.
43. Page (ed.), *Critical Heritage*, 48.
44. Ibid. 41.
45. Ibid. 77.
46. Ibid. 74–5.
47. Gladstone's diary, quoted in Amy Cruse, *The Victorians and their Books* (London: George Allen and Unwin, 1935), 322.
48. *Saturday Review*, 25 Aug. 1860, 249.
49. Ibid. 249–50.
50. 'The Enigma Novel', *Spectator*, 28 Dec. 1861, 1428.
51. Mansel, 'Sensation Novels', 483.
52. Ibid. 495.
53. Alexander Smith [unsigned], 'Novels and Novelists of the Day', *North British Review*, 38 (1863), 184.
54. *Athenaeum*, 2 June 1866, 732.
55. *Westminster Review*, Oct. 1866, 270.
56. *The Times*, 3 Oct. 1868, 4.
57. *Lippincot's Magazine*, Dec. 1868, 679.
58. *Saturday Review*, 9 July 1870, 52–3.
59. Ibid. 53.
60. J. A. Noble, 'Recent Novels', *Spectator*, 26 Jan. 1889, 120.

CHAPTER 4. Masters, Servants, and Married Women

1. *All the Year Round*, 1 (1860), 396.
2. Ann Cvetkovich, 'Ghostlier Determinations: The Economy of Sensation and *The Woman in White*', *Novel*, 23 (1989), reprinted in Lyn Pykett (ed.), *Wilkie Collins: Contemporary Critical Essays* (Basingstoke: Macmillan, 1998), 111.
3. John Kucich, *The Power of Lies: Transgression in Victorian Fiction* (Ithaca, NY: Cornell University Press, 1994), 88.
4. This quotation is from the version reprinted as 'Laid up in Lodgings' in *My Miscellanies*, 226.
5. Anthea Trodd, *Domestic Crime in the Victorian Novel* (Basingstoke: Macmillan, 1989), 8.
6. Kucich, *Power of Lies*, 81–2.
7. Ibid. 102.
8. *Iolani, or Tahiti as it was*, ed. Ira B. Nadel (Princeton: Princeton University Press, 1999), 20.
9. Jenny Bourne Taylor, *In the Secret Theatre of Home: Wilkie Collins, Sensation Narrative, and Nineteenth-Century Psychology* (London: Routledge, 1988), 72.
10. *Household Words*, 13 Dec. 1856, reprinted in *My Miscellanies*, 419.
11. R. Barickman, S. McDonald, and M. Stark, *Corrupt Relations: Dickens, Thackeray, Collins and the Victorian Sexual System* (New York: Columbia University Press, 1982), 111.

12. *All the Year Round*, 21 Jan. 1860, 291.
13. Quoted in Catherine Peters, *The King of Inventors; A Life of Wilkie Collins* (London: Secker and Warburg, 1991), 320.

CHAPTER 5. Sex, Crime, Madness, and Empire

1. W. R. Greg, 'Why Are Women Redundant?', *National Review*, 14 (1862), 453.
2. Margaret Oliphant, unsigned review, *Blackwood's*, Aug. 1863, 170.
3. *Athenaeum*, 2 June 1886, 732.
4. See R. D. Altick, *The Presence of the Past: Topics of the Day in the Victorian Novel* (Columbus: Ohio State University Press, 1991), 54 ff. Mrs Sarah Rachel Leverson, known as Madame Rachel, had a shop in New Bond Street in London where she sold beauty products. It was also rumoured that she provided other services for women—such as abortion.
5. Jenny Bourne Taylor, *In the Secret Theatre of Home: Wilkie Collins, Sensation Narrative, and Nineteenth-Century Psychology* (London: Routledge, 1988), 217.
6. Convicts who were transported to Australia were required to perform forced labour for public works or 'assigned' individuals. A ticket of leave enabled them to work outside of this system, on condition that they continued to live in a particular area and report regularly to the authorities.
7. See Taylor, *In the Secret Theatre of Home* and Deborah Wynne, *The Sensation Novel and the Victorian Family Magazine* (Basingstoke: Palgrave, 2001).
8. Taylor, *In the Secret Theatre of Home*, 103.
9. 'M.D. and MAD', *All the Year Round*, 22 Feb. 1862, 103.
10. Taylor, *In the Secret Theatre of Home*, 171.
11. Stephen D. Arata, 'The Occidental Tourist: Dracula and the Anxiety of Reverse Colonization', *Victorian Studies*, 33 (1990), 623.
12. Lillian Nayder, *Wilkie Collins* (New York: Twayne, 1997), 107.
13. Tamar Heller, *Dead Secrets: Wilkie Collins and the Female Gothic* (New Haven: Yale University Press, 1992), 146.
14. Patrick Brantlinger, *Rule of Darkness: British Literature and Imperialism: 1830–1914* (Ithaca, NY: Cornell University Press, 1988), 200.
15. 'A Sermon for Sepoys', *Household Words*, 27 Feb. 1858, 244.

CHAPTER 6. Psychology and Science in Collins's Novels

1. 'Magnetic Evenings at Home', *Leader*, 17 Jan. 1852, 63.
2. Quoted in Jenny Bourne Taylor, *In the Secret Theatre of Home: Wilkie Collins, Sensation Narrative, and Nineteenth-Century Psychology* (London: Routledge, 1988), 57.
3. Jenny Bourne Taylor and Sally Shuttleworth (eds.), *Embodied Selves: An Anthology of Psychological Texts, 1830–1890* (Oxford: Clarendon Press, 1998), 3.

4. William B. Carpenter, *Principles of Mental Physiology, with their Application to the Training and Discipline of the Mind and the Study of its Morbid Conditions* (1874), quoted in Taylor, *In the Secret Theatre of Home*, 60–1.

5. John Abercrombie, *Inquiries Concerning the Intellectual Powers and the Investigation of Truth* (Edinburgh: Waugh and Innes, 1830), 37.

6. Ibid. 289.

7. See Taylor and Shuttleworth, *Embodied Selves*, 69.

8. Ann Cvetkovich, 'Ghostlier Determinations: The Economy of Sensation in *The Woman in White*', *Novel*, 23 (1989), reprinted in Lyn Pykett (ed.), *Wilkie Collins: Contemporary Critical Essays* (Basingstoke: Macmillan, 1998).

9. 'Madness in Novels', *Spectator*, 3 Feb. 1866, 135–6.

10. H. L. Mansel [unsigned], 'Sensation Novels', *Quarterly Review*, 113 (1863), 482–3.

11. George Robinson, *On the Prevention and Treatment of Mental Disorders* (London: Longman, Brown, Green, Longman and Roberts, 1859), 7.

12. Review of Forbes Winslow, *On Obscure Diseases of the Brain*, in *Edinburgh Review*, 113 (1860), 526.

13. William Tuke founded The Retreat, an asylum for insane Quakers near York in 1792. His son Samuel published a history of The Retreat, describing the humane, 'moral management' method, in 1813.

14. Collins in a letter to Surgeon-General Charles Alexander Gordon, quoted in Wilkie Collins, *Heart and Science*, ed. Steve Farmer (Peterborough, Ontario: Broadview, 1999), 17.

15. 23 June 1882, reprinted in *Heart and Science*, ed. Farmer, 370.

16. *Academy*, 28 April 1883, 290, reprinted in Normen Page (ed.), *Wilkie Collins: The Critical Heritage* (London: Routledge and Kegan Paul, 1974), 213.

17. A. C. Swinburne, 'Wilkie Collins', *Fortnightly Review*, 1 Nov. 1889, reprinted in Page (ed.), *Critical Heritage*, 261.

18. Catherine Peters, *The King of Inventors: A Life of Wilkie Collins* (London: Secker and Warburg, 1991), 299.

CHAPTER 7. Recontextualizing Collins

1. *The Times*, 12 Dec. 1871, quoted in Catherine Peters, *The King of Inventors: A Life of Wilkie Collins* (London: Secker and Warburg, 1991), 334.

2. Quoted in Wilkie Collins, *The Moonstone*, ed. Steve Farmer (Peterborough, Ontario: Broadview, 1999), 613 n. 1.

3. *Athenaeum*, 22 Sept. 1877, 381.

4. Quoted in Peters, *King of Inventors*, 361.

5. *Bioscope*, 16 Jan. 1913, p. xxxiv.

6. *Daily Telegraph*, 3 Oct. 1966.

7. *Monthly Film Bulletin*, Oct. 1934, 82.

8. At time of writing these include: *My Lady's Money*, *'No Thoroughfare' and Other Stories*, *The Biter Bit and Other Stories*, *A Rogue's Life*, *The Legacy of Cain*, *The New Magdalen*, *The Evil Genius*, *Jezebel's Daughter*, *'I

Say No', *The Two Destinies*, *Fallen Leaves*, and *The Frozen Deep/Mr Wray's Cashbox*.

9. Sayers, Introduction to *The Moonstone* (London: J. M. Dent, 1944), p. vi; quoted in Farmer's edn., pp. 13–14.

10. James Wilson, *The Dark Clue* (London: Faber and Faber, 2001), 19.

11. Norman Page (ed.), *Wilkie Collins: The Critical Heritage* (London: Routledge and Kegan Paul, 1974), p. xiii.

12. Harry Quilter, 'A Living Story-teller', *Contemporary Review*, April 1888, reprinted in Page (ed.), *Critical Heritage*, 230.

13. Ibid. 233.

14. Ibid. 230.

15. Ibid. 241.

16. Ibid. 246, 244.

17. Ibid. 244, 245.

18. *Spectator*, 28 Sept. 1887, reprinted in Page (ed.), *Critical Heritage*, 250.

19. *Fortnightly Review*, 1 Nov. 1889, reprinted in Page (ed.), *Critical Heritage*, 257.

20. Ibid. 260.

21. Ibid. 261.

22. Ibid.

23. Andrew Lang, 'Mr Wilkie Collins's Novels', *Contemporary Review*, Jan. 1890, reprinted in Page (ed.), *Critical Heritage*, 267.

24. Swinburne in Page (ed.), *Critical Heritage*, 255 and 263.

25. Quilter in Page (ed.), *Critical Heritage*, 229.

26. *Bookman*, 35 (1912), 571.

27. Walter C. Phillips, *Dickens, Reade, and Collins: Sensation Novelists* (New York: Columbia University Press, 1919), 186.

28. T. S. Eliot, 'Wilkie Collins and Dickens', in *Selected Essays* (London: Faber and Faber, 1932), 464.

29. Ibid. 460.

30. Ibid. 465.

31. Ibid. 469.

32. Malcolm Elwin, *Victorian Wallflowers* (London: Cape, 1934), 226.

33. Ibid.

34. Thomas J. Hardy, *Books on the Shelf* (London: Philip Allan, 1934), 223 and 226.

35. Robert Ashley, 'Wilkie Collins Reconsidered', *Nineteenth-Century Fiction*, 4 (1950), 265–73; 'Wilkie Collins and the Detective Story', *Nineteenth-Century Fiction*, 6 (1951), 47–60.

36. Bradford Booth, 'Collins and the Art of Fiction', *Nineteenth-Century Fiction*, 6 (1951), 131–43.

37. Robert Ashley, *Wilkie Collins* (London: Barker, 1952), 5.

38. Ibid.

39. Ibid. 127.

40. Kathleen Tillotson, 'The Lighter Reading of the Eighteen-sixties', Introduction to Wilkie Collins, *The Woman in White* (Boston: Houghton Mifflin, Riverside Edition, 1969), pp. ix and xx.

41. Tillotson, 'The Lighter Reading of the Eighteen-sixties', p. xxi.
42. William Marshall, *Wilkie Collins* (New York: Twayne, 1970), 5, emphasis added.
43. Ibid.
44. In Jerome H. Buckley (ed.), *The Worlds of Victorian Fiction* (Cambridge, Mass.: Harvard University Press, 1975).
45. John R. Reed, 'English Imperialism and the Unacknowledged Crime of *The Moonstone*', *Clio*, 2 (1973), 281.
46. Ibid. 284.
47. Page (ed.), *Critical Heritage*, 32.
48. Lillian Nayder, 'Wilkie Collins Studies: 1983–1999', *Dickens Studies Annual*, 28 (1999), 258.
49. Jenny Bourne Taylor, *In the Secret Theatre of Home: Wilkie Collins, Sensation Narrative, and Nineteenth-Century Psychology* (London: Routledge, 1988), 31.
50. Ibid. 1.
51. Jonathan Loesberg, 'The Ideology of Narrative Form in Sensation Fiction', *Representations*, 13 (1986), 117 and 116.
52. Tamar Heller, *Dead Secrets: Wilkie Collins and the Female Gothic* (New Haven: Yale University Press, 1992), 8.
53. Alison Milbank, *Daughters of the House: Modes of the Gothic in Victorian Fiction* (Basingstoke: Macmillan, 1992), 14.
54. Patricia Miller Frick, 'Wilkie Collins's "Little Jewel": The Meaning of *The Moonstone*', *Philological Quarterly*, 63 (1984), 318.
55. Ashish Roy, 'The Fabulous Imperialist Semiotic of Wilkie Collins's *The Moonstone*', *New Literary History*, 24 (1993), 657–81.
56. Deidre David, *Rule Britannia: Women, Empire, and Victorian Writing* (Ithaca, NY: Cornell University Press, 1995).
57. Jaya Mehta, 'English Romance; Indian Violence', *Centennial Review*, 39 (1995), 620 and 621.
58. Lillian Nayder, *Wilkie Collins* (New York: Twayne, 1997), 101.
59. See Nayder, *Dickens Studies Annual*, 28 (1999), 304.
60. Ann Cvetkovich, 'Ghostlier Determinations: The Economy of Sensation and *The Woman in White*', *Novel*, 23 (1989), reprinted in Lyn Pykett (ed.), *Wilkie Collins: Contemporary Critical Essays* (Basingstoke: Macmillan, 1998), 111.
61. Anthea Trodd, *Domestic Crime in the Victorian Novel* (Basingstoke: Macmillan, 1989), 103.
62. Elizabeth Rose Gruner, 'Family Secrets and the Mysteries of *The Moonstone*', *Victorian Literature and Culture*, 21 (1993), reprinted in Pykett (ed.), *Wilkie Collins: Contemporary Critical Essays*.

FURTHER READING

CONTEXTUAL MATERIAL

(a) The literary context

Altick, Richard D., *The English Common Reader: A Social History of the Mass Reading Public* (Chicago: Chicago University Press, 1957).

—— *The Presence of the Past: Topics of the Day in the Victorian Novel* (Columbus: Ohio State University Press, 1991).

Brantlinger, Patrick, *The Reading Lesson: The Threat of Mass Literacy in Nineteenth-Century British Fiction* (Bloomington: Indiana University Press, 1998).

Gilmour, Robin, *The Victorian Period: The Intellectual and Cultural Context of English Literature, 1830–1890* (London: Longman, 1993).

Griest, Guinevere, *Mudie's Circulating Library and the Victorian Novel* (Newton Abbot: David and Charles, 1970).

Hughes Linda K., and Lund, Michael, *The Victorian Serial* (Charlottesville: University Press of Virginia, 1991).

Hughes, Winifred, *The Maniac in the Cellar: Sensation Novels of the 1860s* (Princeton: Princeton University Press, 1980).

Jordan, J. O., and Patten, R. L. (eds.), *Literature in the Marketplace: Nineteenth-Century British Publishing and Reading Practices* (Cambridge: Cambridge University Press, 1995).

Miller, D. A., *The Novel and the Police* (Berkeley: University of California Press, 1988).

Pykett, Lyn, *The Sensation Novel from 'The Woman in White' to 'The Moonstone'* (Plymouth: Northcote House, 1994).

—— 'Sensation and the Fantastic in the Victorian Novel', in Deidre David (ed.), *The Cambridge Companion to the Victorian Novel* (Cambridge: Cambridge University Press, 2001), 192–211.

—— 'The Newgate Novel and Sensation Fiction, 1830–1868', in Martin Priestman (ed.), *The Cambridge Companion to Crime Fiction* (Cambridge: Cambridge University Press, 2003), 19–40.

Sutherland, J. A., *Victorian Novelists and Publishers* (London: Athlane, 1976).

—— *Victorian Fiction: Writers, Publishers, Readers* (Basingstoke: Macmillan, 1995).

Trodd, Anthea, *Domestic Crime in the Victorian Novel* (Basingstoke: Macmillan, 1989).

Wynne, Deborah, *The Sensation Novel and the Victorian Family Magazine* (Basingstoke: Palgrave, 2001).

(b) Protest and reform

Brantlinger, Patrick, *The Spirit of Reform: British Literature and Politics, 1832–1867* (Cambridge, Mass.: Harvard University Press, 1977).

Vernon, James, *Politics and the People: A Study in English Political Culture c. 1815–1867* (New York: Cambridge University Press, 1993).

(c) The law, crime, criminality, and policing

Emsley, Clive, *Crime and Society in England, 1750–1900* (London: Longman, 1996 [1987]).

Holcombe, Lee, *Wives and Property: Reform of the Married Women's Property Law in Nineteenth-Century England* (Oxford: Martin Robertson, 1983).

Shanley, Mary Lyndon, *Feminism, Marriage, and the Law in Victorian England, 1850–1895* (Princeton: Princeton University Press, 1989).

Wiener, Martin, *Reconstructing the Criminal: Culture, Law and Policy in England 1830–1914* (Cambridge: Cambridge University Press, 1990).

(d) Gender and sexuality

Adams, James Eli, *Dandies and Desert Saints: Styles of Victorian Masculinity* (Ithaca, NY: Cornell University Press, 1995).

Davidoff, Leonora, and Hall, Catherine, *Family Fortunes: Men and Women of the English Middle Class, 1780–1850* (Chicago: University of Chicago Press, 1987).

Mason, Michael, *The Making of Victorian Sexuality* (Oxford: Oxford University Press, 1994).

—— *The Making of Victorian Sexual Attitudes* (Oxford: Oxford University Press, 1994).

Miller, Andrew, and Adams, James Eli (eds.), *Sexualities in Victorian Britain* (Bloomington: Indiana University Press, 1996).

Mangan, J. A., and Walvin, J. (eds.), *Manliness and Morality: Middle-Class Masculinity in Britain and America, 1800–1940* (Manchester: Manchester University Press, 1987).

Nead, Lynda, *Myths of Sexuality: Representations of Women in Victorian Britain* (Oxford: Blackwell, 1988).

Tosh, John, *A Man's Place: Masculinity and the Middle-Class Home in Victorian England* (New Haven: Yale University Press, 1999).

—— and Roper, Michael (eds.), *Manful Assertions: Masculinities in Britain Since 1800* (London: Routledge, 1991).

Vickery, Amanda, 'Golden Age to Separate Spheres? A Review of the

Categories and Chronology of English Women's History', *Historical Journal*, 36 (1993).

Walkowitz, Judith, *Prostitution in Victorian Society: Women, Class and the State* (Cambridge: Cambridge University Press, 1980).

Weeks, Jeffrey, *Sex, Politics and Society: The Regulation of Sexuality in Britain Since 1800* (London: Longman, 1981).

(e) Social class

Joyce, Patrick, *Visions of the People: Industrial England and the Question of Class* (Cambridge: Cambridge University Press, 1991).

—— (ed.), *Class* (Oxford: Oxford University Press, 1995).

Reader, W. J. *Professional Men: The Rise of the Professional Classes in Nineteenth-Century England* (London: Fontana, 1988).

Stedman Jones, Gareth, *Outcast London: A Study in the Relationship Between Classes in Victorian Society* (Oxford: Clarendon Press, 1971).

Vincent, David, *Literacy and Popular Culture: England 1750–1914* (Cambridge: Cambridge University Press, 1989).

(f) Religion

Cockshut, A. O. J. (ed.), *Religious Controversies of the Nineteenth Century: Selected Documents* (London: Methuen, 1966).

McCleod, Hugh, *Religion and Society in England, 1850–1914* (London: Macmillan, 1996).

Moore, James R. (ed.), *Religion in Victorian Britain: Sources* (Manchester: Manchester University Press, in association with Open University Press, 1988), vol. iii.

Parsons, Gerald (ed.), *Religion in Victorian Britain: Traditions* (Manchester: Manchester University Press, in association with Open University Press, 1988), vol. i.

—— (ed.), *Religion in Victorian Britain: Controversies* (Manchester: Manchester University Press, in association with Open University Press, 1988), vol. ii.

(g) Empire and race

Bolt, Christine, *Victorian Attitudes to Race* (London: Routledge and Kegan Paul, 1971).

Brantlinger, Patrick, *Rule of Darkness: British Literature and Imperialism, 1830–1914* (Ithaca, NY: Cornell University Press, 1988).

Malchow, H. *Gothic Images of Race in Nineteenth-Century Britain* (Stanford, Calif.: Stanford University Press, 1996).

Mukherjee, U. P., *Crime and Empire: The Colony in Nineteenth-Century Fictions of Crime* (Oxford: Oxford University Press, 2003).

Stepan, Nancy, *The Idea of Race in Science: Great Britain, 1800–1960* (Hamden, Conn.: Archon Books, 1982).

(h) Science and psychology

Oppenheim, Janet, *'Shattered Nerves': Doctors, Patients, and Depression in Victorian England* (Oxford: Oxford University Press, 1991).

Scull, Andrew, *The Most Solitary of Afflictions: Madness and Society in Britain, 1700–1900* (New Haven: Yale University Press, 1993).

Taylor, Jenny Bourne, 'Obscure Recesses: Locating the Victorian Unconscious', in J. B. Bullen, (ed.) *Writing and Victorianism* (London: Longman, 1997).

—— and Shuttleworth, Sally (eds.), *Embodied Selves: An Anthology of Psychological Texts, 1830–1890* (Oxford: Clarendon Press, 1998).

Winter, Alison, *Mesmerized: Powers of Mind in Victorian Britain* (Chicago: University of Chicago Press, 1998).

CRITICISM

(a) Articles or chapters about individual novels or specific areas of Collins's work

Allan, Janice M., 'Scenes of Writing: Detection and Psychoanalysis in Wilkie Collins's *The Moonstone*', *Imprimatur*, 1 (1996), 186–93.

Ashley, Robert, 'Wilkie Collins Reconsidered', *Nineteenth-Century Fiction*, 4 (1950), 265–73.

—— 'Wilkie Collins and the Detective Story', *Nineteenth-Century Fiction*, 6 (1951), 47–60.

Balée, Susan, 'Wilkie Collins and Surplus Women: The Case of Marian Halcombe', *Victorian Literature and Culture*, 20 (1999), 197–215.

Bernstein, Stephen, 'Reading Blackwater Park: Gothicism, Narrative and Ideology in *The Woman in White*', *Studies in the Novel*, 25 (1993), 291–305.

Booth, Bradford, 'Collins and the Art of Fiction', *Nineteenth-Century Fiction*, 6 (1951), 131–43.

Duncan, Ian, '*The Moonstone*, the Victorian Novel and Imperialist Panic', *Modern Language Quarterly*, 55 (1994), 297–319.

Fass, Barbara, 'Wilkie Collins' Cinderella: The History of Psychology and *The Woman in White*', *Dickens Studies Annual*, 10 (1982), 91–141.

Frick, Patricia Miller, 'Wilkie Collins's "Little Jewel": The Meaning of *The Moonstone*', *Philological Quarterly*, 63 (1984), 313–21.

—— 'The Fallen Angels of Wilkie Collins', *International Journal of Women's Studies*, 7 (1984), 342–51.

Horne, Lewis, 'Magdalen's Peril', *Dickens Studies Annual*, 20 (1991), 259–80.

Kucich, John, 'Competitive Elites in Wilkie Collins: Cultural Intellectuals and their Professional Others', in his *The Power of Lies: Transgression in Victorian Fiction* (Ithaca, NY: Cornell University Press, 1994), 75–118.

Loesberg, Jonathan, 'The Ideology of Narrative Form in Sensation Fiction', *Representations*, 13 (1986), 115–318.

MacDonagh, Josephine, and Smith, Jonathan, ' "Fill Up All the Gaps": Narrative and Illegitimacy in *The Woman in White*', *Journal of Narrative Technique*, 26 (1996), 274–91.

Mangum, Teresa, 'Wilkie Collins, Detection, and Deformity', *Dickens Studies Annual*, 26 (1998), 285–310.

Maynard, Jessica, 'Telling the Whole Truth: Wilkie Collins and the Lady Detective', in Ruth Robbins and Julian Wolfreys (eds.), *Victorian Identities: Social and Cultural Formations* (Basingstoke: Macmillan, 1996), 187–98.

Mehta, Jaya, 'English Romance; Indian Violence', *Centennial Review*, 39 (1995) 611–57.

Michie, Helena, ' "There is no Friend Like a Sister": Sisterhood as Sexual Difference', *English Literary History*, 56 (1989), 401–21.

Milbank, Alison, 'Breaking and Entering: Wilkie Collins's Sensation Fiction', and 'Hidden and Sought: Wilkie Collins's Gothic Fiction', in her *Daughters of the House: Modes of the Gothic in Victorian Fiction* (Basingstoke: Macmillan, 1992), 25–53, 54–7.

Nayder, Lillian, 'Robinson Crusoe and Friday in Victorian Britain: "Discipline", "Dialogue", and Collins's Critique of Empire in *The Moonstone*', *Dickens Studies Annual*, 21 (1991), 213–31.

—— 'Wilkie Collins Studies: 1983–1989', *Dickens Studies Annual*, 28 (1999), 257–323.

Perkins, Pamela, and Donaghy, Mary, 'A Man's Resolution: Narrative Strategies in Wilkie Collins' *The Woman in White*', *Studies in the Novel*, 22 (1990), 392–402.

Reed, John R., 'English Imperialism and the Unacknowledged Crime of *The Moonstone*', *Clio*, 2 (1973), 281–90.

—— 'The Stories of *The Mooonstone*', in Nelson Smith and R. C. Terry (eds.), *Wilkie Collins to the Forefront* (New York: AMS Press, 1995), 91–100.

Roy, Ashish, 'The Fabulous Imperialist Semiotic of Wilkie Collins's *The Moonstone*', *New Literary History*, 24 (1993), 657–81.

Schmitt, Cannon, 'Alien Nation: Gender, Genre, and English Nationality in Wilkie Collins's *The Woman in White*', *Genre*, 26 (1993), 283–310.

Surridge, Lisa, 'Unspeakable Histories: Hester Dethridge and the

Narration of Domestic Violence in *Man and Wife*', *Victorian Review*, 22 (1996), 102–26.

Welsh, Alexander, 'Collins's Setting for a Moonstone', in *Strong Representations: Narrative and Circumstantial Evidence in England* (Baltimore: Johns Hopkins University Press, 1992), 215–36.

(b) Books and edited collections on Collins's work

Gasson, Andrew, *Wilkie Collins: An Illustrated Guide* (Oxford: Oxford University Press, 1998).

Heller, Tamar, *Dead Secrets: Wilkie Collins and the Female Gothic* (New Haven: Yale University Press, 1992).

Nayder, Lillian, *Wilkie Collins* (New York: Twayne, 1997).

O'Neill, Philip, *Wilkie Collins: Women, Property and Propriety* (Totowa, NJ: Barnes and Noble, 1988).

Pykett, Lyn (ed.), *Wilkie Collins: Contemporary Critical Essays* (Basingstoke: Macmillan, 1998).

Rance, Nicholas, *Wilkie Collins and Other Sensation Novelists: Walking the Moral Hospital* (Basingstoke: Macmillan, 1991).

Smith, Nelson, and Terry, R. C. *Wilkie Collins to the Forefront: Some Reassessments* (New York: AMS Press, 1995).

Taylor, Jenny Bourne, *In the Secret Theatre of Home: Wilkie Collins, Sensation Narrative, and Nineteenth-Century Psychology* (London: Routledge, 1988).

WEBSITES

COLLINS

http://www.deadline.demon.co.uk/wilkie/wilkie.htm   Paul Lewis's Wilkie Collins website is an excellent place to start. It has lots of useful information and images of the author and his contemporaries, plus information about and links to other websites on Collins, as well as links to e-texts of most of Collins's published work.

http://lang.a-u.ac.jp/~matsuoka/collins.html   Another excellent Collins site with useful links.

http://www.rightword.com.au/writers/wilkie/   David   Grigg's   Wilkie Collins Appreciation Page.

http://members.aol.com/MG4273/sensatio.htm   A site on British sensation fiction maintained by Michael Grost; has some useful summaries and analyses of some of Collins's novels.

GENERAL VICTORIAN

http://lang.nagoya-u.ac.jp~matsuoka/victorian.html   Probably the most comprehensive guide to websites offering information on Victorian literature and culture.

http://landow.stg.brown.edu/victorian/victor.html   The Victorian Web, an Overview has links to material on political, social, and economic history, gender matters, philosophy, religion, science and technology, and the visual arts as well as material on authors and genres and links to e-texts.

FILM AND TELEVISION ADAPTATIONS

Armadale (US; director Richard Garrick, 1916).

Basil (US; director Radha Bharadwaj, 1997).

The Dead Secret (US; director Stanner E. V. Taylor, Monopol, 1913).

The Moonstone (US; Selig Polyscope, 1909).
The Moonstone (France; Pathé, 1911).
The Moonstone (US; director Frank Hall Crane, 1915).
The Moonstone (US; Monogram, director Reginald Barker, 1934).
The Moonstone (GB; BBC TV, producer Shaun Sutton, 1959).
The Moonstone (GB; BBC TV, director Paddy Russell, 1972).
The Moonstone (GB; BBC TV, director Robert Bierman, 1996).

A Terribly Strange Bed (US; TV, 1949).
A Terribly Strange Bed, in *A Trio for Terror* (US; director Ida Lupino, 1961).
A Terribly Strange Bed (Poland; director Witold Lesiewicz, 1968).
A Terribly Strange Bed (GB/US; Anglia Television/CBS-TV, director Alan Cooke, 1974).

The Woman in White (US; Tannhauser, 1912).
The Woman in White (US; Gem, 1913).
The Woman in White (GB; director Herbert Wilcox, 1929).
Crimes at the Dark House (loosely based on *The Woman in White*; GB; director George King, 1939).
The Woman in White (US; director Peter Godfrey, Warner Brothers, 1947).
The Woman in White (GB; ABC TV, director Herbert Wise, 1957).
The Woman in White (US; The Dow Hour of Great Mysteries, director Paul Nickell, 1960).
The Woman in White (GB; BBC TV, director Brandon Acton Bond, 1966).
La Femme en Blanc (France; ORTF, director Pierre Gautherin, 1970).
The Woman in White (GB; BBC2 TV, director John Bruce, 1982).
The Woman in White (GB/US; BBC/Carlton, director Tim Fywell, 1997).

INDEX